JUDITH, thirty-six, is a very successful writer, but regularly, every two months, she becomes depressed and irritable, tends to oversleep, and when she tries to write just stares into space.

CARL, an internationally known business executive, every now and then becomes despondent, loses all confidence in himself, and threatens to resign.

AMY, a "Super Mom," has tremendous energy for managing her children, holding down a job, cleaning her house by 7 A.M., and sending her immaculate kids off to school. Yet there are times when she withdraws, gets physically ill and depressed, and ends up in the hospital.

All of these people go through periodic surges of
elation and despair.
All of these people, says Dr. Fieve, suffer from
MOODSWING
a debilitating condition that afflicts more than
twenty million Americans. . . .

Dr. Fieve on Depression

MOODSWING
(Revised and Expanded Edition)

Ronald R. Fieve, M.D.

BANTAM BOOKS
NEW YORK · TORONTO · LONDON · SYDNEY · AUCKLAND

This edition contains the complete text of the original hardcover edition.
NOT ONE WORD HAS BEEN OMITTED.

MOODSWING
A Bantam Book / published in association with William Morrow & Company, Inc.

PUBLISHING HISTORY
Morrow edition published October 1975
Morrow revised edition / April 1989
Macmillan Book Club edition / November 1975
Psychology Today Book Club edition / November 1975
Psychotherapy & Social Science Book Club edition / December 1975
Bantam edition / October 1976
Bantam Revised edition / September 1989

ISBN 0-553-27983-1

Published simultaneously in the United States and Canada

PRINTED IN THE UNITED STATES OF AMERICA

OPM   15   14   13   12   11   10   9   8   7

For Katia
Lara and Vanessa

CONTENTS

INTRODUCTION

When I wrote *Moodswing* some fourteen years ago, it was to tell the story of my search for antidepressant treatments to alleviate those suffering with manic and suicidal feelings and of the breakthrough that my use of lithium achieved.

But in the decade and a half since *Moodswing* was written, the treatment of mental illness has undergone major changes. No longer are most depressions treated with long and expensive courses of psychotherapy. And so it is time to bring that story up to date, to show how treatment of chemical imbalance has progressed.

New modes of health care have sprung up. Specialized clinics for depression and drug abuse, bulimia, alcoholism, and panic disorders are treating patients far more efficiently than before, because antidepressants are taking the place of long expensive courses of psychotherapy. The hour spent talking weekly to the psychiatrist has been replaced by a fifteen-minute visit once a month with a biological psychiatrist, at which time blood levels of drugs are tested and side effects checked. Instead of probing childhood traumas with an analyst, the patient now discusses present stresses with a psychologist or social worker and meets with a peer support group. The cost is far less, and the improvement is greater.

We have been searching for biological markers to give the clinician a blood or urine test by which to determine whether major depressive disorders are present, and there is already a reliable one for in-hospital settings. The genetics of manic depression are being researched in a number of clinical laboratories throughout the world, including my own at·Columbia University and at the Foundation for Depression and Manic Depression in New York City.

And there have been major advances in diagnosis, including the concept of *dual diagnosis,* the notion that the patient has an underlying major psychiatric illness, superimposed on which is another major illness, that of alcohol or substance abuse. The biggest problem facing psychiatry in the late 1980s is substance abuse. But many people suffering from such abuse are actually victims of an underlying depression or panic disorder they may be trying to blot out with their drugs or alcohol. In most cases, once the underlying disorder is treated with antidepressants, the substance abuse, which is usually slow and difficult to cure by itself, can be eradicated more easily.

The concept of depression is being expanded to include more than a blue mood and crying or suicidal thoughts. Today we are seeing more and more patients with mild chronic depression and lack of pleasure in life. These are suffering from a very harmful form of depression called *dysthymia,* literally "bad mood." These people are usually chronic underachievers, unhappy on the job and at home, who may not recognize that they have treatable depression.

As for lithium, it has gained worldwide use and popularity since *Moodswing* was first written. It is now the standard treatment for manic depression and many other forms of depression in clinics and private practices throughout America and most of Europe. Its use has helped patients and their families avoid untold weeks and years of suffering. I would estimate that the use of psychotherapy and psychoanalysis to treat depressed patients has decreased by at least 50 percent.

The outlook for the patient suffering from depression is bright, for he or she is experiencing a treatable biochemical imbalance. It is not only childhood experience, but body chemistry that can affect mood state, and many different kinds of drugs are available for short- or long-term therapy. And these new compounds have fewer side effects and faster action.

No one needs to live with depression. Most depressions are curable with the right treatment. If you or someone you care about is suffering from painful or even suicidal depressed feelings, I recommend consulting a biological psychiatrist.

There is more hope than ever for the millions who suffer from the debilitating emotional illness of mood disorders—and in this revised edition I have tried to share it all with you.

MOODSWING

ONE

The Chemical Revolution

What is being done today for people who are overcome by feelings of low energy and depression? What happens to the superachievers in business, politics, and the arts whose extremes of elation become irrational and psychotic? What is the promise of the revolutionary chemical treatments now available in psychiatry for depression and elation?

Depression is the most common psychiatric problem for which people seek help, and it may have caused more anguish and suffering throughout the world than any other medical or psychiatric illness. Because of its pleasurable aspect, elation has been less talked about, and regarded as an illness only in its most immoderate forms.

Moods of deep depression and elation were described by Old Testament writers and by early Greeks and Romans. Philosophers, historians, poets, and novelists have accepted mental depression that returns from time to time as a part of the human condition, ranging from inexplicable moments of misery or joy to prolonged periods of extreme despondency or elation indicating serious mental derangements. Disorders of mood throughout the centuries have been misdiagnosed and, at the very least, unsuccessfully treated until recently. Those that have not led to suicide have often remained uncontrollable, even in the hands of experts.

What I have to say in the pages to follow may startle many

who believe primarily or exclusively in the psychological approaches to depression. Anyone who has kept abreast of the new chemical advances for treatment and prevention of mood disorders, however, will know that we are now undergoing our third and most spectacular revolution in the treatment of emotional states. In particular, we are witnessing for the first time a major chemical breakthrough with the lithium treatment and prevention of manic depression and recurrent depression. These chemically treatable mood disorders can now be easily recognized in normal people, and are characterized by what I refer to as a recurrent *moodswing*.

I have treated thousands of patients with moodswing, first as a psychoanalyst and in later years as a psychopharmacologist—a psychiatrist who approaches emotional disorders with drugs to alter or correct abnormal or faulty body chemistry. When the primary treatment of manic depression or recurrent depression has required the patient to talk with me about his problems— the so-called psychotherapeutic or psychoanalytic approach—in my experience not very much has happened.

The first time I became aware of the perplexities of manic depression was in the fall of 1954, during my fourth year of psychiatric clerkship at the Harvard Medical School. I was assigned to treat a thirty-three-year-old woman in a deep and uncommunicative depression. Since the principal teaching at that time was psychoanalytic, I spent most of my evenings in the library reading Freud, hoping that I would discover some explanation for the unwillingness of my patient to talk with me. Daily I sat with her for at least an hour, probing all the possible reasons why she might be so deeply hurt, saddened, and depressed, but all to no avail.

To my great astonishment one morning, I returned to have another psychotherapy session with her, and she was not the same despairing, noncommunicative woman I had known. Instead, I was confronted with a wild, talkative, and seductive female who had changed dramatically overnight. In her new, elated manic state, her activity was unstoppable. For two weeks nothing I did had any effect on calming her ecstasy, other than the use of heavy sedatives and restraints that were temporary and relatively ineffective. After several consultations with senior psychiatrists, electroshock treatments were ordered, and for the first time as a student I observed the effects of this therapy—a dramatic, although brief, one-month remission of her symptoms. Then once again she switched into her deep and suicidal depressed state. I remember feeling perplexed and confused, and I considered it a personal defeat. After months of my trying to help this patient, a cure I had hoped to bring about had not been achieved at all. Instead, a harsh, drastic, mechanical shock machine, rather than a warm, understanding human relationship, had been necessary to relieve her acute suffering; even so, no long-range cure had been effected; her depression had recurred.

During the years that followed, I completed a medical internship and residency in New York. While I was going through three years of psychiatric residency at Columbia-Presbyterian Medical Center and the New York State Psychiatric Institute, I rarely met with the diagnosis of manic depression again. It had virtually disappeared. During the 1950s most cases of excitable, talkative, and elated behavior were being diagnosed as schizophrenic. The new phenothiazine tranquilizers, effective in schizophrenia and some excited states, were being given exclusively.

From 1959 until mid-1970 I was in charge of the acute psychiatric service at the New York State Psychiatric Institute, and word had spread from Australia and Denmark of promising results from the use of lithium carbonate in treating manic depression. Researching the world literature on lithium was a relatively easy task in 1959, since it consisted of only a few reports from abroad. I soon read that lithium carbonate was a simple white powder found in mineral water and rocks, a naturally occurring salt similar to table salt. I found that it could be given to excited manic patients by mouth in capsule form. And according to the reports by its Australian discoverer, John F. Cade, it would calm manic excitement in five to ten days.

My first research trials of this drug on hyperactive and elated manics resulted in a dramatic calming of their symptoms. Furthermore, with the correct dosage of lithium, there seemed to be no side effects, unlike the chemical straitjacketing of the patient which often resulted from use of the major tranquilizers. I had seen this latter effect in acutely agitated patients for whom massive doses of tranquilizers were required, to slow them down and induce sleep. In the process, side effects—retarded body movement, a masklike face with little expression, a zombielike appearance—were usually evident. Manic patients calmed on lithium, in contrast, were perfectly normal. Their overactivity, talkativeness, seductiveness, playful tie pulling, and high energy levels were quickly dampened, and they were ready for discharge in a few weeks. Previously, these same patients had received months and years of electroshock therapy, multiple drugs, psychotherapy, and psychoanalysis. During the three years I spent in psychiatric training, the additional five years of formal psychoanalytic training, and the years I have spent in psychiatric research, I have not found another treatment in psychiatry that works so quickly, so specifically, and so permanently as lithium for recurrent manic and depressive mood states.

While working with lithium, I have also watched the alcoholic's high, followed by his crash into depression, which resembles and is therefore often confused with the manic-depressive cycle. Studies now indicate that manic depression and alcoholism go hand in hand and may be related genetically in the same family tree. Furthermore, over the years, it has become apparent that cocaine, heroin, alcohol, marijuana, amphetamines, and sleeping pills are frequently used by depressed people in our society in an attempt at self-treatment of their mood disorders. Instead of curing the depression, these drugs worsen it, and add the dangerous problems of alcoholism and drug addiction.

A new and thought-provoking aspect of moodswing occurred to me for the first time in 1960, when a manic-depressive business tycoon attempted suicide and was persuaded to see me by his concerned brother-in-law. I had been told that his moodswing was on a forty-eight-hour cycle, with depressed days and euphoric days alternating. Impeccably dressed, he first came to my office in one of his highs. His rapid, articulate speech, his perceptiveness, and his astounding success in business were characteristic of the positive side to cyclic illness—moodswing—that produced the high energy and relentless drive in many key people in our society, the superorganizers and go-getters. These often brilliant men, I began to surmise, were milder versions of the wild manics on the ward, and in the sixties they were diagnosed simply as "hypomanic [less manic] personalities who get depressed." They always drove themselves too hard and cashed in on their highs. They sought help only when things fell apart, after they went too high—to the point of being irrational and psychotic—or when they were in their alternately and inevitably depressed moods.

Wild horses could not drag in these charismatic manic-depressives for treatment when they were on top of the world and accomplishing so much. Those with creative talent seemed to be most productive and creative during high moods. During lows their literary, artistic, or business blocks would force them to withdraw, take vacations, or go into hospitals. Their depressions were quietly hushed up by colleagues, family, or members of the board. Their depressed phases were treated in the 1960s with the new antidepressant drugs or electroshock therapy. These men and women then returned as if nothing had occurred. They inevitably had to disappear once again at an unpredictable moment. They were the life of the party, and they loved to take risks, gamble, and manipulate. Their roller-coaster careers reflected their manic-depressed moods. They gravitated toward the top of organizations, if lack of tact with colleagues did not sabotage their advancement in the hierarchy.

Early in my experience I treated a number of these dynamic people for ordinary recurrent depression. They seemed to snap out of their depressions after long and protracted periods of ineffective psychotherapy or effective shorter courses of antidepressant drugs. At the time I wrote, "The patient is now well and cured from his depression." During these so-called well periods, which I did not recognize at the time as mild, hidden highs, interesting things happened. If they were businessmen, they were exceptionally good at making deals. If they were salesmen, they were at the top of the force. If they were cabbies, they seemed to be the most exuberant, cigar smoking, and story-telling of the lot. Between their depressive phases, these patients were extremely effective in their functioning. Only when one of them used poor judgment while in an elated mood would it become obvious that I was dealing with a clear-cut case of manic depression. But in the less intensive forms of mania—the recognizable hypomanias as well as the hidden ones—this particular behavior seemed in many cases to be normal and extremely adaptive. I began to wonder what was so bad about being a mild manic-depressive if one could feel so well and achieve so much. These mild to moderately high moodswings, which did not go too far, enabled many of my patients to become superhustlers between their depressions; and in a society of hustlers, which New York City is, these individuals usually rose to the top. In short, where they had traditionally been viewed by family, friends, other physicians, and myself as normal individuals with recurrent depressed moods, it was now evident that they were in fact mild cases of manic depression. I observed that these mild highs were often an asset and not a liability, which the diagnostic labels "mania" and "hypomania" always imply. I could not find a psychiatric label for this "effective hypomanic" state, indicating its positive and adaptive aspects. Furthermore, the concept of hypercompetence due to mild elation was hardly noted in the psychiatric literature.

Over the years, my experience with lithium in treating mild to severe manic-depressives and patients with simple recurrent depression has convinced me that lithium not only effectively normalizes the manic state, but also prevents or dampens many future lows of manic depression and recurrent depression. Lithium is the first truly prophylactic agent in psychiatry to control, prevent, or stabilize the future lifetime course of a major mental illness.

The first revolution in psychiatry began with the work of Philippe Pinel in 1791. Later, as chief psychiatrist and neurologist of the Salpêtrière Hospital in Paris, he reformed the treatment of the mentally ill by introducing liberal principles in the organization and administration of mental hospitals. For the first time in history, through Pinel's efforts, the mental hospital became the main therapeutic tool for helping mental patients. Pinel rejected the use of chains and beatings as methods of treating mental illness, measures that had been employed liberally since early Roman times. Bloodletting and sudden ducking in ice-cold water, he felt, induced a medical delirium more serious than the delirium of the mentally ill patients themselves. Excited manic patients, in particular, were subjected to these treatments until Pinel's revolutionary changes began to occur. Pinel's humane approach and his theories of hospital management are still valid today in the contemporary community mental-health center. His primary contribution was to change society's attitude toward the insane so that patients were considered sick human beings, deserving and requiring medical treatment. He asserted that it was impossible to determine whether mental symptoms resulted from the mental disease itself or from the effects of the chains on the patient.

Even though the mentally ill had not been tortured at the stake for some time, their condition during most of Pinel's life—in "the Century of Enlightenment"—was still agonizing. If mental patients were not hospitalized, they could be seen wandering aimlessly through the countryside, beaten and ridiculed. In England as early as 1403, the insane were frequently interned and brutalized at Bethlehem Hospital, or "Bedlam," as it was called. This famous insane asylum was a favorite Sunday excursion spot for Londoners who came to peer through the iron gates at the unfortunate patients.

Whether in Paris, London, Philadelphia, or New Orleans, if a dangerous madman had no relatives he would be placed in prison. The inhumanity with which the mentally ill were treated was probably due to complete ignorance of the nature of mental illness, deep dread of the insane, and the belief that mental disease was incurable. Excited patients were locked naked in narrow closets and fed through holes from copperware attached to chains. Straitjackets attached to walls or beds were used to restrain patients, since it was believed that the more painful the restraint, the better the results, particularly with obstinate psychotics. Attendants were often sadistic individuals of low intelligence who could find no other employment. Pinel revolutionized this state of horror for the mentally ill.

*   *   *

Around 1900, when Sigmund Freud ushered in the second revolution in psychiatry, the role of the psychiatrist remained frustrating. He could classify the psychoses and predict their course better than his predecessors a century before, but he still suffered from the same ignorance of the causes of mental illness and basically had to resort to crude and miserable methods of treatment. Freud (1856–1936) was undoubtedly the most renowned of all psychotherapists and psychoanalysts of the late nineteenth century. Originally he had been a neurologist, and he never gave up the idea that all psychological illness must in the end be attributable to an organic process that would one day be treatable with chemical therapy.

Since at that time basic research in the neuroses and psychoses had not yielded any positive biological clues, Freud resolved to confine his work to the purely psychological level. As a young psychotherapist, Freud made a pilgrimage to the French town of Nancy to learn from his teacher there the method of hypnosis for treating the neuroses. Freud synthesized the ideas of the great neurologists and hypnotists of France into a theory of personality that soon became an international movement. He developed the theory of the unconscious and the concept of mental repression and its role in neurosis. For him symptoms were substitute gratifications. The psychotherapist's task was to get the patient to express unconscious feelings and uncover repressed memories that were causing the neurotic conflict. His new technique of uncovering the unconscious through the process of free association of thoughts and the analysis of dreams he called *psychoanalysis*. He soon became convinced that all neuroses had at their basis sexual problems and experiences in childhood. Freud invented the concept of *libido*, a vague term that referred to sexual energy. He also formed the concept of the *Oedipus complex*, the key to all neuroses, in which the unconscious problem of a neurotic male was an unresolved sexual attachment to his mother. A similar problem in neurotic females was termed the *Electra complex*.

Freud felt that the therapeutic force in analytic treatment was the phenomenon of *transference*, in which the patient redirected toward the psychoanalyst many of his previous feelings and ideas associated with his parents and other significant figures of his past. Freud attempted to apply psychoanalysis to the psychoses, but he found that they were not very accessible. He also attempted to apply psychoanalysis to explain art and religion as well as war and culture. Soon in some countries psychoanalysis became a substitute religion, a church with a dogma, like other scientific movements such as Marxism and Darwinism.

Although it is easy now to look back and mention only the shortcomings of the psychoanalytic revolution in psychiatry, it was of fundamental importance, if only because doctors began to listen to what their patients had to say. Furthermore, the psychoanalytic movement represented important progress beyond simply observing, describing, and listing the outward symptoms of mental illness, in which the causes were so poorly understood and the treatments unavailable. It was in large part responsible for the development of a feeling of expectancy and optimism on the part of psychiatrists, patients, and society throughout the early decades of the twentieth century.

The third revolution in psychiatry was initiated in the 1950s, with the introduction of the potent antipsychotic phenothiazine tranquilizers and reserpine treatment of the emotionally ill. Psychiatric hospitals that began to employ these chemical treatments reported a decrease in the use of physical restraints, electroshock therapy, hydrotherapy, insulin coma, and other physical methods of treatment. A reduction in patients' violence and agitation and an increase in the discharge rate of chronic patients hitherto considered hopeless cases began to be achieved. The widespread success with chemical agents in the late fifties precipitated government and private funding for intensive research to find additional psychoactive drugs—and the new science of *psychopharmacology,* the chemical treatment of emotional states, was born. Since then prolonged hospital treatment for mental disorders has become obsolete and emphasis has shifted to outpatient prophylaxis and maintenance therapy with the goal of keeping the patient well and in the community.

In 1955, for the first time in one hundred years, the number of patients admitted to psychiatric hospitals in the United States began to decline. Since then, despite a steady increase in the number of admissions, a decrease in the mental-hospital populations in America has continued. Yet the number would have doubled had it not been for the introduction of the antipsychotic phenothiazine tranquilizers in the early fifties.

Additional drugs were soon developed by the pharmaceutical industry after the serendipitous discoveries of the tricyclic antidepressants and the monoamine oxidase inhibitors. These two classes of chemical compounds, both highly effective in the treatment of depression, were discovered in 1956 and marketed in the late 1950s. Since the advent of the third chemical revolution in psychiatry it has been estimated that psychotropic drugs have been used for the treatment of at least five hundred million patients around the world by 1969. Since then the figure has at least doubled.

Lithium carbonate had already been discovered as a treatment for mania in 1949, and its modest use and development had preceded the advent of the tranquilizers and antidepressants by three and seven years respectively. Because its use was discovered by an unknown psychiatrist working alone in a small hospital in Australia, it was not of any great interest to most American psychiatrists. In the 1950s they were totally immersed in Freudian psychiatry, to the extent that not only all of the neuroses but many of the psychoses were still being treated with psychological or "talking therapies." After Cade's initial report in 1949 lithium was principally developed in Denmark by Mogens Schou beginning in 1954. Thereafter his and other reports followed from abroad throughout the ten-year period of 1949 to 1959. In 1958 I first began to study lithium clinically at the New York State Psychiatric Institute. A Texas team of psychiatrists began somewhat later. After a decade of trials by these and other groups in the United States and abroad, the American Psychiatric Association's Lithium Task Force ultimately recommended it to the Food and Drug Administration for therapy of mania in 1969, twenty years after its discovery.

Research in psychiatry has proceeded so rapidly over the past twenty-five years that modern clinical practice employing lithium as well as other chemotherapeutic agents only now is beginning to catch up to the research findings. There are still psychiatrists in America who blatantly underdiagnose depressive and manic-depressive moodswings, frequently lumping them into the wastebasket concepts of schizophrenia, neurotic depression, and other poorly defined disorders. These misdiagnosed patients receive treatments for schizophrenia, usually phenothiazine tranquilizers, or for neurotic depression, often years of analysis or psychotherapy.

The use of lithium constitutes a turning point in the mental-health field and, at least in Australia and Europe, can be said to have truly initiated the third revolution in psychiatry. A breakthrough has finally been achieved in the treatment and prevention of one of the world's major mental-health problems, moodswing, in the form of manic depression and the genetically related form of recurrent depression.

When Thomas Eagleton, the vice presidential candidate in 1972, made news with his history of depressions and electroshock treatments, the American Medical Association asked me to organize a symposium on depression. This meeting was planned so that knowledge of this illness could be pooled and the American people could be educated as to what it was, where to get help for it, and what were the latest research findings and most effective treatments.

During my work on this project it seemed most likely, as in the cases of so many other supersuccessful people who had become depressed, that Senator Eagleton might, in fact, be a hypercompetent or "effective hypomanic" between depressions, and his moodswings might be viewed from a treatment-and-prevention standpoint as potentially responsive to lithium and thus manic-depressive.

Again, the high might not be recognized but hidden, only to be manifested in the adaptive, hard-driving, and energetic ways of his past political career, attributes traditionally viewed by Americans as ideal for positions of leadership. The effective high had not been thought of as the opposite pole to his depressed moodswing. Eagleton's high-drive level, his rapid ascendancy, and his admitted failure to pace himself were characteristic of the positive side of an effective, and often hidden, hypomanic mood state. His lows had on several occasions been too low to disguise. The hospital admissions and electroshock treatments for his depressed phases were the only aspects that had been known and publicized.

Armed with this hypothesis of Eagleton, I began looking into the moods of great men and highly creative individuals of the past—political, literary, and financial. Many of these people revealed a common pattern of moodswing in their personal and professional lives, not unlike that of Senator Eagleton. During their highs they were fascinating achievers, often worrisome but dynamic and creative leaders. During their lows, instead of being recognized as depressed, they were exhausted men of battle, viewed as "physically run-down" and fatigued. The lives of these men confirmed what I had suspected twelve years earlier in the case of the forty-eight-hour manic-depressive business tycoon.

The lithium breakthrough has brought all of these fascinating pieces of the puzzle together. It has clarified the fact that major mood disorders may at times be advantageous and productive—and can be stabilized by a simple, naturally occurring substance. Furthermore, findings point to the fact that mania and mental depression must be due to biochemical causes handed down through the genes, since they are correctable so rapidly by chemical rather than talking therapy.

This revelation, which is now gaining wide acceptance in most scientific circles around the world, also calls for social change. It is bound to change the diagnostic styles and treatments in modern American psychiatry and bring psychiatry back into medicine, from which it has strayed for seventy years. Diagnoses of manic depression and recurrent depression are already on the increase. Millions of cyclically depressed people if stabilized on lithium could lead normal lives after years of waste and suffering. Most young manic-depressives could look forward to normal lives if maintained on lithium, just as diabetics and cardiacs can when maintained on insulin or digitalis.

I want to emphasize, however, that lithium is no panacea. It should not be given for all forms of depression or for other forms of mental illness in which careful research trials evaluating its effectiveness have not been performed. It cannot be given indiscriminately, since the patient and his or her blood chemistries must be watched closely by a physician or in a lithium clinic where expertise in the diagnosis of mood disorders and the use of lithium and other drugs is available. A full medical evaluation and a careful descriptive diagnosis of moodswing in either its manic-depressive or recurrent-depressive forms must precede the initiation of lithium therapy. To clarify who should receive lithium, I want to present a more complete account of moodswing, how I diagnose it, and how my patients describe it in their own words.

T W O

Moodswing

HOWARD HUGHES SPENDS THREE MILLION PURCHASING TV STATION TO SEE SIX A.M. COWBOY MOVIES, reported *The New York Times* on March 20, 1974.

Many people who read about this extravagance thought of it as the whim of a wealthy eccentric. I considered it the typical act of a manic business tycoon with enormous energy that kept him up most of the night, since manics need very little sleep. If Hughes couldn't sleep from 1:00 to 6:00 A.M. (when his staff and the local Las Vegas television station KLAS tuned out), why shouldn't he think manic and buy the station, especially if old cowboy and airplane movies gave him pleasure while the rest of the world slept?

People also speculated that Hughes's disappearance from civilization and his solitary, withdrawn existence expressed the wishes of an eccentric who wanted privacy, or of a man who was physically ill. I would venture that this somber and secretive side of his life-style revealed the typical pattern of a severe, prolonged depression.

Who are the manic-depressive personalities in past and modern times? How can we recognize them through their achievements and disasters? How much promiscuity, how many extramarital affairs and ruined marriages have oversexed, high-energy manic personalities perpetrated behind the scenes, undiagnosed and untreated? Who can we recognize as manic among

15

the driven businessmen, reporters, and publishers who work until midnight every night, needing no more than a few hours' sleep, somehow managing to sandwich in a family life? How can we recognize manics or depressives in the gallery of theater personalities, in the political arena, among students, professional men, housewives, and laborers? How can we diagnose ourselves to find out if we have the manic-depressive personality type?

William Inge, the famous playwright, killed himself. So did Sylvia Plath, promising novelist and poet, at a time when her work was being widely acclaimed. Joshua Logan, famous director-playwright-producer, and coauthor of *South Pacific,* for which he won a Pulitzer Prize, had directed an earlier hit, *Charley's Aunt,* during a high that followed a serious depression. During the depression he had directed a failure. Buzz Aldrin's drive took him all the way to the moon—how high can one get? During the months following the moon landing, Colonel Aldrin became depressed and was admitted to a mental hospital.

Which of us doesn't know and marvel at that incredible Super Mom who rarely sleeps, has tremendous energy, works for hours taking care of the children, while holding a part-time job, contributing time to charities, getting to bed at 1:00 A.M. and up again at six, cleaning the house by seven, before taking the kids to school? But what about her sudden disappearance or unexplained illness, while the rest of the family has to take over the household and she withdraws, seems to be sick physically and depressed for months on end? What about the mental problems in her family that were always hidden? The uncle who spent his entire life in the hospital; the cousin who died mysteriously in her early twenties—it was rumored by some that she had hanged herself?

One of my patients, an attractive forty-five-year-old housewife, described her moods in the following way:

"When I start going into a high, I no longer feel like an ordinary housewife. Instead I feel organized and accomplished and I begin to feel I am my most creative self. I can write poetry easily. I can compose melodies without effort. I can paint. My mind feels facile and absorbs everything. I have countless ideas about improving the conditions of mentally retarded children, of how a hospital for these children should be run, what they should have around them to keep them happy and calm and unafraid. I see myself as being able to accomplish a great deal for the good of people. I have countless ideas about how the environment problem could inspire a crusade for the health and betterment of everyone. I feel able to accomplish a great deal for the good of my family and others. I feel pleasure, a sense of euphoria or elation. I want it to last forever. I don't seem to need much sleep. I've lost weight and feel healthy and I like myself. I've just bought six new dresses, in fact, and they look quite good on me. I feel sexy and men stare at me. Maybe I'll have an affair, or perhaps several. I feel capable of speaking and doing good in politics. I would like to help people with problems similar to mine so they won't feel hopeless.

"It's wonderful when you feel like this, but it's devastating once you go into a depression. The feeling of exhilaration—the high mood—makes me feel light and full of the joy of living. However, when I go beyond this stage, I become manic, and the creativeness becomes so magnified I begin to see things in my mind that aren't real. For instance, one night I created an entire movie, complete with cast, that I still think would be terrific. I saw the people as clearly as if watching them in real life. I also experienced complete terror, as if it were actually happening, when I knew that an assassination scene was about to take place. I cowered under the covers and became a complete shaking wreck. As you know, I went into a manic psychosis at that point. My screams awakened my husband, who tried to reassure me that we were in our bedroom and everything was the same. There was nothing to be afraid of. Nevertheless, I was admitted to the hospital the next day."

This is a sensitive self-appraisal of the subtle changes that occurred in my patient from a feeling of well-being and mild elation to a fully developed manic psychosis that required hospitalization. From her description it is apparent that the earliest symptoms of the mild manic state are pleasant ones, including a surge of confidence and a capability that are desirable among normal people. Millions of people experience this mild, pleasant high, but it usually does not last for long; it can develop into an overt manic state, in which judgment is lost, or more frequently it switches into a mild to deep depression.

This same patient of mine, after coming down from a high on lithium treatment, described her depressed moods as "my real problem." She dismissed her highs as pleasurable and entirely normal. She told me about the agonizing black moods that had haunted her past during a subsequent interview in my office.

"My first depression came out of the blue and occurred when I was twenty-five. Prior to this I had been overly happy, elated because of having given birth to lovely twins a month earlier. At first I tried to keep my mind occupied by keeping busy around the house, cleaning, and taking care of the babies. However, I soon had no enthusiasm for anything. I seemed to get no pleasure out of living. I had no feeling toward the babies or my other two children. I tried to do extra things for the children because I felt extremely guilty about my lack of feeling. I would do everything in the house quickly and then would find myself with nothing to do. I had no interest in any outside activity or any project which would be of great interest to me in a normal frame of mind. I couldn't concentrate. My mind seemed to be obsessed with black thoughts. My husband took me out frequently to take my mind off things, but even that was an effort for me."

The feeling of gloom and lack of energy that she described to me is typical of a postpartum chemical or metabolic depression seen as part of the depressed phase of manic depression (called *bipolar* manic depression) or recurrent depression without highs (called *unipolar* recurrent depression). The term *metabolic* indicates that the depression is caused by an abnormality in the body's chemistry, or metabolism, and not by stress or problems in living. These depressed feelings sometimes go on and on in patients, much to the perplexity of everyone, without the slightest insight on the part of the patient or the family. These are the symptoms characteristic of a depressive illness requiring the intervention of a psychiatrist, who, by using lithium and antidepressant drugs, can bring about a remission of most of these depressive symptoms in several weeks, in addition to preventing their recurrence.

While sitting across from me in my office, this same patient described how her postpartum depression ultimately affected her whole existence:

"As time passed, these feelings of despair and uselessness increased. I lost ten pounds and had no appetite. I would try to sleep away time but found myself unable to. I had terrible dreams and would wake up often throughout the night with a feeling of panic in the pit of my stomach. This feeling of anxiety was always present, and for no good reason it continued to get worse. I found myself not wanting to go back home when I went out to try to shop, yet I couldn't be alone. No matter what I did, I couldn't concentrate except on questions such as, What is the matter with me? Am I going insane? What have I done to deserve this? What sort of punishment is this? I felt that my appearance had severely changed. I felt old and unattractive. I had no sexual desire and became more and more guilty about my lack of sexual interest in my husband. I wondered if I was already going through the menopause. Could the change of life come on at such an early age and make me feel such profound depression and anxiety?"

Anxiety and depression, terms that are used almost interchangeably in common parlance, are in reality two different conditions. Anxiety is much more easily recognized. The psychological components of anxiety—uneasiness, apprehension, nervousness, tension—show up physically in a rapid heart rate, profuse perspiration, clammy hands, and fidgety actions. Depression, on the other hand, is characterized by apathy, a lack of pleasure, diminished energy, low self-regard, and, in more serious cases, an inability to cope with even bare essentials like getting to the office and clothing and feeding oneself. It manifests itself physically in disturbed sleeping and eating patterns, as it did in this patient. Her loss of weight and trouble falling asleep are hallmarks of a depressive disorder.

Anxiety and depression are not mutually exclusive. In fact, they often appear together. Depression is almost always accompanied by anxiety, although the reverse is not necessarily true.

The depressed individual knows that he or she is not operating normally but doesn't understand why. My patient's frustration at her continued inability to cope created more and more anxiety, which, in turn, undermined any remaining confidence. An altogether vicious cycle followed.

The combination of anxiety and depression confuses not only the sufferer but, too frequently, his physician as well. Often the anxiety will be noticed but not the underlying depression; it goes undetected. The overlay of anxiety often masks a patient's more serious depressive condition. Tranquilizers, sedatives, or barbiturates may take care of the surface anxiety but do nothing for the underlying problem of depression. The patient remains depressed and needs antidepressant drug treatment and lithium in many cases, if the depression is recurrent.

This same patient wept and told me of the crisis that finally led to hospitalization:

"Eventually I found myself going to sleep earlier at night and wanting to sleep as much as possible. This was the only way my mind would stop thinking the same anxious thoughts over and over again. Shortly after this I began to feel physically ill, my appetite got worse, and my smoking increased. My stomach began to trouble me, and I developed severe daily headaches. One day on awakening I found myself unable to get out of bed. Because I felt physically sick and unable to care for my family I began to think that I had a virus and asked my husband to call the family doctor. He gave me a thorough physical exam with blood tests and urinalysis, and found nothing wrong, but I persuaded him to treat me for a virus anyway. He didn't mention that this might be a *masked* or *hidden depression,* with anxiety and physical pain my only complaint.

"Several days later, after taking medication, I felt no better, and I awoke the next morning and felt that I didn't want to live. Nothing in life seemed important or worthwhile, and I thought of ways to commit suicide. These thoughts racked my entire body with fear. I knew then that I was not physically sick and that I had to reach out for another kind of help. I told this to my husband and saw my physician again. Upon hearing what I had to say, this time he prescribed an antidepressant and a tranquilizer. He didn't seem to know too much about what depression was or what kind of medication was needed. He recommended that I see a psychiatrist, which, of course, I couldn't possibly do. After taking the medication for one day I felt even worse. If I had to see a psychiatrist, it meant that I was probably going insane, and this thought made me even more frightened. It was more than I could stand. The fear of being mentally ill was so horrible that I decided to take my entire bottle of sleeping pills rather than face the shame of being a mental patient."

My patient's history is fairly typical of that of the millions of Americans every year who need psychiatric or medical help for symptoms of depression, but who are often too frightened to ask for help. Millions will go to their general practitioners for complaints that we know can now be diagnosed as masked depression, or depression that disguises itself in the form of some psychosomatic illness. The unknowing physician who saw this woman missed the diagnosis of depression until he was called back a second time and clear depressive complaints including suicidal feelings were related. Losing a patient such as this by suicide is not uncommon if the diagnosis of masked depression is missed.

Twenty million Americans a year—10 percent of the population of the United States—experience a clinically depressed mood and never know just what it is they are experiencing, where or when to seek help for it, or even if help exists. If they do go for help, often they do not find it. Or they may be given the wrong kind of treatment; this type of depression should now be treated primarily and rapidly with antidepressants rather than with prolonged counseling of psychological therapy.

Statistics on manic moodswings don't seem to exist other than in the form of rough estimates from the Department of Health and Human Services that indicate that probably in any one year between two and four million Americans will have attacks of elation, some mild but others serious enough to warrant outpatient psychiatric help or inpatient psychiatric hospitalization. Many of the milder high states will be beneficial and appropriate to the individual, enabling him to achieve much of value by means of his driven, manic energy. There is always the danger, however, that the manic highs will go too far and cause devastating results to family and society in various ways: financial extravagance, reckless driving, promiscuity, misdemeanors, felonies, and other acts against society because of lack of judgment and poorly directed energy during the highs. A depression almost always follows. Alcohol and drugs are often a complication.

Another one of my patients, a young secretary thirty-three years old, was ill for a week before I was forced to admit her to a psychiatric hospital. During her early school years she had been outstanding as a student, and later she decided to do secretarial work rather than go on to college. She developed many avocational interests including ballet, reading, and languages. Several days before I admitted her for treatment, her friends noticed that she was going out every night, dating many new men, attending church meetings, language classes, and dances, and showing a rather frenetic emotional state. Her seductiveness at the office had resulted in her going to bed with two of the available married men, who didn't realize that she was ill. She burst into tears on several occasions without provocation and told risqué jokes that were quite out of character. She became more talkative and restless, stopped eating, and didn't seem to need any sleep. She began to talk with religious feeling about being in contact with God and insisted that several things were now necessary to carry out God's wishes. This included giving herself sexually to all who needed her.

When she was admitted to the hospital, she asked the resident psychiatrist on call to kiss her. Because he refused to do so she became suddenly silent. Later she talked incessantly, accusing the doctor of trying to seduce her, and began to talk about how God knew every sexual thought that she or the doctor might have. Several days later on the psychiatric ward, she developed a great excitement and overactivity. She said she had so much to do that she no longer had time to eat. After five days of starvation she required tube feeding. Large doses of medication were needed to calm her agitated state. She entered a phase of great physical activity. She paced the floor and went into patients' rooms, causing considerable disturbance. She was distractible, misidentified people, and was disoriented in time and place. Her condition seemed to approach a state of ecstasy when she sang religious hymns and unabashedly stripped in front of everyone. Once she became violent and struck another patient. On another occasion she broke the window in her room. After three or four days, when her delirious manic state was still not calmed with antipsychotic medication, she was given electroshock treatments, which elicited an immediate response. Since she had had two previous manic attacks similar to this one, she was placed on four capsules of lithium daily and stabilized clinically by regulating her blood lithium level over the next two weeks. Subsequently she was discharged and came to me as a private patient for monitoring in a well and normal mood state.

The more typical milder manic states that occur in a large percentage of the population are never reported to psychiatrists or physicians at any time since they are so pleasurable. It is understandable why people wish to prolong highs and become angry with anyone who wants to treat them or suggests that they "are going too fast" or "doing too much in life."

One twenty-eight-year-old New York socialite told me during a consultation:

"In one of my productive highs that sometimes last six to twelve months, I was head of a charity ball and planned a dinner for close to three hundred people. I found that I was able to organize it myself, plan the menu, and personally call all of the invited guests. This was in addition to caring for my four small children, a large house in the country, and an apartment in New York. The dinner turned out to be a grand success and I received numerous compliments as to how well I had managed so much. In other highs it seemed that I had enormous amounts of energy, but I didn't have quite the same ability to direct and channel my energies into something worthwhile, as I did during that particular occasion. I don't know what makes the difference. Some highs have led to a helpful and creative life with useful accomplishments, and other highs to destructive behavior, hospitalization, and embarrassment to my family and friends.

"As the years have passed, it seems that I have had urges to start many projects simultaneously when I get to feeling so well. When my highs are racing too fast, many of these projects don't reach completion. I am too distractible; there is always something else to do. Too many demands seem to be placed on me by my family and friends. Too many opportunities seem to crop up on all sides. On several occasions I went on shopping sprees, buying and charging at any store I walked into. On one occasion I bought ten fur coats at Bendel's and of course they all had to be returned. On another occasion I wasn't so lucky. I ran up charges of forty thousand dollars on my husband's credit cards within a week. We couldn't return these goods and they all turned out to be useless things that I had just kept on buying compulsively during my state of elation. My husband finally caught up with this charging before it caused him further embarrassment and serious financial loss."

The excessive buying sprees, gambling, and other extravagance characteristic of many manics are calamities to those families who cannot afford this kind of manic behavior. Among the more affluent, the constant compulsive spending and traveling sprees are less noticed and in some instances become almost a normal style absorbed within the family pattern. Thus, many well-to-do husbands tolerate the excitement and stimulus of a chic wife constantly going on shopping binges, bringing home literally dozens of new articles and changes of clothing that can never be utilized. Many such men and women frequently travel back and forth to weekend havens of foreign capitals. Jet travel unleashes much of the energy of these wealthy manics whose way of life demands constant movement.

The many subtle faces of mania, as well as the many faces of depression in its milder states, are difficult for the medical profession, including psychiatrists, to diagnose and treat. How does one diagnose the compulsive gambler, with his passionate love for frenetic activity? He spends his entire paycheck on the latest race and seldom wants to come for treatment, even if seriously depressed. What diagnosis does one give the tycoon with incredible energy who has driven himself up the business ladder to head five major corporations? He has been more successful in business than his competitors through his shrewd bets, his investments, and his manipulations of people. His energy has appeared to remain stable through the years, mostly on the high side, with very few dips into depression. Will a severe depression eventually hit once he reaches the pinnacle of achievement and success in his field? Or, as in the case of some men, will it come after retirement?

What about the millions of people who just seem to be getting on in life, with day-to-day, humdrum existences in which they don't seem to have any energy for anything—the apathetic, the bored, those who don't seem to be getting any pleasure out of living? Many of these people I now recognize in my office as suffering from mild forms of chemically treatable depression. Their only complaint is a chronic lack of optimism, or failure to get much pleasure out of anything. One to six months later these moody people often seem to swing back to their normal, optimistic selves without treatment. They undergo a spontaneous, mild, chemical moodswing.

How many confusing explanations of these personalities have been forthcoming from psychoanalysts, sociologists, theologians, and experts on psychological consequences of urbanization? Researchers in mood disorders are beginning to study many of these individuals who are in reality only mildly depressed, or dysthymic, because of abnormal body metabolism or chemical imbalance rather than particular circumstances in their lives. How many have biological depressions that will respond to mild doses of lithium or the latest antidepressant drug? How far do subtle forms of moodswing go, and what are the numerous ramifications? What are the symptoms and precursors of the highs and lows of adulthood, in childhood and adolescence? The moodiness of some adolescents, the acting out against authority, the getting into heavy drugs—are these early signs of adult depression or manic depression? How many speed freaks, early alcoholics, or potheads are depressed adolescents or young adults attempting to narcotize themselves out of their depression into highs? How many are simply seeking relief from painful depression?

One of my patients, an eighteen-year-old college student, was seen in the emergency ward and sedated for hysterical crying after a suicide attempt. The surgical resident had to suture the radial artery in his left forearm as he lay in a weakened and depressed state, surrounded by pools of blood. He was first discovered by a roommate, who had seen his withdrawn behavior and loss of interest in school develop during the last semester. He had begun skipping classes, staying in bed, and not eating. These were the only signs that were noticed. His interest in dating had also stopped, but no one seemed to see that all these symptoms were indicative of a serious depression.

One broker patient of mine has so much energy, so many facts at his command that he has tripled most of his clients' accounts, including his own. He gets things done. Some of the office personnel jokingly say, "He's a maniac," while he proudly smiles.

Another broker patient of mine was that way before the market collapsed. He was respected as the sharpest, cleverest, and most energetic man in the firm. He stopped his lithium, got high, and went too far too fast, manipulating clients' stocks and overinvesting his and clients' money, so that bankruptcies occurred. Ultimately he was fired from his job and had to settle the liens of his clients for money he had lost when he had exercised poor judgment. Although his family urged him to return for treatment, he refused and subsequently shot himself.

These case histories of my patients reinforce the startling statistics that depression and manic depression occur in at least 3 to 4 percent and possibly as high as 8 to 10 percent of the general population. How many of these people would benefit by treatment? Recognition by the public and medical profession of altered mood states and their successful control and prevention with lithium and antidepressants remains behind the research advances of the last twenty years.

I have been concerned as to how one might go about disseminating information about the new chemical treatments in psychiatry so that the gap between research findings and their application to patient care can be closed. Since lithium has been used for treating manic depression for over thirty years in Europe and is not yet recognized adequately or used sufficiently in the United States, a brilliant and talented American who happened to be one of my patients suggested that he might help close the gap by telling his story of the manic depression that plagued him throughout thirty years of his creative life. His dramatic story follows. It raises the question I am often asked: Does lithium affect creativity? This is one of the most important questions I want to answer.

THREE

Moods and Creativity

I believe that depression is terrifying; and elation—its non-identical twin sister—is even more terrifying, attractive as she may be for the moment. But as she goes higher, man is even more dangerous than when in the depths of the depression. However, I'm sure that the thing that is almost as much or more of a menace to the world today is the stupid, almost dogged ignorance of these illnesses; the vast lack of knowledge that they are able to be treated and the seeming ease of the cure, the simplicity of bringing them under control.

In 1973 my patient Joshua Logan, the extraordinarily talented director, writer, and producer in the American theater, spoke these words before an American Medical Association symposium on depression, and exposed his personal history of manic and depressive moodswings, from which he had suffered for over thirty years.

My first impression was that something had sneaked up on me. I had no idea I was depressed, that is, mentally. I knew I felt bad, I knew I felt low. I knew I had no faith in the work I was doing or the people I was working with, but I didn't imagine I was sick. It was a great burden to get up in the morning and I couldn't wait to go to bed at night, even though I started not sleeping well. But I had no idea I had a treatable depression. I had no idea it was anything like a medical illness. I thought I was well but feeling low because of a hidden personal discouragement of some sort—something I couldn't quite put my finger on. If anyone had told me that I could walk into a hospital and be treated by doctors and nurses and various drugs and be cured I would have walked in gladly and said, "Take me," but I didn't know such cures existed. I just forced myself to live through a dreary, hopeless existence that lasted for months on end before it switched out of the dark-blue mood and into a brighter color. But even then I didn't know I had been ill.

My depressions actually began around the age of thirty-two. I remember I was working on a play, and I was forcing myself to work. I couldn't work well. I directed a very elaborate musical comedy on Broadway, and on a pre-Broadway tour during the time I was in this depression. I can remember that I sat in some sort of aggravated agony as it was read aloud for the first time by the cast. It sounded so awful that I didn't want to direct it. I didn't even want to see it. I remember feeling so depressed that I wished that I were dead without having to go through the shame and defeat of suicide. I couldn't sleep well at all, and sleep meant, for me, oblivion, and that's what I longed for and couldn't get. I didn't know what to do and I felt very, very lost. I remember I asked a friend of mine who was with the company manager to walk around the block with me during lunch because I didn't want to have to converse with the cast lest they sense my feelings. I told my friend that the play was awful. He said, "No, no. It's not so bad. I don't know what's the matter with you, you're looking at things wrong. Come on now, just buck up."

It seemed to me that all friends of the average human being in depression only knew one cure-all, and that was a slap on the back and "Buck up." It's just about the most futile thing that could happen to you when you're depressed. My friends never even hinted to me that I was really ill. They simply thought that I was low and was being particularly stubborn and difficult about things. If anyone had taken charge and had insisted that I go to a mental hospital, I probably would have gone straight off. Instead they simply said, "Please don't act that way. Please don't look at your life so pessimistically; it's not so bad as you think. You'll always get back to it. Just buck up." Finally, as time passed, the depression gradually wore off and turned into something else, which I didn't understand either. But it was a much pleasanter thing to go through, at least at first. Instead of hating everything, I started liking things—liking them too much, perhaps, I swung into a different mood altogether, which I didn't understand, nor did anyone else. At first people thought I was drinking, even though I was seldom around any bar, and I wasn't seen to take a drink of alcohol in front of anyone, so they couldn't quite explain it that way. And yet I was fairly flamboyant in my thoughts, imagination, and speech without really being dangerous. I was certainly very active mentally and physically. I lost weight, dropped down almost overnight to my best weight, like a fighter in good trim. I put out a thousand ideas a minute: things to do, plays to write, plots to write stories about.

I decided to get married on the spur of the moment. I pursued a girl, talked to her a lot, and talked persuasively to her parents. I swamped them with favors. She was so beautiful and lovely that I practically forced her to say yes. Suddenly we had a loveless marriage and that had to be broken up overnight.

By this time even my mother, sister, and family doctor were quite certain there was something wrong. One day two psychiatrists from a nearby hospital in Westchester were sitting in my apartment when I came home. One of them said to me, "You're in the midst of a very serious nervous breakdown." This was my first major state of manic elation, that at first had seemed so pleasant and productive. At that point I wasn't sleeping at all. Whether I needed it or not, I didn't want to be curtailed or put into a hospital. I can only remember that I worked constantly, day and night, never even seeming to need more than a few hours of sleep. I always had a new idea or another conference. I directed another play which should have taken at least a month or five weeks. I directed it in two weeks, including two previews. It was a revival of the famous old farce *Charley's Aunt,* which is a pretty manic play to begin with. And it introduced to the world José Ferrer, who has a high-flying quality about him, always. It also introduced me to my present wife, who was to play the real aunt. It was an exhilarating time for me. I was extremely productive, perhaps overly so, but it was the best thing I think I've ever done in my life. I doubt if I've ever had the freedom of thought and unfettered ideas which really connect with an audience that I had during that time. When the notices came out, I was considered "discovered." They had never talked about direction in any of my plays until then. Suddenly I was a famous man, and I was shot into an even higher mood state. It finally went too far. In the end I went over the bounds of reality, or law and order, so to say, I don't mean that I committed any crimes, but I could easily have done so if anyone had crossed me. I flew into rages if contradicted. I began to be irritable with everyone. Should a man, friend or foe, object to anything I did or said, it was quite possible that I could poke him in the jaw. I was eventually persuaded by the doctors that I was desperately ill and should go into the hospital. But it was not, even then, convincing to me that I was ill.

There I was, on the sixth floor of a New York building that had special iron bars around it and an iron gate that had slid into place and locked me away from the rest of the world. I had made a deal with the doctor who had finally got me into the hospital. He had had to promise that I would not be put into any special ward or be locked up in any way. I looked about and saw that there was an open window. I leaped up on the sill and climbed out of the window on the ledge on the sixth floor and said, "Unless you open the door, I'm going to climb down the outside of

this building." At the time, I remember feeling so powerful that I might actually be able to scale the building. I
was in a psychotic high. They immediately opened the
steel door, and I climbed back in. That's where manic
elation can take you.

Over the succeeding years, including four in the Army, I
had mild moodswings, but no major disruptions. During
this part of my life and later, I had a course of psychotherapeutic and psychoanalytic treatment with Dr. Lawrence
Kubie. He turned out to be a great friend and helped me
with many of my own personal problems that had grown
out of my hospitalization and my extraordinary success.
Without his help, and the help of several other psychiatrists, my freedom to express myself may well have been
curtailed. But a few years later, without apparent warning,
I again found I was getting ill. This time I was doing a
play with an important cast. All through this period I had
been doing plays, in fact, my most successful ones. *Mister
Roberts* and *South Pacific* were written during a happy period, but I felt nowhere near as high as I had been when I
was really in a manic state. I was happy with my work, but
never manic until many years later—thirteen years after my
first hospitalization—when I was directing this new play.
Suddenly, I had so many things crowding in on me,
including a new movie career that was starting, and I
found that again I was ill. This time there was a crisis in
my work. I left the play and went to a hospital in New
Orleans where I was given electroshock treatments—six of
them—and came out in a very short time, better than
when I had gone in. After that I went through years of
work in pictures and plays when sometimes I was slightly
high and productive, and sometimes I was slightly low.
But by this time they had begun to learn about various
drugs.

I visited psychiatrists three and four times a week, and at
various times I took antidepressants to elevate my mood
and tranquilizing drugs to reduce it. But it was only
toward the end of this last career of mine, which was

mostly in motion pictures, that I began reading about lithium, which might actually stabilize the highs and lows that I had suffered from for years. I have now been taking lithium carbonate for four and a half or five years, and I've not been conscious of the slightest highs or lows out of what would be considered a normal proportion. And yet, I seem to be as productive as I've ever been. I've collaborated this past year on two different musical comedies, and I'm writing my own autobiography. It's been a rewarding and enjoyable experience.

Joshua Logan was referred to me by the brilliant and prolific dean of American psychoanalysis, Lawrence Kubie. Kubie had been one of my favorite teachers at Columbia ten years earlier. Like Freud he had an appreciation of the undiscovered biological bases for major mental illness. Even so, he remained doggedly faithful to the psychoanalytic explanation of manic depression up until the time of his death in 1973. In a letter to me several weeks before he died, he criticized the biochemical theory of manic depression as explained by me on a national television program:

> . . . you make it appear as though an illness which was strongly colored by affective [i.e., mood] disturbances was an independent entity instead of being something which usually evolves out of untreated or unsuccessfully treated neurotic roots. In short, almost all depressions and/or elations are neurotonogenic [i.e., neurotic in origin] and any effort to make manic-depressive conditions out to be independent entities is misleading.

I couldn't have disagreed more, but I replied:

> From the work we have done here it is my belief that there is a group of manic-depressives which have a strong genetic loading [i.e., predisposition] and another group that may be more environmentally determined. My impression is that lithium treatment dramatically eradicates or at least

markedly attenuates over 80% of future highs and lows in this heterogeneous group of manic-depressives. Some of these, of course, are still left with personality disorders requiring psychotherapeutic or at times analytic treatment.

When I wrote this letter it was apparent that the biochemical revolution in American psychiatry was already under way. Psychiatry was suffering from an identity crisis and was going through a difficult transition. Even today many psychiatrists, psychologists, and psychoanalysts, agree with Kubie and cling to the psychoanalytic explanation of the major mood disorders despite compelling scientific evidence to the contrary. The medical model with an emphasis on heredity and brain chemistry is obviously replacing it, and it is giving way. Brain scientists and psychiatric researchers know this, but the average patient and the public do not. Nevertheless, Logan's success story with lithium made millions of people aware of the new, fast, and safe drug treatments available.

Not all manic-depressives are as creative as Logan, and of course not all creative people are manic-depressive. But when we look at the number of artistically gifted people like Joshua Logan who have been cursed with emotional problems, there seem to have been more who have had them than not. Moodswings, especially depression, alcoholism, suicide, and drug taking, have seemed to plague creative people in particular. The number of modern writers alone who have committed suicide includes Ernest Hemingway, Virginia Woolf, Hart Crane, Vachel Lindsay, John Berryman, and Anne Sexton, as well as those I have already mentioned, to name only a few. Why should these especially gifted individuals decide to end their lives? Robert Lowell, Theodore Roethke, and Graham Greene survived shattering depressions. Dylan Thomas, Brendan Behan, Thomas Wolfe, and F. Scott Fitzgerald seem to have committed suicide with alcohol. The list is so long and the events of their lives so discouraging that one can't help but wonder if there is some connection between creativity and severe emotional disorder.

Genius and insanity have been keeping company for at least two thousand years. Aristotle associated creativity with epilepsy and melancholia, or depression. Of those who were eminent in philosophy, politics, poetry, and the arts, Aristotle wrote, "All had tendencies toward depression." In *The Anatomy of Melancholy,* which first appeared in 1621, Robert Burton was concerned about madness and creativity. He believed "the vile rock of melancholy" to be one of its milder but most frequent forms. Of its victims he wrote, ". . . they can think of nothing else, continually suspecting, no sooner are their eyes open, but this infernal plague of melancholy seizeth on them, and terrifies their souls. . . ."

Insanity was considered akin to genius up to the end of the nineteenth century. Probably the greatest boost for the mad-genius stereotype came from the Romantic movement. Romanticism began, it has been said, with Goethe's *The Sorrows of Young Werther,* a book that was banned soon after it appeared in 1774 because it precipitated a rash of suicides among young men all over Europe in emulation of the blighted young genius hero. Every Romantic poet considered it *de rigueur* to be, if not an outright madman, at least a conspicuous sufferer. Hence Byron's prose, Shelley's flights of fancy and histrionic suicide, Coleridge's gloom and opium, De Quincey's drug addiction. These poets capitalized on the fact that they were sick. Suffering was associated with art—an attitude toward creativity that many still have today.

Around the turn of the century a large number of pseudoscientific studies of "genius" were turned out by respectable English, German, and French psychologists. Some of these studies had an unpleasantly eugenic or superrace ring. Many of them traded on two thousand years of accumulated anecdotes about geniuses, stories that were something less than reliable. To be inspired and to be creative was to be mad. The more gloriously abnormal the better.

Havelock Ellis contradicted this speculation in 1904, when his famous work *A Study of British Genius* was published. It was a history of 1,030 famous geniuses from the beginning of Britain's history, compiled from the *Dictionary of National Biography.* He found that only 4.2 percent (44 cases out of 1,030) could be called insane, a proportion not too far from that of the emotionally ill in the general population. "We must put out of court," Ellis wrote, "any theory as to genius being a form of insanity."

Another reason that the link between genius and insanity persists in many minds is that creative people do behave in ways out of the ordinary. In this respect, the unusually talented artist genius is often confused with the emotionally disturbed person. The former is usually set apart from the group at a rather early age, and his or her interest in artistic endeavors commences earlier than that of others. The early aloneness and nonconformity lead to earlier psychological problems. The pattern of most artists' lives falls out of cycle with that of ordinary people, since artists often continue to be productive without considering the usual human needs or time schedules. Many artistic geniuses have no skill in dealing with the outside world, other than through their creative media. When there is recognition of their special creative language, they tend to come to life and be responsive to others.

Creative people are inclined to be individualists, and there is a tendency for others to interpret their unusual behavioral patterns as emotional disturbances rather than as unique behavior of people of potential genius. Their single-mindedness of endeavor is also characteristic of many psychiatric conditions. However, in the emotionally disturbed neurotic or psychotic, these endeavors are usually unintelligible and disorganized. A well-organized artistic production does not result. In contrast, the extraordinarily talented person, no matter how bizarre his ideas, usually finds someone who can understand the thrust and genius of his work.

Of course, there have been many geniuses who were psychotic. It does not follow, however, that because some artists develop psychosis or neurosis, all others have this same potential. The offbeat nature of the artist's thinking, his or her unrelatedness to conventional thought or achievements, and quite often the disturbing elements in the artist's work combine to sustain the myth that a genius is also *mad*.

Some psychologists and psychiatrists study creativity and its problems exclusively. A whole psychiatric subspecialty of creativity management has sprung up, largely in response to the demands of industry for creative thinkers. Creativity cultivators have innovated think tanks to stimulate creative ideas, tests for screening out noncreative employees, and programs in schools to encourage creative children. For many people creativity has been encouraged because it is economically advantageous. Business will tolerate nonconformity, even with personality maladjustment, if it means a gain in creativity leading to a gain in profit.

Some recent creativity studies show that creative individuals tend to be eccentric, erratic, out of the ordinary, and in particular more prone to emotional problems than the general population. Nancy Andreasen surveyed the emotional problems of fifteen writers from the University of Iowa Writers' Workshop, the staff of which had formerly included authors Robert Lowell, John Cheever, Kurt Vonnegut, and Paul Engle. The identity of the writers in Andreasen's study, however, was confidential. Her survey revealed that the writers had a much higher incidence of psychiatric disorders than either the normal control group or the general population. Out of the fifteen writers, nine had seen a psychiatrist, eight had been treated with drugs or psychotherapy, and four had been hospitalized. Only four of the control subjects had seen a psychiatrist, three had been treated, and none had been hospitalized. There was a significantly greater proportion of alcoholism (40 percent), drug taking, and moodswings in the university's creative-writer group than in the control group. Andreasen admitted that the sample was small. Nevertheless her conclusions do raise several interesting questions about mood and creativity.

In a follow-up study fifteen years later, Andreasen compared thirty writers at the Iowa Writers' Workshop to thirty nonwriters with similar intelligence and economic background. She tested for creativity, depression, manic depression, alcoholism, suicide, drug abuse, and schizophrenia in all of the subjects as well as in their parents and siblings. The results showed a higher incidence of affective disorders among the creative group, although no more than an average amount of schizophrenia. Eighty percent of the writers had had at least one episode of manic depression or depression, compared to only 30 percent of the nonartistic group.

Andreasen also found that first-degree relatives of the writers were more creative and had more moodswings than the relatives of nonwriters. Almost half the writers reported having highs and lows; only 10 percent of the nonwriters had these so-called bipolar moodswings. In fact, during the investigation two of the writers suffering from depression committed suicide. Andreasen hypothesized from this study that moodswings and creativity run in families, and both appear to be genetically inherited. She concluded that "affective disorder may produce some cultural advantages for society as a whole, in spite of the individual pain and suffering that it causes."

Another recent study seems to corroborate a link between creativity and mental disorders. Psychologist Kay Jamison interviewed forty-seven well-known British painters, writers, and sculptors, and found that eighteen of these highly gifted creative artists had either been hospitalized for moodswings, treated with lithium, or given electroshock therapy for depression. This high rate of mood disorder (38 percent) is more than six times that of the general population.

Both these recent studies support the connection between manic-depressive moodswings and creativity, a link that was initially pointed out in a research study by Philip Politan and myself and is illustrated throughout this book. I believe there is often a positive benefit for the individual, the family, and society from the milder forms of manic depression and hypomania. This advantage is often overlooked by psychiatrists, who see only the anguish, pain, and totally disruptive aspects of this illness.

I have found that creative people are usually more vulnerable emotionally than the rest of us. Since their productivity benefits us all, anything emotional that interferes with their creativity deprives all of us. Creative persons seem to lack adequate means to protect themselves, not only from the outside world, but also from themselves. When they want to go for help, they are usually afraid that the psychiatrist or the treatment will affect adversely their ability to create.

Creativity is a delicate balance easily disturbed, as anyone who has had a writer's block can testify. The challenge is to encourage creativity and maintain that delicate equilibrium at optimum efficiency, so that the artist can remain extraordinarily open to new things.

Several of the writers who studied at the University of Iowa described experiences of being flooded with emotional stimuli that they were unwilling or unable to block off. This flooding resulted in a confusing variety of conflicting passions, ideas, and diversions. Some of the writers complained that excessive sociability was a problem. They needed substantial blocks of time and isolation from human contact to accomplish their work. Their tendency toward unconventional or restless behavior—a greater incidence of experimentation in sex, frequent moving from place to place, a tendency to try a variety of different jobs, and a considerable amount of marital difficulty—may also reflect the ease with which they were flooded with stimuli from the world to which they had to respond. Indeed, their frequent use of marijuana and alcohol, which basically act as central-nervous-system depressants, may reflect their search to decrease the multiple stimuli that they found difficulty in filtering out.

There is a school of thought that maintains that creativity is simply a response to emotional pain. Anxiety, maladjustment, conflict, in this view are the wellsprings of art. The idea that art is compensation, or born out of conflict, is a tenet of Freudian psychology. The early Freudian view of creativity as compensation for or sublimation of aggressive and sexual impulses, or as sublimation of mothering impulses (artists do conceive, gestate, generate their works), in recent decades has been toned down. The notion that creativity is simply a compensation for unconscious urges is a tiresome piece of reality-twisting in the service of an over-rigid conceptual scheme. The older psychoanalytic theories provided an ingenious gallery of unconscious reasons to explain the drive to create. But the Freudian view of art as compensation is, I feel, fundamentally negative. It says essentially that art is rooted in sickness. It ignores the possibility that the artist may need to create for reasons other than pathological. It neglects the pleasure inherent in creating that others don't seem to extract from this activity. It discounts the irrepressible urge to express oneself that most people's genes don't seem to contain.

From treatment experiences with creative individuals who are also depressed or who have manic depression, I would conclude that individuals are creative despite their disorders, but certainly not because of them. Clinical psychiatric evidence suggests that, in both neurotic and psychotic artistic geniuses, the work is usually mildly to severely impaired during the active neurotic and psychotic processes. Particularly during psychotic illness, disorganization, depression, withdrawal, isolation, and rage may combine with paranoia so that the consequences are a complete devitalization of the artist's work. In this respect, psychiatrists report that the remarkably gifted individual who has a severe emotional illness constantly struggles, sometimes unsuccessfully, to keep his or her illness from interrupting and eroding sustained creative concentration. During the psychotic process the artist is most often unable to turn the illness to creative use; and the pattern followed is one of labored, noncreative repetition with a resulting dull, unintelligible meaning to the art and a lack of organization to the end product.

There is, however, most artists will admit, a definite association between moodswings and creativity crossing back and forth over the fine lines that separate the pathological, the normal, and the helpful or adaptive mood state. Often the latter is a mild high, but in some instances it is mild depression or a moodswing with alcohol that some artists claim facilitates the creativity.

Kubie, in his definitive work on creativity, *Neurotic Distortion of the Creative Process,* explains that conflicts are inevitable in the process of maturation, since the human being is so complicated. He adds that for some people conflicts manifest themselves as neurotic symptoms, while for others conflicts manifest themselves as creativity. The implication is that when an artist can't create, he is "neurotic," but when he can, he is simply "gifted." After having treated dozens of highly creative people in my practice over several decades, I have found that there is more than a simple chance association between high levels of creativity and the highs of some manic-depressives. In many creative individuals, there is a pattern to their creative surges and creative blocks that is similar to the manic-depressive's highs and lows. A person experiencing a bout of creativity tends, like the hypomanic, to resist all efforts to corner or restrain him, or to relate his personal ideas or plans to a doctor or a friend, before the creative act or project is completed. The similarity between the swings of creativity and unproductiveness of most artists and the swings of elation and depression in manic depression is striking.

Many of the world's great artists have been manic-depressive or, less frequently, simply manic. Their bouts of creativity almost inevitably coincide with the manic phase. These periods tend to be staggeringly productive. The manic artist, producing at white heat, is unstoppable, often performing the work of two people.

Handel was notorious for his major moodswings, and is known to have written his gigantic oratorio, *The Messiah,* in six weeks. Another musician, Rossini, spun out *The Barber of Seville,* one of the major operas of the nineteenth century, in thirteen days. Critics have computed that it would take almost thirteen days simply to copy the score. Rossini's musical career peaked with *The Barber of Seville,* but he then went on to a dry spell that lasted some fourteen years. During this time he produced nothing. When he began to compose once again, the work was of inferior quality.

The composer Robert Schumann was manic-depressive, and his cycles of creativity are documented. During 1840 and 1849 he was elated for the entire year, and these were the peak years of his musical output. When Schumann was in a deep depression, he stopped composing altogether. In 1844 he remained depressed for the entire year and wrote almost nothing. In 1854, after his major creative phase, he tried to drown himself in the Rhine, but was rescued, only to spend the remaining two years of his life in the hospital.

Honoré de Balzac, a classic manic-depressive, wrote *Cousin Bette* in an unbelievable six weeks. Balzac's life was typically manic, as were the content and volume of his writings. He spent money recklessly and was always in debt; he frequently stayed up all night without sleep, surviving on black coffee. When he was not on a buying spree he was on a writing spree. The orgies of work alternated with orgies of pleasure. When he worked, his program was dinner at 6:00 P.M. bed until 1:00 A.M., work until 8:00 A.M., rest until 9:30 A.M., then a cup of coffee and work again until 4:00 P.M., at which time he might receive visitors. This pace he could keep up for weeks, with alternate periods of eating and fasting binges when he would gain or lose twenty pounds within a short period of time. Only a manic could execute something so grandiose as *La Comédie Humaine*, ninety novels and stories in which two thousand important characters appear and reappear. He was also involved in a project to melt the silver out of the slag heaps of Roman mines in Sardinia.

Occasionally, Balzac would abandon his schedule of work to pursue Mme. Evelina Hanska all over Europe. For two years before he died he lived with Mme. Hanska on her estate in the Ukraine. He married her in March 1850, brought her back to Paris in May, and died in August in a state of manic exhaustion at the age of fifty-one.

Another artist with manic-depressive cycles, although with medical complications, was Vincent Van Gogh. Van Gogh reported "furies of painting" when he would not eat or sleep for days on end. His paintings were produced in cycles. These bouts of creativity were exciting and rewarding when the high did not go too far. Van Gogh's difficulty was complicated by the fact that not only did his depressions paralyze him, but his manic state often gave way to severe paranoid rages that prevented him from working. Van Gogh had manic attacks that required hospitalization in 1888, 1889, and 1890. Interspersed among these hospitalizations he had periods of lucidity when others took him to be perfectly sane—the well-known, normal interval phases of the manic-depressive cycle. Depressions usually followed Van Gogh's violent manic attacks. Around 1888 he experienced a productive hypomania, and after completing some two hundred paintings within a very short time, he had a disagreement with Gauguin, who wanted him to run off to the

South Seas. It was then that Van Gogh attacked Gauguin with a razor, and that was followed by the famous episode in which he cut off his own ear. His second hospitalization was at St. Rémy for a violent attack of paranoid mania. He finished another 150 paintings thereafter, but all of his most important works in later life were painted between paranoid attacks when he was completely in charge of himself. His third hospitalization was for attacking his friend Dr. Gachet with a revolver. Two days later he shot himself.

Perhaps the best-known modern manic-depressive writer is Ernest Hemingway, whose adventures during his highs and lows made national headlines. His career illustrates the benefits and pitfalls of the creative manic-depressive. Hemingway's constitution was such that his abundant energy made it excruciating for him to stay still. When he was not writing, he was fighting, or deep-sea fishing, or hunting—doing anything so long as it involved movement. Hemingway's terrifically active periods alternated with his depressions. Whatever he did, he did violently. When he was depressed, self-doubt would overcome him. Hemingway's heavy drinking during most of his adult life might be considered his own form of self-treatment. For a period of forty-two days, while he was a correspondent in the Second World War, he slept only two and a half hours a night.

Hemingway's first serious depression after the First World War, came when a woman rejected him, and he then broke off all close ties, including with his family. In 1925 he worked furiously on *A Farewell to Arms*. Beginning in 1926 he fell into a depression that lasted for nineteen months. Later he wrote Scott Fitzgerald, "I am no longer in the bumping-off stage." But what he called his "black-ass days" increased in frequency after the Second World War. Hemingway had a sense of mission or a sense of himself as the hero. In his manic periods he would become convinced that he was immortal. The number of his injuries sustained in various plane crashes, automobile collisions, and fist-fights are legion. He was extremely disciplined as a writer and could work from dawn to noon or 2:00 P.M., then go out fishing or hunting and still be ready to go at two the next morning, when everyone else was too exhausted to move. Toward the end of his life his rages and elated spirits were always likely to cost bystanders their front teeth. In 1960 he was hospitalized. This must have been most difficult to accomplish since he had always hated psychiatrists. He is known to have had three courses of electroshock treatment later at the Mayo Clinic. He became paranoid toward the end and thought that the Internal Revenue Service was out to get him. According to his brother's biography, he killed himself because his body, always important to him, was falling apart. The likelihood is, however, that he was also drinking and in another serious depression as well. His brother described him as a consummately impulsive individual all of his life, who talked constantly and was without inhibition. Like Van Gogh, he became violent with others, and finally with himself. Hemingway's mood disorder was complicated by the fact that he styled himself "the American male hero," and tried to live up to this self-imposed image. His father had also committed suicide.

It is curious that manic grandiosity, when associated with people like Hemingway, Theodore Roosevelt, or Churchill, is grandiosity with a basis in fact. They *are* the biggest, bravest, and most powerful men in the world. For these few a delusion of grandeur coincides with the actual state of things; and if it does so, is it really a delusion? Psychiatry fails to provide the answer, since there is no psychiatric label for delusional grandiosity that grows into reality.

The cycle of rest and creation of the artist resembles that of manic depression, and manic depression my occur more frequently in creative people. Being a manic-depressive, however, does not make one a great artist, although every manic, when in a high, feels inspired. Mild elation or hypomania can give the needed extra boost to creative people, although it certainly isn't sufficient in itself to make the ordinary man creative. Creativity is probably a delicate special balance of talent, discipline, and inherited chemical energy. It flourishes when combined with the right enviromental conditions. Manic elation, then, is not creativity. But in small doses it certainly helps by sustaining the great effort that is usually required to perfect something really innovative. There is a fine and at times invisible line between mania and creativity.

When an artist comes for help and is diagnosed as manic-depressive, with true psychotic ups and downs associated with his art, then what? Since mood and energy are so bound up in creativity, where and how does the psychiatrist draw the line as to when to treat and when not to treat? When the artist is about to kill himself? When his family interferes because they can't tolerate it any longer? When he himself asks for help? Does the physician who treats the artist and decides to subdue the highs and lows subdue the creativity as well? This is what my highly creative patients demand to know. The possibility that the psychiatrist may interfere with the creative gift is the principal reason that artists are suspicious about most psychiatrists. Most artists fear that psychiatric treatment will deprive them of their talent, either by the "talking cure" or by a type of pill that will turn them into contented, well-adjusted, and unproductive people. The antipathy between the artist and the psychiatrist is stronger than that between the nonartist and the psychiatrist, since the artist, like the psychiatrist, is a specialist in human emotions. He is a highly independent person whose stock-in-trade is also the psyche and who is used to handling it by himself and in his own way. The creative artist with disabling moodswings would seem to have the choice of suffering a great deal or seeking help. If he decides on the latter, what are his options?

Traditional options for the emotionally disturbed artist have been psychotherapy and psychoanalysis, and the controversy has long been waged over whether psychoanalysis "adjusts" the creative individual out of his creativity or frees him from his neurosis so that his creativity is enhanced. With respect to neurotic conflict, Dr. Lawrence Kubie says neurosis only hinders creative output, and that removal of the neurotic conflict through psychotherapy or analysis constitutes the principal scientific approach to managing neurosis in creative individuals. The conflict that has arisen, however, is that if the creative person who is neurotic is treated for his neurosis, will his creativity really increase, as Kubie says it will, or will it decrease, or remain unaffected? If he is made into a well-adjusted person, is society robbed of the benefits of his illness and his creativity?

For individuals truly creative to begin with, I have found that freeing up the neurotic conflict by whatever means that works—psychoanalysis, psychotherapy, or drugs—enhances the creative spark as well. I believe that creativity, if it is there to begin with, is much too strong to be affected adversely by these treatments. Psychoanalysis or psychotherapy does not actually dry up artistic creativity and in some instances it probably helps. It should be noted that many creative people do not seek help until their gifts have already been severely impaired.

But what are the effects of the mood-changing drugs on creativity? In my experience, they restore it when it has been impaired by abnormal moodswings of psychotic elation or immobilizing depression. An unusual story of a creative patient may tell us something about drugs and creativity when scientific studies are lacking.

Late one evening, around eleven o'clock, I received a strange phone call from officials at O'Hare International Airport in Chicago. I was told that a Boeing 747 bound from New York to San Francisco was about to make an unscheduled landing because of one passenger, a middle-aged gentleman. He had not tried to hijack the plane, the security officer assured me. Nor had the disturbance reached a point of real violence. However, he had been walking up and down the aisles of the plane in a state of great excitement and elation, trying to hold an evangelical prayer meeting. Finally, it had been necessary to restrain him forcibly with the aid of several passengers, who were probably quite content with the theological doctrines they already held.

The man had given the officials my name and my unlisted telephone number in New York, which was rather unusual, since I had never met him. I soon recognized, however, that this was the same patient who was supposed to have had an appointment with me earlier that afternoon but had not appeared. His wife had flown him over from England for a consultation. Because of his state of manic elation that had been building up dangerously over the past months, she had contacted me previously by letter, warning me of the difficulty she might have in bringing him to my office. Later I learned that at the last moment before our appointment the patient had eluded his wife, saying he was going down to the lobby of their hotel for a paper. Instead, he had taken a cab to Kennedy Airport and boarded a plane for the West Coast. It was now depositing him in Chicago, to the great relief of the other passengers.

The O'Hare police captain asked me several questions, which were difficult to answer. Fortunately a report had arrived two days earlier from a hospital in London, and I had had the opportunity to read it.

"Is this man dangerous, Doctor?" the police captain asked. "Should he be brought to the local precinct for booking or is he sick enough to be taken to a mental hospital?"

I paused before I answered these questions and recalled the contents of the hospital report. Previously the patient had been hospitalized for two manic episodes and a suicidal depression. I advised the officer to take him to the nearest psychiatric hospital, where he could undergo a complete medical and psychiatric examination. "Certainly he ought to be hospitalized voluntarily tonight and evaluated," I said. "If he is a danger to himself or others and refuses, he should be examined by two physicians with the possibility of commitment." I assured the police officer that I would get in touch with the patient's wife in her New York hotel, since she had not yet called me. According to his case history he had outwitted many doctors in the past, and I felt that once again I was in for a full night of playing the "manic game," which would mean long-distance telephone treatment, talking to police officers, hospital psychiatrists, the patient's wife, and probably the patient himself.

I retrieved his history from my files that same night. I read that the patient, in his late sixties, was a well-known and extremely gifted modern painter. In his early school years he had been a remarkable student and had shown a gift for watercolor and oils. Later he had studied art in Paris and married an English girl he had met there. Eventually they had settled in London.

Ten years later, when he was thirty-four years old, he had persuaded his wife and only son to accompany him to Honolulu, where, he assured them, he would be considered famous. He felt he would be able to sell his paintings at many times the prices he could get in London. According to his wife he had been in an accelerated state, but at that time the family had left unsuspecting, believing with the patient in their imminent good fortune. When they arrived they found almost no one from the art world that he was supposed to know. There were no connections for sales and deals in Hawaii that he had anticipated. Settling down, the patient began to behave more peculiarly than ever. After enduring several months of the patient's exhilaration, overactivity, weight loss, constant talking, and unbelievably little sleep, the young wife and child began to fear for his sanity. None of his plans materialized. After five months in the Pacific, with finances growing thin, the patient's overactivity subsided and he fell into a depression. During that period he refused to move, paint, or leave the house. He lost twenty pounds, became utterly dependent on his wife, and insisted on seeing none of the friends he had accumulated in his manic state. His despondency became so severe that several doctors came to the house and advised psychiatric hospitalization. He quickly agreed and received twelve electroshock treatments, since the psychiatrist was not familiar with the use of antidepressant medications. The shock therapy temporarily relieved his depressed state. Soon afterward he began to paint again and to sell his work modestly. Recognition began to come from galleries and critics in the Far East. Several reviews acclaimed his work as exceptionally brilliant.

This was the beginning of the lifelong career of his mood-swing. While still in Honolulu, he once again became severely depressed, requiring electroshock treatments. Four years later he returned to London in a high. In this manic state he spent his carefully accumulated lifetime savings, took on several mistresses, divorced his wife, gave away paintings, and gambled. He began to be obsessed by religion and mysticism, and felt he could communicate with the universe through his paintings. When this manic period subsided and he surveyed the wreckage of his life, an eight-month interval of normal mood followed, after which he again switched into a profound depression. During this normal phase he recognized that paintings accomplished during the psychotic high were not as good as he had thought them to be.

During this rebound normal period, he met and married his second wife, who said that at the time he was enthusiastic and irresistibly charming but not in any sense abnormal mentally.

Despite the fact that he was now beginning to achieve international renown for his canvases, he began to feel plagued with frequent and severe suicidal depressions. During these periods he withdrew, refused to paint, lost weight, and slept sixteen hours out of twenty-four. He said that he no longer wanted to live. On one occasion his wife found him walking naked in the middle of the night, about to take a bottle of sleeping pills. This depression lifted spontaneously after six months.

Once again, his wife persuaded him to see a doctor, and he was treated with psychic energizers. He complained that he was being straitjacketed and refused to take any more. He remained despondent throughout the summer and fall and could not work. When winter approached, he agreed to try antidepressants again. When his blood pressure was monitored by his psychiatrist it was found to be very low, since the antidepressant dosage had been raised by the patient without consulting the doctor. He soon developed the idea that the doctor was trying to kill him with drugs, and he refused to take further treatment.

Following his depressed periods he felt normally productive and then mildly elated. Gradually and inevitably these productive periods merged into episodes of manic excitement, when he became so high that the form and content of his oils appeared confused and unintelligible. During these highs he was quarrelsome and restless, constantly picking fights with art dealers and moving furniture and family about. He took advice from no one. He talked constantly, slept hardly at all, and entered a state of ecstasy that was a trial for everyone around him. He wrote insulting poems and letters to old friends and even people he did not know. Then he would become overly sentimental and call friends out of the past. He spent all day on the telephone with them. He accused his wife of trying to lock him up and refused to see a psychiatrist, fearing that he would take his high away. He courted dangerous situations constantly during his highs, and he frightened most of those around him. On several occasions he had delusions that he was God. This was the manic psychosis that was diagnosed after forceful removal from the 747 and hospitalization in the Chicago clinic.

During his hospital stay in Chicago he responded well to his first trial with lithium, and his blood lithium reached a satisfactory level within two weeks. His sleep improved and his manic high subsided within the first two weeks. During the next two weeks his excitability began to increase once again, while doctors noted that his blood lithium had mysteriously dropped.

An astute nurse discovered that he had thrown his pills down the toilet. Once his lithium level was brought up to its therapeutic range a second time, his high again subsided and he was discharged, after he gave me his firm promise that he would keep taking lithium and be properly monitored by me.

After returning to New York to see me, he indicated that he was anxious to continue with lithium treatment. He was fearful, however, that it might interfere with his creativity. He told me that during his mild highs, which generally lasted two to four months, he was extremely productive and painted dozens of canvases. Some critics had remarked that these paintings were different and must have come from different "periods of inspiration." They were superior to the fragmented paintings that came during frankly manic, psychotic states.

My patient admitted to me that when his mild highs became too great and expansive, he could not paint well since he was restless and easily distracted. He would think he had done something original only to discover later that his "inspiration" was ridiculous. His political and religious theories suffered from the same lack of critical perspective during his psychotic highs. He would conceive them in a flash of enthusiasm only to discover later that they were absurd.

The patient and I agreed that he would continue on lithium in England, with the understanding that he would keep me posted. I referred him to a London psychiatrist for monthly blood lithium monitoring, and he returned home.

Because this patient was a creative artist, I was most interested in his own self-evaluation on and off lithium. He told me by letter that lithium removed the anguish that he used to feel just under the surface when he was taking tranquilizers and sleeping medications, during high or low mood states. He described his manic states in retrospect: "Basically I must draw this conclusion: In a manic phase one becomes infinitely more virtuous, pure in spirit, and consequently stronger in one's opinions and convictions. All of that is most contagious, and it is felt by those around you and makes them tend to follow you as their leader unless you get too high."

He recalled his manic state in the Chicago hospital by letter in the following way:

> While in my manic state in the hospital with several depressed patients surrounding me, patients seemed to improve from their depression, making me feel that a manic patient may be therapeutic for others who are less witty, passive, and in depression themselves.
>
> During a manic phase I feel a strong sense of freedom, of independence, of outspokenness, but a freedom most of all.
>
> I feel no sense of restriction or censorship whatsoever. I am afraid of nothing and no one. During this elated state, when no inhibition is present, I feel I can race a car with my foot on the floorboard, fly a plane, when I have never flown a plane before, and speak languages I hardly know. Above all, as an artist I feel I can write poems and paint paintings that I could never dream of when just my normal self. I don't want others to restrict me during this period of complete and utter freedom. This is the way I feel during an uninhibited manic high. Afterward when I am in the middle or in a low, I know that my judgment has previously been impaired. I know that during the high I was a threat to my own existence and to others around me. Later, when I evaluate my paintings during these periods, I don't

like them even though while working on them I sometimes reached such a point of ecstasy that I felt I could communicate with God.

Next year this artist will have his tenth major international showing, but his exhibition will be something of a first. It will contain paintings finished over the last three years while he has been on lithium carbonate. He has dubbed this his "lithium period."

Moods, energy states, and creativity are thus inextricably linked together. When abnormally low or high moods or periods of energy occur in the creative artist, his creative work will suffer. Should he or should he not go for help? What kind of help should he request? From what kind of psychiatrist? I have tried to answer these questions for artists with disabling major moodswings, who, I believe, should be treated sensibly with antidepressants and lithium stabilization. The evidence is that overall creative output becomes more consistent with lithium and it does not interfere with the quality of the work. Artists with minor highs and disabling lows might consider doing nothing or having only the depressions treated with mild doses of antidepressant drugs. It may be that when symptoms of moodswing are not really debilitating or destructive, lithium and antidepressant drugs are inadvisable.

It is incumbent upon the psychiatrist to evaluate all patients carefully in terms of their lifelong adaptation to a chronic, recurrent mood disorder, especially those with earning potential during mild hypomanic phases. If the high is productive of success and well-being without serious annoyance to anyone, I try to determine whether or not it is therapeutically wise to leave it alone. The depression that is painful and disturbing to everyone, especially the patient, can be treated as a separate entity. Psychiatrists must consider each patient individually to determine whether prophylactic use of lithium carbonate is really in the patient's best interest. Some artists become so accommodated to their mild highs and lows that they consider these episodes as basic facets of their personalities and really want no change in their way of life. These patients should be left alone. Neither lithium nor antidepressants should be given.

F O U R

Wall Street Wizards and the Midas Touch

Manics love to gamble. They love the excitement of it. The stock market, racetrack, roulette wheel, cards, slot machines—whatever the game, the manic enjoys the rush and thrives on the tension, and he finds that this form of quick gratification suits his impatient temperament precisely. He has to wait all week for a paycheck, but only two minutes for a horse race. A manic has schemes to beat the Dow Jones, the dealer, the house, the track, or the numbers. He will manipulate for the sheer joy of manipulating, nonstop for twenty hours a day. He may—in headlong pursuit of success—cheat, lie, and steal without anyone realizing what he is doing. In fact, when he gambles, he gets so caught up in his machinations, so stimulated by the wheeling and dealing, that he turns other people on, catches them up in his fantasies of instant millions and the Midas touch.

When he is winning, the manic gambler feels high. He believes he is making things happen. No wonder other players gather around his table and the room fills with excitement. Here, in the making, is the myth that keeps the gambler going; his run of luck is his positive reinforcement to continue.

The money itself is often secondary. Some gamblers gamble for the thrill of winning, and not necessarily for gain. Money is only a symbol for the gambler, a medium of exchange or a token that assures him his high is working for him. Most gamblers will say they gamble because they want the money, or they like the fun of it. In their heart of hearts, they like the high feeling they associate with the thought, I've got to go down and beat this game and master it. Often they will try until their dying day.

Most manics also love power. When every life situation becomes a game of skill—and of course the gambler tends to dismiss chance—the gamester is forever wheeling and dealing to find the perfect system, the perfect scheme to make a killing. In his actual gambling the manic gambler may have an advantage, just as in life he may have an advantage over others who are not so full of drive. His enthusiasm and confidence tend to weight games of skill in his favor. If he is playing poker and he is on top of the world, chances are he can bluff the rest of the table with a pair of tens and they will buy it. He throws himself energetically into whatever he is playing and figures out angles well in advance. He isn't just betting, as the rest of the world is; he is making an informed guess.

Compulsive gambling seems to be more frequent among the relatives of manic-depressives than in the general population. Unable to stop once they start playing, compulsive gamblers often wreck their finances, marriages, and careers. They play all night; and they play all weekend. George Winokur, professor of psychiatry at the University of Iowa, feels that this suggests a genetic link between manic depression and gambling. It may be similar to the link between manic depression and alcoholism, which compulsive gambling with its binges resembles.

The compulsive gambler, although less interested in money than in satisfying his compulsion, is basically different from the professional gambler. The professional gambler—for instance, a croupier or dealer—is cool and deliberate. He is calculating rather than compulsive. He doesn't go on gambling binges. Since it is his means of making a living, he is usually business-like about it, and he tends to look down on the compulsive gambler, who is unable to control himself.

Not all gamblers are manic-depressive, and not all manic-depressives gamble. When those who gamble are up too high, they go too far and overextend themselves, err in their judgment, and go into serious debt. When this happens, they may switch into deep depressions and suffer terrible moods of remorse, self-hatred, and self-recrimination. It is difficult to tell how much the financial loss itself contributes to the switch into the depressed phase. The stress of the loss may precipitate some depression that follows the high. But poor judgment during the elated mood is usually the cause of the extravagance; and the depression, with or without financial reversal, inevitably follows.

In times of despair the manic-depressive gambler thinks he has thrown his family into bankruptcy, when in fact he may have lost only two hundred dollars in a Saturday-night pinochle game. The depressed businessman may have an unshakable conviction that he teeters on the brink of bankruptcy when business is actually pretty good. These near-psychotic delusions are simply the opposite side of the coin of the grandiose delusions of the manic state. Delusions of poverty among the depressed and manic depressed are in fact quite common. Typically, the depressive will not spend. He wants to keep everything, since he is afraid he is going bankrupt; he pulls everything in toward himself and hugs it desperately.

The life-style of the manic-depressive who is in a high tends to be a glorious scattering of money. He looks for new and interesting ways to spend it. He goes on buying sprees for the sheer joy of spending. At times he is on the brink of being out of touch with reality. The extreme example is the man who threw fifty thousand dollars out of his window in mid-Manhattan and called his bank to send over more. This is rare, but it has happened. At the other end of the spectrum—and it could be the same high-flying philanthropist when he is down—is the depressed character who tries to slit his wrists when he thinks of his extravagance and is overwhelmed by self-disgust for even normal spending, as if it were some unspeakable perversion. In this state he wishes for a well-aimed bolt from the blue to strike him dead. Men like this have blown their brains out because of real or imaginary financial catastrophes.

In the middle is the mild manic, or hypomanic. He is not out of touch with reality. In fact, he is more in touch with what is going on than most others. The hypomanic tends to develop a sixth sense about gambling, because he may be open to grasping the thousands of small controlling factors that can win or lose a game. He is hypercompetent and jumps into every situation that he wants to control. For him knowledge is power. He is hyperperceptive as well as hyperaggressive and hyperactive. He is tuned in to the games going on behind the games. He has a tremendous advantage, as long as he doesn't overextend and start showing poor judgment by going too high. He will be a gambler par excellence if he can maintain that mild high mood; and he might also, if he desires, be an extraordinary businessman.

But when does betting on the market or on the horses go beyond the norm, and enter the realm of pathological gambling? The question is a critical one, since the estimated number of pathological gamblers in the United States is one to two million and growing yearly. The American Psychiatric Association's *Diagnostic and Statistical Manual of Mental Disorders III Revised* (also known as the *DSM III-R*) describes the pathological gambler as having at least four of the following symptoms:

1. Frequent preoccupation with gambling or with obtaining money to gamble.
2. Frequent gambling of larger amounts of money or over a longer period of time than intended.
3. A need to increase the size or frequency of bets to achieve the desired excitement.
4. Restlessness or irritability if unable to gamble.
5. Repeated loss of money by gambling and returning another day to win back losses ("chasing").
6. Repeated efforts to reduce or stop gambling.
7. Frequent gambling when expected to meet social or occupational obligations.
8. Sacrifice of some important social, occupational, or recreational activity in order to gamble.
9. Continuation of gambling despite inability to pay mounting debts, or despite other significant social, occupational, or legal problems that the person knows to be exacerbated by gambling.

When I first interview a patient with a possible gambling problem, I ask: How often do you play cards for money? Bet on sports? Use a bookie? Play the stock market? Use slot machines or other gambling devices? What is the highest amount of money you've ever gambled in one day? Did your parents have a problem with their own gambling? Did you ever feel guilty about your gambling, or receive criticism for it? Do you have arguments with friends or family over the way you handle money? Have you ever missed work (or school) because of gambling? Have you borrowed money to gamble, and if so, where or from whom? Have you ever gambled more than you intended to?

The compulsive gambler may partake in card games, stock options on Wall Street or bet on horses, dogs, sports, dice games, bingo, bowling, or pool. A gambling patient usually denies that he or she is a pathological gambler, but the family is quick to diagnose the patient as such, usually after a financial crisis.

In many of these individuals, their pathological gambling is readily apparent, but the underlying depression or manic depression they may be suffering from is often hidden. Frequently there is a history of several threats of or even attempts at suicide, accompanied by drug or alcohol abuse in the patient or his family.

If a psychiatric evaluation shows that a man or woman is a pathological gambler, what treatments are possible? And how good are they? On the whole, psychotherapy and group therapy do not seem to get lasting results, although they have not been fully evaluated with scientifically designed studies. Behavioral modification techniques with aversion or desensitization therapy have been used with mixed results. The group approaches that have been successful are those such as Alcoholics Anonymous and Gamblers Anonymous.

Structured inpatient hospital treatment programs lasting about one month have also been tried for the problem of pathological gambling. These programs are modeled after established programs for substance abuse and alcoholism. The results have been encouraging. Dr. Julian Tabor at the Veterans Administration

Medical Center in Cleveland reported that 56 percent of their sixty-six patients said they were still not gambling six months after they were released from the hospital. These patients also participated in Gamblers Anonymous, which was clearly a major factor in helping them to abstain.

In many of my gambling patients, I have found a family history of depression or manic highs. In these patients, I use lithium and/or antidepressant drugs to improve the results of behavioral or group therapy. When moodswings are present in the patient or relatives, the chances of a dramatic improvement are much higher, since the underlying mood disorder can be treated. In the families of manic-depressives, I also often find relatives who suffer from compulsive gambling as well as alcoholism, drug abuse, and suicidal behavior.

In my opinion, therefore, many compulsive gamblers are suffering from treatable moodswings in conjunction with their gambling. The gamblers may think they are depressed because they've lost a large sum of money, or they may think they are elated because they've won, but they are actually going through lows and highs that are independent of whether they've won or lost. Gambling belongs to the genetic spectrum of mood disorders, which means that it is related biochemically and genetically to other mood disorders, such as depression and alcoholism. Several large families with gamblers and manic depressives are being studied by our research group and when these studies are completed the genetic relationship should become clearer.

Pathological gamblers do financial damage to both themselves and their families. Many "ordinary" businessmen, however, gamble large sums every day routinely as part of their jobs. If they are good at risk taking they may become phenomenally high-paid entrepreneurs or Wall Street moguls. Institutionalized gambling fuels the erratic ups and downs of the stock market. Alexis de Tocqueville understood correctly 150 years ago that America is a nation of gamblers when he said, "The whole life of an American is passed like a game of chance, a revolutionary crisis, or a battle." Gambling is a fact of American life. And it is a fact of American business.

Most particularly, the analogy has been made between gambling and the backbone of our economy, the stock market. The resemblances are perhaps too obvious to need restating. Richard Ney wrote in *The Wall Street Jungle*, "Some people claim that 'investment advisor'—which is what I am—is just a high-class name for a croupier. I agree. I deal in a big floating crap game, one that is played every week in the richest and most exclusive casino in the world: the New York Stock Exchange."

The stock market is no hallowed, dignified retreat for quiet business; it is a madhouse, and many of the gamblers there are high. It is an elegant, high-stakes version of the casino, and its habitués, like the Las Vegas junketeers who come on weekends from all over the country, feed off one another's moods. Even more than the less respectable forms of gambling, the stock market offers overcharged manic personalities a chance for the battles they crave; it is an arena in which these men and women can unleash their tremendous energy while they enjoy a cleansing type of strife and release. If they could not discharge this energy somewhere, what would they do? They might just as well turn over a million dollars while they are at it.

I don't mean that all involved in the stock market are gamblers; they are not. One has to distinguish between the long-term investor—hardly ever buying or selling, but depending upon eventual growth or dividends to give him income—and the speculator. The former simply minimizes the gambling aspects by becoming a sleeping partner in a running business. But if someone constantly moves in and out of the market looking for a quick profit, then he is just as much a gambler as the person who bets on the horse race.

One manic broker patient of mine is so enamored of the investment battle that he is up every morning raring to go at five o'clock, even though the exchange does not open until ten. Before dawn one morning during an "up" market, his wife discovered him in their Jacuzzi whirlpool bath turned up full blast, carrying on with other early birds over the telephone. There he sat shouting, planning deals as the noisy water swirled around. Most of his colleagues were probably still asleep. "I do this every morning," he explained. "It warms me up for the fights later in the day."

On Wall Street the mood may be manic, normal, or depressed. Certainly the analogy between high and low moods in humans and the market is something to think about, since the mood of the country certainly affects the market. Perhaps because the stock exchange operates on "panic and greed," as one cynical investor put it, the market is an extraordinarily moody place. However, the relationship between the moods of investors and the moods of the market is not clear.

If high finance is anywhere open to suggestion, it is in the area of conglomerates and takeovers. Never before has so much wealth been spun out of so little. In fact, the conglomerates might be called tributes to the power of suggestion. They are vast empires built out of wheeling and dealing and wishing. In a sense the conglomerate can be said to be the epitome of the "manic art form." It embodies perfectly the manic's love of money and manipulation. It is manic grandiosity institutionalized, and it combines the love of gambling and the buying spree. It specializes in the complex process of acquisition. Indeed, acquisition is the only reason for its existence.

This love of wheeling and dealing for its own sake—above and beyond the need for money—is a classical manic symptom. I have patients who are extraordinarily successful businessmen, brokers, and financiers. When they are too high, they love to pit one topflight law firm against another in long, drawn-out litigations. These manics want to get their way through legal channels if need be. They love to see the fur fly between the senior partners of competing law firms who have often been seated at the same dinner party the night before. They can afford the legal fees of five hundred dollars an hour.

The manic entrepreneur may see himself as a sort of corporate bullfighter, waving a red cape at the old Wall Street brokerage houses and law firms. Like the manic gambler, the manic businessman has an advantage over his competitors if he is not too high. Being hyperenergetic and hyperperceptive, he can create dynasties and empires because he is more alert and has more energy than the rest.

The manic businessman, when he is high, finds out the many details of management and ferrets out hidden government information. He is first in the office, bright-eyed at seven o'clock, and stays late every night after everyone else has gone home. James Ling, "the Merger King," used to work out at his gym every morning until the rest of the world got up. Harold Geneen, a former chairman of ITT Corporation, not only used to drive his people all day in marathon meetings, but, when they gratefully collapsed at 10:00 or 11:00 P.M., he would return to his office and start whirling his way through the ten overstuffed suitcases that served him as briefcases.

Manic businessmen have an almost pathological fear of vacations. Why shouldn't they? Hyperactive, they find enforced leisure a form of torture. The late Charles Bluhdorn, a former chairman of Gulf and Western Industries, was a case in point. "My wife thinks I'm nuts because I don't know how to relax," he complained, "but when you are building something you are spinning a web and you tend to become a prisoner in the web." He didn't want to get one inch away from that web. He had an almost mortal fear of vacations. Once, when his wife dragged him to Mexico, he raced back the next day because the phone service to the States was so bad. Another year, in St. Moritz, he slipped on the snow and cut his leg before he even got his skis on. Retreating to a round of telephone calls, he developed laryngitis. "It was a pitiful situation," one friend sighed. "Charlie Bluhdorn, his leg in a cast, unable to talk."

Manic businessmen frequently have a good case of telephonitis; they don't feel right unless they have six or seven overseas calls coming in, and as soon as they come in the office they will grab any telephone anywhere and start dialing. Some of my patients have come into my office and grabbed the phone off the desk to ask for the overseas operator, or to dial Chicago or Los Angeles. They can't help themselves. The wife of William Zeckendorf, Sr., was reported to have said, "From the time he gets up in the morning he's on the telephone—while he's dressing, at breakfast, in the car, in the office, as soon as he gets home, right up until he goes to bed."

Telephoning is only part of the manic's usual need to talk. Clinically, this results from his "flight of ideas and distractibility," and is called "a rush of speech" in its extreme form; it's an inability to stop talking. But if a person is only hypomanic, his constant chatter may charm a captive audience. How else could he swing those fabulous deals on the strength of his sales pitch alone?

It would be a mistake to think that all successful hustlers and multimillionaires are manic; they're not. Some are simply highly ambitious, compulsive, possibly neurotically driven men, who tend to kill themselves working. Admittedly, some are just plain normal, although being called this would probably insult many. However, chances are that the people who thrive on their overwork are at least slightly high. And if they handle your personal portfolio, they can either make or break you.

Golf for most manics is too slow, although they may fake liking the game to clinch a business deal. They can't stand creeping around at someone else's pace, putting a little ball in a hole for four hours. They would much prefer belting out a few good sets of tennis, trapshooting, or even bashing a punching bag. And, of course, these men are twitchy; they're probably moving metabolically about a third or a half again as fast as most of the people around them. Just as a child with his higher rate of metabolism feels restless when he is told he must sit still, so the manic gets impatient faster than the rest of us with idleness. Time rushes for the manic; there is never enough of it as long as he is busy. When I have asked manic-depressive patients what their greatest need in life is, they have usually answered, "More time." Even those manics who appear cool on the surface often race underneath, and it may show up in their passion for strenuous physical sports.

The very successful businessman tends to be single-minded in his acquisitions. He is competitive and compulsive. He would like to do everything himself. Harold Geneen, for instance, did his best to run the billion-dollar ITT empire like a one-man operation. The supersuccessful businessman is probably very extroverted; at least superficially, he is very little given to introspection. He is often, however, a solitary person who lives for his moneymaking as a gambler lives to gamble; he probably substitutes moneymaking for what the rest of the world calls living.

William Zeckendorf moved Denver a half-mile, he used to say proudly. And, despite economic disaster that destroyed his empire, he could tell a reporter, "Why, we're responsible for three billion dollars' worth of construction in North America. And we're still here to tell the story." Of course, Zeckendorf went overboard with projects like the one to buy Yonkers Raceway and convert it into a year-round sports arena topped by a 450-foot dome that would make it the largest roofed structure in the world. This project was not completed, but his $75 million Counthouse Square in Denver *was* built.

The manic's energy is invaluable. It can be great for lighting fires under people and getting things started. The drawback is that he doesn't always know where to stop. He often overextends himself only to fall disastrously. Zeckendorf did exactly that. He bogged down financing a real-estate project of mind-boggling dimensions. Ultimately, his refinancing didn't come through.

The difference between success and failure in people like these may come down to whether the manic businessman has the sense to surround himself with the proper cautious advisers or with yes-men. Zeckendorf did not have such advisers; he was pretty much a one-man operation. Charles Bluhdorn, on the other hand, who was generally felt to be "eccentric" on Wall Street was, according to a *Life* reporter, able to "surround himself with brilliant youthful lieutenants, expert in areas where he realizes he is abysmally deficient." In his gusto for making deals, the reporter wrote, Bluhdorn sometimes pushed beyond good sense. "Once during a flight he developed a ravenous urge to buy the airline. He rushed back to New York intent on doing it. 'No, Charlie,' his boys told him, 'the airline's too small and has too much competition.' "

Charlie Bluhdorn was a typical high-powered manic. As a schoolboy in Vienna he was such a hellion that his father sent him away to an English school. He came to New York at sixteen and worked for a cotton-brokerage firm for fifteen dollars a week. He took a sixty-dollar-a-week job for an exporter-importer in a shabby one-room office. When his boss left him in charge while he was in Europe, Bluhdorn took over and was soon selling lard to Brazil, and spaghetti and malt to Italy. He did

$1 million worth of business the first year. When only twenty-one, he went to Washington and talked the secretary of commerce out of restricting his export quota for malt. At twenty-three he went into business for himself and was soon importing $1 million worth of coffee a day. He began speculating in commodities, sometimes winning and sometimes losing. Later he went into automotive replacement parts, bought Michigan Bumper, merged it into a Houston auto-parts firm, and renamed the company Gulf + Western. He subsequently began selling $100 million worth of auto parts annually. With this as a base he began to buy companies in other fields—hundreds of them. When buying New Jersey Zinc, for instance, he was able within a few days to negotiate a loan for $83 million—one of the largest ever, and more than three times Gulf + Western's net worth at that point. His splashiest buy was Paramount Pictures. He financed *The Godfather* and *The Godfather Part II*.

In a magazine article on him, an associate was quoted as saying:

> Bluhdorn never walks, but runs. He is like a racehorse. Put him on the track and he runs a great race. But somebody has to lead him back to the stable, cover him with a blanket, and give him some food.
>
> He is unstoppable, and gets violent verbally frequently. Wall Street calls him "the Mad Austrian," because of his highs. The Street distrusts him, perhaps sensing intuitively . . . that his moods are unpredictable.

"What if he starts thinking he's so smart he doesn't have to listen to anybody, and really goes off the deep end?" asked one stock analyst. "People on the Street are still wary of him, and the minute he falters there'll be the biggest pile of stock being dumped you've ever seen."

A recent giant of Wall Street, Ivan "the Terrible" Boesky, is known to have had the kind of high energy that many tycoons crave. Hard-driven, used to working eighteen- and twenty-hour days as a matter of course, Boesky during his Wall Street days slept about two hours each night, rising at four-thirty each morning. He used a three-hundred-line telephone console to keep his huge information network operating, and carry out grandiose schemes in which he gambled millions of dollars. Boesky had what might be called the "manic advantage" of quick intuition, unbounded energy, and grandiosity. But there is often another side to this energy. It may go too far. Not only did Boesky squander millions of dollars of other people's money in bad arbitrage deals, he broke laws on several occasions.

How much of our national economy is being controlled by high-powered men with manic blinders? Are many of our well-known and much publicized media giants, newspaper magnates, and real estate tycoons in fact both blessed, and cursed with some form of manic depression? In the spotlight during 1988 was John Mulheren, Jr., an extremely aggressive and successful risk arbitrager who was reported to be a manic-depressive whose lithium treatment was interrupted. Two weeks after he stopped taking it, he threatened to assassinate his onetime associate, Ivan Boesky, and was arrested with a weapon. Mulheren's arrest illustrates forcefully the tragic, destructive side of manic depression.

Though being manic can make a man very successful in his field, usually it also means he is manic-*depressive*. There comes a time to pay the piper for the marvelous high.

Almost every manic will sometime, somehow, eventually crash. Then, if he is a gambler, he will probably just stay away from the casinos until he goes up again. That could be why most of the people who are attracted to places like Las Vegas tend to go there during a high. Anyone in the depressed phase of a moodswing has no taste for the bright lights, noisy crowds, chance, and excitement.

If he is a businessman, he is in worse trouble. He will go downhill in his depression the same way, but he won't be able to drop everything and stop going to work. His personality will change in the same serious way. His cheer and talkativeness will evaporate; he will brood on loss, real or imaginary. He may become deluded, feeling that he has no money or that he is going to lose his money, so he draws it in and he won't spend. It may hurt him to buy pencils and stamps. He will avoid risks, even the ordinary risks necessary to his business. Every business is by definition a risk, except, perhaps, the corporate monster that obviates all risk by cornering the market, the suppliers, the jobbers, the raw materials, the competition, and the minds of the consumers.

In a small business, when the boss gets depressed, if he is prone to moodswings, he becomes overcautious, irritable, and stingy. His singular lack of largesse may even be fatal for the company that he may have built up effortlessly in a more expansive mood.

A highly reputable and profitable new computer firm that specializes in software provides consultants for other firms that need them. Essentially it is a one-man operation headed by a patient of mine; he is usually a ball of fire, reviews and clears all contracts for services coming and going. Normally he has an uncanny ability to submit bids that the market will bear but which will yield a profit to his firm. So his profits in this cutthroat business really depend on the accuracy of his judgment. Since he is mildly manic-depressive, when he feels low he feels stingy. Even his most devoted subordinates shake their heads when he handles bids in this condition. They try to reason with him during these times, but even so, he loses customers and consultants and contracts. The staff says his bids run up and down in cycles so regularly every three to six months that they are almost getting used to it, and they try to stagger their contracts accordingly.

How often do we read in the papers about fabulously successful businessmen who have suddenly, for no apparent reason, taken their lives? "He had been very depressed," says the brother of an executive who shot himself. Such items are reported almost monthly. Why should an extremely rich man kill himself? He made millions. He served on the board of four major corporations. He had a town house in the city and a country place on Long Island.

Psychoanalysis has made it fashionable to interpret such luxury suicides by saying that men driven horribly to succeed destroy themselves because of a neurotic fear of success or a neurotic depression that results from the success and its symbolic meaning. They are said to have been compensating and to have been fired with neurotic ambition. If they don't kill themselves with heart attacks, they try the real thing.

For some this may be true, but how often are suicide and deep depression simply neurotic reactions to success? It is my feeling that if the family histories of these suicidal depressives were fully known, one would frequently find in their family pedigrees many instances of mood disorder. Although it may help certain men rise to the top of the heap, mood disorder may also bring them down and sometimes their relatives with them— down into despair, to the point at which they must simply end their pain. This mood disorder is primarily chemical and genetic in origin, either way. There is no other "primary" reason for it, environmental or otherwise, although major stresses may trip off the genetic vulnerability and biochemical mechanism responsible for the moodswing. Depression, other suicides, and alcoholism are common in such family trees. Naturally, not every fabulously successful corporate executive will try to kill himself or have a brother who does so. But there seems to be a clustering of depression, drug abuse, alcoholism, and moodswing in the family histories of suicides.

Jack Dreyfus, chairman of the Dreyfus Fund, has said that he had a strange form of "electrical" disorder. For years while he was making millions, no one knew he wished he could die and escape his misery.

I was anywhere from a little depressed to quite deeply depressed most of the time. There was an ever-present feeling of fear which varied in intensity during the day, and my mind was preoccupied with pessimistic and frequently angry thoughts. I had minor discomforts, chronic pains in the neck, and mild stomach upset. The happiest part of the day was the times when, with the help of sleeping medication, I was asleep. When I awoke in the morning, I was at my best. Usually around dusk a little depressive cloud would descend on me and my hands and feet would get extremely cold.

The depressive side of moodswing is painful and difficult to control or conceal. It impedes fast action and judgment. It introduces terrible pessimism and self-doubt into situations in which these indulgences can be fatal. The cartoon of the Wall Street banker poised for a dive off his window ledge has been familiar enough since 1929 and 1930. It has enough of a basis in fact, however, to deserve serious attention—and particularly so during actual market recessions. During the thirties there were many suicides when banks and businesses failed. It is not unusual even today for an uncommonly successful businessman to contemplate killing himself when he loses his fortune. But why should he get so depressed over money? one might ask; some men have made fortunes and lost them over and over again. Which came first in a financial suicide? the biological psychiatrist wonders. Was it the chemical moodswing to a deep depression, or was it the actual loss of the fortune? I maintain that the high often prompts a reckless loss of money; and suicide is a consequence of what is now called *double depression:* the combination of the depression, which would have occurred anyway, and the reaction to the loss.

Losing a great deal of money is difficult for most people—but suicide? It hardly seems worth it. Are the feelings of worthlessness and hopelessness and despair independent of the financial disaster? A depressed millionaire who feels he is bankrupt and has nothing to live for may be many times more liquid than most of us.

Whether depression is chemical in origin, reactive, or a combination depends on the individual and his personal situation. Reactive depression is a normal response to a loss; it usually goes away. Its seriousness is in proportion to the impact of the loss and it rarely leads to suicide. Unipolar recurrent depression and bipolar manic depression do not behave this way. Patients with these depressions also seek reasons. Failing to understand that there may be a physical basis, they search for an external cause and find convenient reasons. The suicide risk in people with chemical depressions of this nature is the highest of any psychiatric state.

When the papers reported, 60-STORY PLUNGE KILLS CHAIRMAN OF BILLION-DOLLAR CONGLOMERATE, associates said he had been working sixteen to eighteen hours a day for the last several weeks, becoming "severely depressed because of the tension." I feel that he suffered from a devastating failure in his brain's biochemistry.

FIVE

Biological Clocks: Seasonal and Premenstrual Depressions

In 1960 I began treating a forty-eight-hour manic-depressive businessman. For twenty-four hours he would be elated, driving, up all night, talking incessantly, and making business deals on the telephone. During the next twenty-four-hour period he would switch into a depressed, pessimistic mood and barely be able to make it to the office. At work he would hide from his peers, refuse to take telephone calls, and shy away from all responsibility. These moodswings continued regularly for years, documented by his faithful secretary. She had virtually devoted her life to protecting this volatile man from the disasters of his rapid mood changes. During his up days he would turn the whole office on and stimulate client accounts. During down days he would lose business and puzzle everyone by his withdrawn behavior. His forty-eight-hour cycle became so predictable that his secretary charted his highs and lows, scheduling his calendar for new contacts and tough business deals on his good days, and shielding him from any demands when he was down. Because she protected him during depressed days and encouraged him on euphoric days, he had been able to achieve startling success in business. Clients saw him only in his gregarious, persuasive mood.

Manics, like the forty-eight-hour businessman, typically think and act with such ingenuity they make one smile and want to go along. They persuade the innocent who want to believe, and they often accomplish their goals. Yet manic enthusiasm often leaves one with the feeling that the means to the end are too superficial, if not bizarre, and that something in the scheme is not quite right.

During one of his up days it occurred to the forty-eight-hour businessman that he could use antidepressant drugs to get through his depressed days. By stabilizing his moods he thought he could enhance his business productivity. He therefore arranged a luncheon at his Wall Street club, inviting several key members of the pharmaceutical industry. At the meeting he proposed drug control of mood cycles in business leaders. He argued that this might lead indirectly to drug control of business cycles and the market. His goal, he explained, was to make "leaders out of laggards," using a nonaddictive, safe, antidepressant treatment to pick up business leaders' moods on depressed days. Quixotic as it was, his program somehow persuaded one of his guests— the president of a pharmaceutical company who was rather manic himself—to let him have some ten thousand free samples of a well-known antidepressant drug for a "controlled test." Armed with his samples, he kept them all and medicated himself. He took the pills on his depressed days, and every other twenty-four hours he swung into his usual manic high. Unfortunately, what his scheme did not take into account was that most antidepressants not only alleviate the depressive phase of a mood cycle, but they also accentuate the high. In his case the depression was eliminated, but the highs became so severe that they reached the point of manic psychosis. Not only was obtaining antidepressants by pull rather than by a doctor's prescription clearly illegal, but using them without medical supervision was dangerous.

It was at this point that I saw the patient for the first time. His up-down, self-medication regimen had made him a borderline manic-psychotic. He did not come willingly. Most manics don't. He was forced into seeing me by relatives who threatened him with hospitalization if he continued to refuse treatment.

When I entered my office he was sitting at my desk making long-distance telephone calls. He apologized for taking this liberty and sat down to tell his story in the third person, as if he were talking about someone else. He was charming and spoke rapidly. He addressed me by my first name. He obviously liked the idea of running his own "pill show" and controlling his own mood destiny. He was pleased that the lows in his forty-eight-hour cycle had been moderated by his do-it-yourself medication program. He was even happier that his highs had become higher. He saw no need to consult me as a patient, but clearly wanted me as a friend instead. He thought he was doing extremely well and was only there to appease his relatives. He invited my wife and me to dinner, saying he had several good stock tips for me, which I politely declined.

Attempts like this to buy off the doctor are common among manic patients, who try to avoid the patient role whenever possible. It was only because of insistence on my part and on the part of his family that he agreed to take lithium.

In the course of his lithium treatment the forty-eight-hour cycle diminished. However, he remained in his enthusiastic state. He was what we call a rapid cycler (four or more episodes a year), and rapid cyclers do not respond to lithium in one or two weeks as other manic-depressive patients do. About 50 percent of rapid-cycling patients require two to twelve months to stabilize on lithium alone. Another 25 percent require the addition of thyroid, a monoamine oxidase inhibitor, or carbazamine, or some other form of step-up treatment in the psychiatrist's last-ditch bag of tricks. The remaining 25 percent are simply tough and refractory to almost anything and these patients may participate in one of our new drug trials (See chapter 15).

Before my forty-eight-hour businessman's cycles had dampened, he brought into my office a prospective bride for my approval. Then fifty-two, he had divorced four previous wives because of "incompatibility." In fact, they were unable to cope with his highs. This time he insisted on getting approval from all fifteen members of his family *and* his psychiatrist. In soliciting everyone's approval he was flattering them, at the same time showing everyone he was capable of "good judgment."

Although few people are forty-eight-hour cyclers like the businessman, all of us recognize that some days go well and others go badly. Moods and behavior change from day to day and week to week—and often in longer cycles, from month to month or yearly. Traditionally, such moodswings are explained as the direct result of pleasant or adverse circumstances in daily life. No doubt external events do affect our moods. However, few of us stop to consider that it is sometimes the other way around. In the high of a chemical moodswing, we have a productive period when everything seems to go right. In low phases we have negative attitudes and adverse results. This is a reality of moodswing that personnel-office managers and industrial psychologists ought to consider.

If we stopped to chart our moods, would we see any regularity in our ups and downs? We all know people with biological mood clocks that help them function best as "day people," while other people are nocturnal, alert at night, and slow and sluggish during the day. There are many chemical clocks in man only now being discovered.

The twenty-four-hour cycle seems to be an important organizing principle in our physiology, since our body temperature, blood pressure, respiration, pulse, blood sugar, hemoglobin levels, and amino acid levels change daily. Strength and weakness vary with the time of day. According to tests administered to jet pilots, mental performances are at their peak between 2:00 and 4:00 P.M., when reaction time is quickest and psychomotor coordination is best. The poorest performances are between 2:00 and 4:00 A.M.

The alteration of sleep and waking usually sets the pace for increases and decreases in metabolism, for bowel function, for kidney activity, for body temperature, and for many other interwoven functions. If we shift our hours of sleep, these functions shift as well. Unfortunately, since the parts of the body shift at different speeds, the heart, kidneys, liver, and adrenal glands may adjust at different rates. This lack of synchronization causes the malaise of jet lag. Evidence that a twenty-four-hour clock exists in all of us is most apparent when we experience this phenomenon. The sleep-wake cycle is especially disrupted in manics who require less sleep, and depressives who are unable to sleep or who sleep excessively.

Daily body rhythms can be affected by drugs, stressful situations, and even excessive noise. Once a mild mood disorder with disturbed rhythms has begun, it tends to be self-perpetuating, since depression and anxiety tend to disrupt twenty-four-hour rhythms further. These conditions are aggravated by an irregular living schedule. In part, the old-fashioned sanatorium rest cure was effective with "nervous" disorders because it put the patient on a regular schedule of sleep, activity, and meals.

Biological clocks can be influenced by external conditions such as weather, the alternation of light and dark, and the length of day. Without environmental cues to time there is a tendency for various body rhythms to become dissociated.

Psychiatric disorders can follow inner clocks that are affected by the environment. Full-moon madness, the source of the word *lunacy,* is one of the earliest confirmations of this. Eskimos, Lapps, and Finns are said to suffer from an annual arctic psychosis, or "winter madness." For a few days some may be clinically insane with hallucinations and paranoid ideas. One explanation is that they may lack calcium, essential for the nervous system, because of the lack of vitamin D caused by insufficient sunshine.

Recent psychiatric research has uncovered another type of seasonal mood disorder, the so-called SAD (seasonal affective disorder). People suffering from it experience seasonal highs and lows, usually winter depression. A middle-aged patient named Ellen has come to my office every February for the last four years complaining that she feels almost suicidally depressed. "I feel sluggish all the time, I can't get out of bed in the morning, and I don't have much interest in my children's goings-on, or even in my husband. It's not like me." But each year as soon as April rolls around with its longer days and more sunlight, she feels like her normal, cheerful self, and has no more depression, until the following winter, when the cycle of low mood begins again.

The vast majority of SAD patients report that their depressive symptoms occur only in the fall and winter. These patients become irritable, oversleep and overeat, usually binging on carbohydrates. A typical biological depressive has moodswings because of faulty body chemistry, but, in contrast to the SAD patient, loses appetite and experiences weight loss.

Dr. Norman Rosenthal, a former student of mine now working at the National Institute for Mental Health, has administered light therapy to more than a hundred SAD patients in the throes of depression. They sit for two to five hours a day in front of special full-spectrum lights that take the place of the rays of the sun and are five times brighter than normal indoor lighting. Rosenthal reports that light treatment relieves depression in about 80 percent of these patients. After two or three days of light treatment the low mood lifts, and thereafter daily exposure to the light is needed to prevent its return. Interestingly, many SAD patients, Rosenthal reports, experience high moods throughout the summer months, sometimes bordering on mania.

Researchers have known for many years that when light strikes the human retina, the pineal gland is stimulated via neural pathways. This stimulation decreases the secretion of melatonin, an important neurohormone. It is possible that melatonin is related to depression in SAD patients, and that light therapy has an antidepressant effect because it alters the amount of melatonin in the nervous system.

Some patients have been reported with reverse SAD: They have summer depressions and hypomania during the fall, winter, and spring. These patients have been treated by manipulating both temperature and light conditions during different seasons of the year.

Most of us are aware that the body's inner clock mechanism is normally affected by many environmental influences. In women the menstrual cycle follows a twenty-eight-day lunar clock. The menstrual cycle is a good example of a normal cycle in which slight imbalances enlarge into many conspicuous symptoms. Probably 60 percent of all women experience some mood change in the cycle, particularly in the four to five days before and during the menses. In the past it was common to suggest that premenstrual symptoms came from resistance to sexual role or from denial of femininity. We now suspect that endocrine imbalances have much more to do with it. These menstrual mood changes may result from disturbances in water and sodium retention, related to abrupt hormonal changes at midcycle.

A small minority of women suffer from premenstrual tension so severe that they become nearly psychotic for a few days each month. Because lithium is thought to act on the cyclical aspects of mood disorders by shifting water and electrolyte (salt) levels, it has been tried for severe premenstrual tension. Early positive results have been obtained with lithium even in stubbornly resistant patients who have not responded previously to antidepressants, estrogen therapy, or electroshock therapy.

Ann, a twenty-eight-year-old married woman and mother of three, was admitted to the emergency ward in a coma due to an overdose of barbiturates taken during her menstrual period. She had a history of unusually severe premenstrual depression, and on three previous occasions she had made similar suicide attempts during her period. Once she slit her wrists; on two other occasions she swallowed one hundred aspirin. All previous suicide attempts were treated as acute medical emergencies, and later she was sent to a psychiatric facility. On each occasion her depression disappeared within several days after her period terminated, and she was discharged to resume her normal activities.

After her first pregnancy she had suffered a postpartum depression characterized by disinterest in the baby, loss of appetite and weight, crying spells, and suicidal wishes. At that time she had developed the conviction her husband no longer loved her. This depression, because of its severity, had required electroshock treatments. During the year following the postpartum depression, she had been weepy and irritable, and suffered mild recurrent depressions that had coincided each time with her menstrual period. Each month she experienced tension, weight gain, and swelling in the abdomen, along with a desire to retreat from the world several days before and during her period. These menstrual depressions frequently kept her in bed for two or three days. They appeared to get more severe as she got older. After each period her symptoms would subside and she would feel perfectly normal for the next twenty-odd days.

Ann's moodswing was probably tripped off by a biological clock mechanism related to the biochemistry of the menstrual cycle. Eventually she was treated with lithium and by the end of a year her monthly depression and irritability disappeared.

Although a number of patients with serious premenstrual depression have responded to lithium, sufficient studies have not yet been completed to conclude that lithium is truly effective for this condition.

Sometimes mild mood disorders appear masked as physical symptoms: migraine, back pain, and plain "fatigue." In extreme psychiatric disorder such as periodic catatonia (schizophrenia), the sufferer swings from a normal state into a hyperexcited violent state, or into a frozen condition that resembles paralysis. The reasons for periodic catatonia are not understood; it may result from faulty metabolism.

In manic depression, mood shifts are accompanied by shifts in body chemistry, particularly in the amounts of salt and fluid in and around cells. Depressed patients studied on metabolic wards have consistently shown that they retain salt and fluid only during their depressed phase. Although lithium's primary action is on salt (sodium chloride), the clock that regulates the physiochemical changes of manic depression is unknown.

Most manic-depressives are not as regular in their mood shifts as the forty-eight-hour businessman. There is no known formula to predict the timing of attacks. In most cases normal intervals become shorter and episodes become longer as the person ages; but they have also been known to discontinue suddenly for months or years. With the widespread use of antidepressant and antipsychotic drugs it is difficult to evaluate the natural course of this periodic disease. Sometimes a so-called neurotic problem that has not responded to psychotherapy is in reality caused by a biological mood clock. I saw one example of this in a young woman with writer's block.

Judith, a thirty-six-year-old mystery-story writer who had written and published ten books, had maintained a predictable two-month cycle for years. She would be manic for one month and depressed the next. She was referred to me for treatment of her rapid cycling moodswings and also for the problem of writer's block, which occurred every other month, disrupting her fiction in a cyclical way. In order to verify her moods I asked to see her weekly.

When she appeared for her appointments, it was apparent whether she was in a high or low mood. During her high month I would first hear her talking rapidly and enthusiastically to the staff and other patients in the waiting area. She acted like a self-appointed group therapy leader, moving about quickly, bubbling with energy, and hardly letting anyone get a word in edgewise. During the up month she talked excitedly about her ideas and her most recent book. She dressed attractively and enjoyed taking part in what she called the "two-month biological clock experiment."

Fortunately her highs were mild and helpful to her writing. The material that poured out of her during her high month was innovative and of high quality. Examples of her mildly manic writing were shown to critics, who praised the smooth flow of ideas, well-drawn characters, and vivid action. One month she went too high and her writing became wild and fragmented.

Every two months she switched dramatically into a depressed, irritable, fearful state. She was late for office appointments or missed them altogether. She complained that instead of needing five hours' sleep and getting up at 6:00 A.M., she would oversleep and linger in bed all day. During her low month the attempt to discipline herself to write resulted only in excuses to avoid sitting down in front of the typewriter. If she did try to write, she stared into space. In her down, blocked periods, she felt she was a phony and a failure as a writer and a woman. She would downgrade the good material that she had previously written. During the depressed month, she appeared tired and disheveled. The only hope she expressed was for the return of her pleasurable and creative high, which always followed.

Since, like the forty-eight-hour businessman, she was a rapid cycler, she was told that her moodswings might require four to twelve months on lithium before stabilization. Owing to her manic impatience, she became discouraged early in treatment and decided to stop lithium during one of her highs. Unfortunately, I have not heard from her since.

Moods like this in some but not all cases are determined by biological clocks. They are the most interesting and easily recognized forms of moodswing.

SIX

Cocaine, Alcohol, and Depression

The first time Steve came into my office he looked like he'd been on a bender, with dark glasses and a two-day growth of beard. He pushed a glossy brochure from a well-known Wall Street brokerage firm across my desk, and pointed to the CEO in the photograph. "It's me," he said.

As a young stockbroker he'd made millions for himself and his clients by masterminding brilliant deals. By the time he was twenty-eight he was a legend on Wall Street. But when he confronted me, he looked almost like a derelict. A few years back, he explained, the market had taken a major dive, and he had suffered enormous losses, worse than the Dow Jones or any of his colleagues. He had panicked and sold too soon, several of his clients had lost millions, and some were now threatening to sue. Most of his larger accounts had transferred to other firms. His Rolls and his Lear jet had been liquidated to raise cash, and he was about to lose his elegant home on Long Island because of liens and his almost nonexistent cash flow.

During the past year he'd become suicidally depressed, lost weight, and lived like a recluse. He disliked answering the telephone because the thought of talking to clients or friends was unbearable. His wife had left him and taken the children; he had no interest in sex anymore.

A few years earlier he'd started using cocaine when he was in a mild slump. He'd gone to a party and tried cocaine for the first time, and it had made him feel more like his usual high-energy self, optimistic and boundlessly confident. "Cocaine is all over Wall Street," he told me. "You wouldn't believe who's using it now. Some guys have messengers going from office to office delivering drugs. Drugs are as easy to get as paper clips. I use a beeper to call my dealer."

Steve had never done drugs in college, and used alcohol only once in a while. He was now spending about two thousand dollars a week on cocaine. For the first time he was "bending the rules" in his work, and had become paranoid: He was afraid he would be arrested by the FBI, and he had received threatening phone calls.

Occasionally a cocaine user can quit by himself, but in most cases that I've seen, hospitalization and detoxification are the only routes that keep the cocaine user from going back to it. A medical program combined with group therapy, individual therapy, and peer assistance groups such as Alcoholics Anonymous or Cocaine Anonymous, has the best success rate in shaking this difficult addiction. But first the user must admit that he or she is an addict. Addiction is defined by the American Psychiatric Association as the inability to stop or reduce use; intoxication throughout the day and episodes of cocaine overdose; impairment of social or occupational function, and duration of disturbance for more than one month. The addict cannot control how much or when cocaine is used. As one user said, "At the end, I was just by myself, doing coke. It was like a noose tightening around my neck. I would just sit in my car and snort coke by myself."

Cocaine can cause seizures, profound low mood, respiratory depression, coronary artery spasm, myocardial infarction and hemorrhage. Ten years ago many users considered it nonaddictive; today we know this is not the case. Cocaine is one of the most addictive substances known to man, and laboratory rats will choose it over food, sex, or any other activity. In one experiment, the animals used cocaine rather than food until they perished of starvation.

We are now in the middle of a boom generation of cocaine users. In 1973 cocaine was used by only 2 percent of people over eighteen in this country. Today it has become an epidemic, even among the upper-middle class. In 1979, 20 percent of medical school students had tried it. By 1984, 40 percent had. According to the National Clearing House for Alcohol and Drug Addiction, by 1986, the year Len Bias, the Boston Celtics' number one draft choice, died of cocaine intoxication, about 25 percent of Americans eighteen to twenty-five years old had tried coke, and one in five of that age group had used it recently. The National Institute of Drug Abuse survey in 1982 found that 21.6 million Americans (one in ten) had tried cocaine, that almost 12 million had used it in 1981, and that 4.2 million Americans used it regularly.

More than 23 percent of all workers in the United States use dangerous drugs on the job, according to a survey conducted by a leading business quarterly. The federal Alcohol, Drug Abuse, and Mental Health Administration widely proclaims that "cocaine is one of the worst drug abuse catastrophes ever to face our nation."

Marijuana is now the most widely consumed illicit psychoactive drug in the United States. There are about 20 million users of marijuana, and 6 million current abusers of cocaine. Over 10 million Americans are using prescription drugs for nonmedical purposes.

This epidemic has brought about a revolution in drug treatment programs. Because so many Americans are now using drugs on the job, many companies are funding drug testing programs for employees and job applicants. A whole new industry based on testing workers has developed. An accurate drug test now costs a company between twenty and forty dollars, but the cost is small compared to the estimated losses from drug-related accidents and increased medical claims. One large auto company found that each employee with an alcohol problem cost it 50 percent more each year in medical claims. Substance-abusing employees are four times more likely to have accidents and twice as likely to miss more than a week of work at a stretch than their drug-free colleagues, and they file more compensation claims. According to the National Institute of Mental Health, United States companies lost about $71 billion in productivity in 1987 to alcohol and drug abuse, up from an average of $30 billion in the mid-1970s. Employers spent another $14 billion in direct health care costs, including treatment and claims processing. Mental health and substance abuse claims account for 28 percent of the insurance claims of one large Massachussetts company. According to the National Triangle Research Institute survey in 1981, losses due to alcohol and drug abuse were over $100 billion a year. In 1982 over $82 billion in accident loss was reported and over half of these accidents were drug- or alcohol-related. About 30 percent of the Fortune 500 companies have employee assistance programs, for they've found that it's cheaper to treat an employee for a drug or alcohol problem than to train a new employee.

Most cocaine users who have tried to quit or cut down by themselves have found that the rebound depression caused by the drug made it impossible. Although the exact mechanism by which cocaine works is unknown, it is thought that its effect moves from the bloodstream to the central nervous system. At first, it increases the action of the naturally occurring chemicals, the neurotransmitters, that stimulate the pleasure centers of the brain. But eventually, the neurotransmitters are too diminished to react, and more cocaine is needed. When the drug wears off, the user experiences a "crash," or low mood that is relieved by taking more cocaine. When the drug is withheld for a longer time, a depression—often suicidal—sets in that may continue for weeks or even months.

The problem is complicated by the fact that about three quarters of cocaine users are so-called polydrug users: While cocaine is used to get the person high, alcohol or a tranquilizer such as Valium, barbiturates, marijuana, or sometimes heroin is taken to counteract the wild stimulant effects of the drug: including seizures, cocaine jitters, or the hyper-high. So the patient may need to be detoxified from several drugs at once.

The addict commonly suffers from sexual problems, such as loss of sex drive or inability to perform, paranoia, inability to concentrate, and loss of memory. And he or she develops a tolerance to the drug: More and more is needed to feel good.

One hospital's cocaine hotline reported that their callers averaged from one to thirty-two grams per week, at about $100 per gram, spending around $650 per week on the average. Almost half the abusers used the drug daily. One quarter had lost their jobs and husbands or wives, almost half reported losing friends, one third lost all financial resources, one in ten had had an accident, one in ten attempted suicide, almost two thirds had violent fights, one in five stole from friends or job to support a habit. More than a third turned to drug dealing.

Not only does cocaine erode the personality, but it often produces acute anxiety and panic, and can lead to a full-blown psychosis complete with hallucinations. When Steve came to see me, he had tried several times to cut down by himself, without success. Controlled use is almost impossible. Once a person has become a user, the only treatment that works is complete abstinence from all drugs, including alcohol. Phasing out slowly, just cutting down, or substituting one drug for another (cross-addiction) just doesn't work.

An inpatient hospital program has a much better chance to succeed in the difficult task of rebuilding a cocaine-devastated life. Steve very reluctantly agreed to enter our program that would require more than a month in a treatment center, with group and individual therapy, peer group meetings, and Cocaine Anonymous meetings. Most important, he would receive medication.

Biological psychiatry has developed a number of treatments that make cocaine and opiate withdrawal easier. Several years ago researchers noticed that patients who were being treated for depression with antidepressants and who also abused cocaine reported that they couldn't get "high" from cocaine when they were taking tricyclic antidepressants. It was then postulated that cocaine depleted certain neurotransmitters in the brain. Since these neurotransmitters were made from the amino acids L-tryptophan and L-tyrosine, a combination of these amino acids plus the antidepressant imipramine or desipramine is used to treat cocaine abusers. For most patients, the treatment "cocktail" blocks the cocaine high, lessening the craving for more of the drug and diminishing the rebound depression that occurs at withdrawal. Our Foundation research team has used the antidepressant desipramine, bromocryptine, lithium, and other medications successfully.

The future looks bright for combination drug treatments against cocaine addiction, provided the patient admits he or she is an addict and is motivated to get help. A cocaine abuser will go through several stages of recovery, beginning with the acceptance of the idea of permanent abstinence.

Steve opted for a twenty-four-hour-a-day treatment program in our mid-Manhattan hospital, which usually costs from $200 to $500 per day, and which is usually reimbursed by insurance. While he was in the hospital, he worked with my multidisciplinary team of doctors and psychologists. The night he was admitted he had a full physical, including a neurological workup because he had had several seizures while on cocaine. His neuroendocrine exam and his blood chemistries were normal. Normal liver and heart function are a sine qua non for any antidepressant drug treatment. Likewise, a strong family support system is almost essential for cocaine abuse recovery. Steve's wife and other relatives agreed to participate in therapy sessions with him. He also agreed to attend Cocaine Anonymous meetings daily, possibly for the rest of his life. These groups of peers who are in different stages of recovery offer support, encouragement, and confrontation that give the addict the strength to stay "clean." Anyone who has not used drugs for two weeks is free to join.

Steve's hospital treatment changed him. "I used to think I was superior to the other people in the hospital because I'd made more money," he told me. "They were losers and I was better because I was living in the fast lane. The group made me face the fact that I was an addict. I've stolen money to get cocaine, and I was hooked. I couldn't quit by myself and I can't stay off it without CA."

Antidepressants and lithium were an important part of Steve's treatment. When he entered the hospital, I immediately prescribed lithium and desipramine. Before he began to use cocaine Steve had had a history of moodswings: periods of high energy and enthusiasm when he didn't need much sleep, when he enjoyed wheeling and dealing in business and had grand schemes for making money. But his wife reported that he had also had periods of despondency and low energy over the years, when he was irritable, had trouble getting out of bed, and showed little interest in his job or family. She remarked that this had been going on long before cocaine entered his life. In fact, as we know, Steve had started to use cocaine as his own self-styled form of medication during one of his periodic depressions. He had needed his high-power "up" self to be able to function well in his multimillion-dollar job. His latest depression had been compounded by the recent financial losses, so that he was suffering from a "double depression," an actual loss combined with a biochemical moodswing. No wonder he tried to revive himself with a central nervous system stimulant.

After almost a month of acute detoxification and stabilization treatment in our hospital, Steve was released with the understanding that he would go to my office for monitoring. At the office he received his medications, had his urine tested three times a week, and went to behavior modification sessions and group sessions, as well as his Cocaine Anonymous meetings. His blood levels for desipramine and lithium were monitored weekly and later monthly. Any new symptoms were reported to me so that I could adjust his dosage if he began to have moodswings.

Our structured after-care program for cocaine, alcohol, or other drugs usually lasts from six to twelve months. Patients are given information about drugs to prevent relapse, including lectures and readings on drug withdrawal, and warned of the course that relapse usually follows, including dreams about taking drugs, the temptation to try another mind-altering drug, the mistaken belief that "a little bit" of cocaine can be used in moderation.

Steve needed to find enjoyable substitutes for drug use, just as he needed to avoid drug-using friends. We find jobs for withdrawn addicts who have become part of our rehabilitation program, to speed their recovery. An exercise program is invaluable in cocaine rehabilitation, since it improves mood and self-image.

"Without cocaine everything looks gray," one woman said, referring to the depression of cocaine withdrawal. The cocaine abuser has a difficult time with rehabilitation, but thanks to antidepressants and lithium, as well as other recent discoveries, the road to recovery is encouraging. Recent research has shown that bromocriptine is helpful to overcome drug addiction. Bromocriptine reduces the amount of dopamine, another neurotransmitter, which helps to reduce the craving for cocaine.

The youngest victims of the drug epidemic have a double disadvantage in kicking the drug habit. A fifteen-year-old-boy named Jason was brought in to see me by his distraught parents. A regular user of marijuana for three years, he had also tried cocaine, crack, and Quaaludes. He had gone to school high on marijuana so many times that the school authorities had alerted his parents. His grades were plummeting, he saw few friends, and stayed in his room smoking pot and listening to music. Once a basketball player, he now socialized mostly with other kids who did drugs.

"I have weird feelings sometimes," he said. "I don't feel I'm a real person. I don't feel like doing anything. The only time I feel happy is when I'm high. I'm spaced out most of the time."

Jason, like many young drug users, suffers from the amotivational syndrome. During crucial developmental years, marijuana use can lead to lack of socialization, and failure to learn elementary skills, discipline, and family values. Since the traditional learning influences of family and church have dissolved in recent decades, the media, videos, and peer pressure provide role models for youngsters that glorify drug use and the quick fix for anxiety and other emotional problems. The National Institute of Drug Abuse did a survey in 1982 of fourteen- and fifteen-year-olds and found that in this country 640,000 used marijuana, 100,000 used cocaine regularly, 100,000 used stimulants like Dexedrine, 50,000 used sedatives, and a staggering 1 million used alcohol regularly. Socially "acceptable" drugs such as cigarettes, alcohol, and over-the-counter diet pills have become "gateway drugs" leading to illicit drug use.

The New York Times reported in 1983 that "marijuana is currently our second largest cash crop nationally, after corn." Attitudes toward all recreational drugs have become more liberal because of more relaxed attitudes toward using marijuana. Sixty-four percent of American young people have tried an illicit drug before they finish high school. One third have used drugs other than marijuana, and one out of every sixteen high school seniors smokes marijuana every day. At least 20 percent have smoked pot daily for at least a month some time in their lives.

Even more sobering, many of these teenagers will go on to harder drugs. Sixty percent of marijuana users do. Mental-health professionals are beginning to see a new generation of adolescent and chronic young adult psychiatric patients: those who are drug-dependent. Stuck in the transition between youth and adulthood, they have ego deficits, difficulty with reality testing, poor impulse control, and moodswings. They are acutely vulnerable to stress. Many of them wander from city to city, are unemployed, and perform at low levels. The most frequent victims are young single males.

Jason was in danger of joining this large population of young adults who have passed through adolescence as regular drug users. Fortunately, his lack of motivation in school, his poor performance and aimlessness alerted his parents before he suffered permanent emotional and physical damage. I recommended that he either enter the outpatient drug rehabilitation program at our Foundation clinic or the private practice. He and his parents came for weekly family therapy sessions, and he received individual counseling. His parents began to understand the pressures that had prompted their son to take drugs in the first place, and the anxiety he often felt about performing in school to please them. Jason was educated about the long-term effects of drug use.

When I questioned him Jason admitted that he also used cocaine, which he had bought from friends, sometimes twice a week. Jason's pattern of drug use is not unusual for his age group. Many teenagers are smoking crack, the cheap and available free-base form of cocaine, which is even more damaging than cocaine hydrochloride. The Institute for Social Research at the University of Michigan conducted a poll among teens that found that only 30 percent of the high schoolers queried believed that experimenting with cocaine was dangerous! One senior in twenty-five had used crack at least once.

Anyone willing to kick the cocaine habit must agree to weekly urine testing. A psychiatrist in the initial consultation must look carefully for signs of underlying depression. If the depression is primary (occurs chronologically before the drug abuse), then it must be treated with antidepressants. A drug abuse patient with a primary depression and secondary drug abuse actually has a better chance of recovery than if the drug addiction is primary. The same is true for an underlying panic or anxiety disorder, which, like the depression, may have prompted self-medication with street drugs.

I often recommend a three- or six-month course of tricyclic antidepressants for a teenager with a drug problem. He or she will sleep better, and have less anxiety facing life stresses during the crucial months of rebuilding a life-style free of drugs. New friends, new hobbies, and new attitudes have to be cultivated during this time. Simply acknowledging the drug use can be stressful in itself, and peer pressure to resume drug taking is immense.

Many students and even some parents and teachers take a cavalier attitude toward marijuana, saying that it's normal for society. I take exception to this, having seen how academic failure affects a child's future. Cannabinoids build up in the brain and body, leading in extreme cases to memory loss, feminization of men, and in decade-long habits, a condition resembling Alzheimer's disease. Milder use can involve chronic insomnia, fatigue, headaches, poor sexual performance, depression, anxiety, irritability, paranoia, as well as loss of interest in activities, lack of concentration, and in some cases, suicide. I have seen apathy and depression on the faces of many of my adolescent patients who are using this drug; I believe marijuana's effects are longterm and it is unquestionably dangerous.

Alcohol joins marijuana and cocaine as one of the most commonly abused drugs in America today. Among high school students surveyed by the National Institute of Drug Abuse, almost three out of four had used it in the previous month; half used it before high school; and one in fifteen used it every day! Among adults, alcohol ranks as the most widely used psychoactive drug. About four out of five adults drink regularly (over 100 million). Since alcohol consumption is an ingrained and acceptable part of most adult life-styles, the onset of alcoholism or "problem" drinking may be difficult to spot. The mechanism of denial makes it easy for many drinkers to rationalize alcohol abuse. In my opinion, alcohol addiction occurs when tolerance and withdrawal are present. Tolerance means that more and more alcohol must be taken to get the desired high. Withdrawal means that if alcohol is not used, the person feels shaky, nervous, oftentimes nauseous, panicky, and loses appetite.

Also typical of alcoholism is the blackout: For the space of one or two hours, or longer, the person has no recollection of where he was, what he said or what he was doing. This may occur once or many times, but if it occurs even once, I diagnose alcoholism.

The onset of alcoholism may take many years. Beer, wine, or hard liquor may be the drug of choice. An ounce and a half of whiskey contains as much alcohol as a twelve-ounce bottle of beer, or five ounces of table wine, and the effect is the same. Beer is metabolized more slowly and intoxication may occur more gradually. Nevertheless, it's the amount of alcohol not the beverage that matters. Intoxication is considered to occur at a blood level of .05 percent, which produces impairment in most people—two bottles of beer, ten ounces of wine, or two ordinary ounce and a quarter drinks.

Alcohol is a central nervous system depressant, which is why many people use it as a tranquilizer at the end of a hard day, or as an assist for tense social situations. The warning signals of psychological dependence are: using it regularly to cope with the stresses and strains of daily living; drinking to relieve boredom or depression; drinking to avoid unpleasant emotional reactions or situations; and drinking in advance of new social situations in order to get prepared psychologically. Psychological dependence can signal growing addiction if a person feels uncomfortable or avoids social situations in which alcohol is not served, or is drinking in advance of a party or meeting in case alcohol will not be available.

Physical dependence involves withdrawal symptoms when drinking stops. These may develop after years or after only weeks of heavy drinking. They include loss of appetite, nausea, anxiety, sleeplessness, severe agitation and irritability, loss of sensation, loss of memory, confusion, tremors, vomiting, illusions, and hallucinations. In advanced cases delirium tremens develops, with tremors, convulsions, exhaustion, and cardiovascular collapse.

The National Institute of Alcohol and Alcohol Abuse defines heavy drinkers as those who have five or more drinks per occasion at least once a week. There are ten to twelve million alcoholics currently in the United States, plus ten million "problem" drinkers for whom alcohol interferes with normal living. According to the National Council on Alcoholism, only 3 percent of alcoholics are on skid row. The rest are in homes, offices, and factories, and at least 50 percent of today's "problem" drinkers are employed.

Health problems abound for alcoholics. They have twice the chance of premature death as nonalcoholics, more chance of liver disease, vitamin deficiency, gastritis, impotence, infections, peptic ulcers, suicide, pneumonia, heart and pulmonary disease, tuberculosis, and epilepsy complications.

The accident statistics are well known: 10 percent of all deaths in the United States are alcohol-related. Sixty percent of all traffic deaths are alcohol-related. Clearly, misusing alcohol can be dangerous. It has caused extreme damage to millions of children, families, and careers. Yet alcoholism is an extremely difficult disease to treat medically. Only as late as 1956 did the American Medical Association succeed in changing the definition of alcoholism to an illness. Previously it was and still is in some places considered a moral laxity or a failure of willpower. Largely through the efforts of Alcoholics Anonymous, which was founded in 1935, alcoholism has lost much of its stigma. Celebrities with drinking problems have publicized their recovery to help bring the disease and its treatment out into the open. Alcoholics Anonymous remains the single successful treatment modality for alcoholism. Rarely can a drinker stop by himself. Neither Freudian analysis nor religious faith have on their own been successful in treating this deadly illness. About 60 percent of alcoholics who join AA remain sober and stay in the program.

Withdrawing from alcohol can often be made easier with antidepressants and lithium, especially if a severe depression sets in when alcohol isn't taken. In many cases alcoholism is not primary but secondary to depression. Before treatment of an alcoholic can begin, the physician must determine whether the alcoholism is the underlying disease, or if it is secondary to another emotional illness, such as depression, drug abuse, sociopathy, or mania. If alcoholism is secondary, the chance of cure is good. Antidepressants and lithium can be used to wipe out the underlying depression, making it easier for the recovering alcoholic to rebuild his or her life. And once the underlying depression is treated, the alcohol is often no longer needed to blunt the emotional pain.

The history of first-degree relatives is also important: Relatives of alcoholics often suffer from alcoholism, suicidal behavior, serious depression, or moodswings. Alcoholism belongs to the spectrum of mood disorders that includes depression. Mania and low mood, some forms of schizophrenia, and suicidal behavior all occur in clusters along with alcoholism in many families. In one case, a grandfather was given shock therapy and committed suicide; his son and daughter had a "drinking problem" and moderately debilitating moodswings, and his granddaughter was hospitalized for alcohol and drug abuse.

This familiar pattern of inherited mood disorders, including alcoholism, has led researchers to search for a genetic link. The high incidence of alcoholism in the families of depressed patients may be transmitted on the X chromosome or on chromosome 11, and much research remains to be done.

Brenda came in to see me because she'd hit bottom socially and financially. Her husband was threatening to leave her. For the past five years she'd been drinking every morning and all through the day. She kept a pint in her glove compartment, had passed out in restaurants, and had recently cut her head in a fall in front of her apartment. A housewife, she didn't need to work, but she found the long hours spent at home now that her children had grown up left her bored and depressed. When she tried to "cut down" to a reasonable three Scotches a day, scheduling herself to begin at five in the evening, she felt even more down in the dumps.

But she had taken the first step toward successful withdrawal: She had admitted that she had a drinking problem. Willpower alone wasn't going to cure it.

It is essential that the alcoholic admit that the drinking problem exists, and that he or she cannot handle it alone. If severe medical and life-style problems exist, hospitalization in a detoxification center is required. Group and individual psychotherapy often involve the family as well as the recovering patient. Alcoholics Anonymous meetings are the sine qua non of treatment; without AA, drinkers go back to drinking.

Most members of AA find that they must attend meetings daily or three or four times a week for about five years, or in many cases for the rest of their lives, to maintain sobriety. Recently polydrug users have begun to appear in AA meetings, especially among the under-thirty group; these are users of alcohol and drugs. Almost no "pure" alcoholics exist among young people anymore, report several leading psychiatrists in the field of alcoholism today. Youth is hooked on booze and other drugs, or only on other drugs. Tranquilizers, cocaine, marijuana, and heroin are the most commonly seen. However, the scope of this national problem has resulted in some innovative and effective new treatments. Antidepressant medication plays a prominent role, as do group therapy and behavior modification. In the next few years, we will see even more effective treatments develop to stem this destructive tide.

SEVEN

Teenage and Adult Suicide

A sad phenomenon of the eighties is the teenage "suicide clusters," groups of teenagers who know each other or know about each other, who choose to commit suicide. Often they have reached stressful points in their lives, either in high school or the early years of college. They may come from affluent or from less well-to-do homes, from homes with caring parents or from broken homes. The majority of these suicides occur under the influence of alcohol or drugs. Many young would-be suicides do not appear to be depressed; they may instead be extremely angry, impulsive, or reckless. In some cases, friends, teachers, and parents have no idea how serious the suicidal intent is until the attempt has been made.

In Plano, Texas, there were eight teenage suicides in one year (1983–84). In Westchester County, New York, there were thirty teen suicides in two years, with five in a twenty-day period in 1984. In Clear Lake, Texas, six teenage suicides occurred in fourteen months in 1983. Their contagious nature is often aggravated by media reporting, as teenagers often mimic what they have seen on TV.

According to the National Center for Health Statistics, the suicide rate among those in the age group from fifteen to twenty-four tripled between 1950 and 1980. Suicide is now the third leading cause of death, behind accidents and homicide, for teenagers and young adults. In 1980, more than fifty-two hun-

97

dred completed suicides were reported among persons aged fifteen to twenty-four, and this number is probably low since— because of the social stigma attached to suicide—it is often reported as an accident, especially if drugs and alcohol are involved.

Some experts claim that one in ten students plans suicide. What we know is that every day one thousand young people in the United States attempt it. Almost all teenagers will have to deal with a severely depressed peer at some time between the ages of fifteen and twenty-five. According to the latest estimates, adolescents make about half a million suicide attempts a year—more than a hundred times the number of reported suicides.

The statistics for combined teenage and adult suicides are also changing: Between 1965 and 1986, about 645,000 Americans completed suicide (an average of three deaths every hour). In 1960, the suicide rate was 10.6 out of every 100,000. In 1970, it was 11.6 out of 100,000, and in 1980 rose to 12.5. Since then it has declined slightly. The peak suicide group used to be the elderly, especially white males over the age of sixty-five living alone. Today the group most at risk is white males aged fifteen to nineteen (9 deaths per 100,000 in 1984); their suicide rate increased by 60 percent between 1970 and 1980, and for white males aged twenty to twenty-four, the rate increased by 44 percent. White males aged fifteen to thirty-nine now account for one third of all suicides in the United States.

There are now three times as many adolescent suicides as there were thirty years ago. Before 1950, three times as many women as men tried to commit suicide but did not complete it while three times more men than women completed suicide. Women employed their traditional methods, such as pills and wrist slitting, while men had recourse to more violent means, such as jumping, shooting, hanging, and stabbing. But as women have become more "liberated," they have used more violent means. Today an increasing number of adult women, especially those under the age of fifty, are committing suicide. On the other hand, among the elderly, the rate has dropped.

There are, as well, the questionable suicides, or "hidden suicides." Some of these are slow suicides, caused by chronic drinking or drug abuse, while others are more rapid, in the form of self-destructive behavior such as reckless driving. They may include the woman depressed over career setbacks who drives her car into a tree, leaving no skid marks; the adolescent who drives beyond the speed limit or accepts dangerous dares; the youngster who abuses drugs and gets into fights with drug dealers and whose body is found floating in the river; the alcoholic who ignores warnings from her doctor that continued drinking will cause fatal liver disease; or the anorectic girl who starves herself to death. If we included these hidden suicides in our statistics, the incidence would be much greater.

What are the causes of suicide? Who is most at risk?

In adolescents, a history of previous suicide attempts is certainly a risk factor, and an indication of feelings of helplessness and hopelessness is a warning of depression. Every teenager undergoes dramatic changes in his or her physical appearance, sexuality, and aggressive feelings. He or she needs to separate from parents and establish friendships with peers, as well as to make choices about a career, yet a period of mourning occurs as ties with parents and childhood are cut.

Because our society has become more rootless in the last thirty years, adolescents have much less family support during their difficult times. According to recent statistics, between 44 and 66 percent of adolescent suicide attempters come from broken homes. Often there are two working parents out of the house. Since one in two marriages ends in divorce, parental separation is common for youngsters. About 80 percent of suicidal teens have lost a parent through death or divorce before age fourteen. In many families there is severe conflict and lack of communication with the adolescent, along with denial that problems exist. And America's present decline of religious and ethical values has meant a spiritual and emotional emptiness for many youngsters.

About 80 percent of adolescent suicide attempts occur when the youngster is depressed; the other 20 percent of teenage attempters show impulse disorders, such as excessive anger and acting out: These latter may threaten suicide in a manipulative attempt to get their own way. But whether the threat is manipulative or not, the family must *always* respond as if it were really going to happen and get professional help immediately. Most suicidal youngsters have suffered a major loss such as parental divorce, a death in the family, moving, breaking up with a girlfriend or boyfriend, social humiliation, or failure at school. To complicate matters most adolescents are introspective and very self-critical.

Blocked communication is frequently a harbinger of a suicidal event. Sociologists report that teenagers today spend an average of fourteen minutes a week talking to their parents, while by the time a teenager graduates from high school he or she will have spent fifteen thousand hours in front of the TV.

Epidemic use of drugs and alcohol has also escalated the teenage suicide rate. When the San Diego County coroner examined 133 suicides of people under age thirty, between 1981 and 1983, 53 percent of the victims were substance abusers (mainly drugs). There is no question that alcohol and drugs contribute to the rapid acceleration of the teen suicide rate by lowering impulse control, increasing depression, and impairing school and social success.

Young people are faced not only with a high degree of stress in school, but also with parental expectations, and their own demands on themselves. School pressure is often underestimated by adults. In one poll, teenagers who were asked what was the major stress in their lives reported it was grades. According to Javad Kashani, University of Missouri professor of psychiatry, as many as one quarter of college freshmen will consider or act on suicidal feelings. It was once thought that blacks had a lower suicide rate than whites, but as young blacks move into urban environments, especially into college and job market pressures, their suicide rate climbs.

Childhood sexual abuse is a leading precursor of suicidal behavior among young teenage girls. In one study, one third of the girls interviewed who had attempted suicide had been victims of childhood incest, particularly by a father. Unwed pregnancy is reported to be the largest contributing factor among teenage girls committing suicide. Often the attempt occurs after they have been totally abandoned by the boy involved.

Other youngsters at risk are those with epilepsy or learning disabilities, such as dyslexia, which are demoralizing, frustrating, and may constantly undermine the young person's self-esteem. Any chronic medical illness that makes a child "different" contributes to an increased suicidal risk—this is true also for adults.

Masked depression in teenagers may take the form of alcohol and drug abuse, sexual experimentation, or trouble with school authorities or the law. Many suicidal teens live in an "emotional refrigerator." They don't feel low, they feel numb. They think their parents only want to hear that everything's fine, and so they learn not to communicate.

Teenagers do not always have a clear idea of the finality of death. They may have a romantic vision of joining dead friends or relatives, or they may believe they will come alive again after seeing their parents weep at the funeral. Teenagers are bombarded by heavy-metal songs glorifying suicide. The rash of teen suicides that occurs after the death of a rock star or movie idol (John Lennon or Marilyn Monroe) has been well documented. In Leominster, Massachusetts in 1984, two fifteen-year-old girls committed suicide in response to a song by Pink Floyd.

Teenagers who consider suicide usually give weeks or even months of warning, although their parents and friends may not realize that until after the fact. For every two hundred teens who attempt suicide, one succeeds; yet of every five who die by suicide, four have made at least one previous attempt.

If a young patient comes to see me, I immediately take a family history to see if there is suicide, depression, manic depression, or alcoholism in the family. If these disorders are present, the risk of suicide in the patient is substantially increased.

Jonathan, eighteen, came to see me after a failed suicide attempt during the fall of his freshman year at college. He had been pushed by his parents to take six courses to prepare for his father's professional career, for which he had neither the interest nor the aptitude required. One Saturday night after studying in the library stacks until eleven, he came back to find himself the only one in his dorm. Feeling isolated and friendless and facing a "hopeless" future, he took two hundred aspirin and five tranquilizers he'd stolen during his previous weekend at home. His parents took his suicide attempt seriously, and brought him immediately to my office. I hospitalized Jon for a complete evaluation, close observation, and treatment.

Michael, a fifteen-year-old boy, attempted to hang himself a year after his favorite uncle committed suicide. The youngster was not able to express his pain and anger to his parents over the loss of his uncle, and he also felt survivor's guilt. The parents had stopped talking to him while they were going through a divorce, and his continuing depression had led to failure in school.

In most suicides the common factors are helplessness and hopelessness. The person suffers from tunnel vision, and cannot see any other option for solving his or her problems. This is the so-called "closed world" of suicide.

Warning Signs in Suicide

Among the 80 percent of suicide victims who give warning signs (statements, cues, or actions) for weeks or months in advance, I find the following the most prevalent signs and symptoms:

1. Weight loss, depression, and frequent moodswings
2. Alcohol and drug abuse
3. Withdrawn, isolated behavior
4. Oversleeping or insomnia
5. Loss of interest and deteriorating performance in job or school
6. Aggression and violent impulsive outbursts

Alcoholism and alcohol use increase the likelihood of suicide. Alcohol increases impulsiveness, depressed feelings, and poor judgment. A report by an NIMH conference stated that 80 percent of adolescents have drunk alcohol just before they made a suicide attempt. Some adults who are usually nondrinkers get drunk before they commit suicide. According to a British study of one hundred suicides, two-thirds suffered from depression. Fifteen percent suffered from alcoholism alone or from alcoholism and depression.

The parent or physician should be alert in the event of any of the following:

1. Loss of an important person or thing: a job, a friend, health, youth, position, stature in the community, a spouse, or even a pet.
2. An angry argument. Many suicides are acts of anger and impulse; teenagers especially may lash out at themselves when frustrated.
3. Episodes of hopelessness and low feelings. The common symptoms of depression—crying, sleeplessness, loss of appetite and weight—are present in at least 75 percent of suicides and suicide attempts.
4. A suicide threat. *Any* mention of suicide should be taken seriously and professional help sought the same day.
5. A sudden change of mood from depression to cheerfulness. Often when the decision to commit suicide has been made, the person shows great calm and peace of mind.
6. Giving away prized possessions such as cameras and jewelry, for no apparent reason. The person may remark that he or she "won't need them anymore."
7. Making a will or other preparations, such as arranging life insurance.

Other warning signs may be behavior changes, such as when a low-keyed student starts acting hyper. If such changes last for more than a week, a teacher or parent should take the student aside and discuss what stresses the student may be under. The student should then see the school psychologist or counselor. Another personality change to watch for is withdrawal from friends and family, as when the teenager begins to spend long hours locked up in his or her room alone listening to music. It is normal for teenagers to have moodswings, but any extremely depressed mood lasting more than several days should be suspect. A suicidal person may also make statements of worthlessness ("I'm no good for anything"; "I'm a burden to my family"; "I'd be better off not around").

Still another suicide warning sign is "accidental" poisoning or accident-prone behavior. Taking an "accidental" overdose of pills or pills in combination with alcohol can be a cry for help, even though the suicidal wish is unclear even to the person. The commonest pills of abuse are aspirin, tranquilizers and sleeping pills, alone, in combination or with alcohol. Statistically, teenagers usually make such "accidental" suicidal gestures two or three times before a serious suicide attempt.

When I see any of these signs in a patient, I treat it as an emergency and family crisis. By questioning the patient directly I try to bring suicidal thoughts and plans out into the open. It is not true that discussing suicide will make the person more likely to attempt it. In fact, when suicidal plans and feelings are discussed in a sympathetic way, the chance of the person committing suicide greatly decreases.

Among teenagers there is a code of secrecy and denial. Most teens will confide in a friend if they feel suicidal, yet almost never volunteer this information to a teacher or parent. Teenagers tend to protect one another's secrets. That is why one of the core tenets of high school suicide-prevention programs is that even if someone is sworn to secrecy about a friend's suicidal plans, he or she must tell a teacher or counselor anyway.

One should be alert to the danger of suicide at the time of apparent improvement, after the deepest depression lifts. Most suicides happen within three months after the worst of the depression is over. Many physicians and counselors have been lured into a false sense of security during this "lag time" when the crisis lessens and the patient seems to feel better. Yet in many cases this is when the suicidal person physically has the strength to carry out self-destruction. The patient must be monitored closely with professional treatment—often including antidepressants and/or lithium, along with psychotherapy.

Most suicidal people are ambivalent about dying. As many as 60 to 70 percent have seen a doctor for medical help within six months of their suicide. One woman who tried to commit suicide by jumping off a bridge wished on the way down she would be rescued. Fortunately, she was picked up by a fisherman. After years of maintenance antidepressant drug treatment for severe recurrent depression, she never tried it again.

In most cases, the suicidal mood is temporary, and so the majority of people who receive help after an attempt don't try again. However, multiple attempts *are* common when there has been no counseling, no intervention by a crisis center, or no long-term antidepressant treatment by a psychiatrist. For biological depression and manic depression, the patient needs continuous preventive antidepressant medications and/or lithium.

Many of my patients are severely depressed and manic-depressive, a group that has the highest incidence of suicide attempters and completers among people with psychiatric conditions. In one study I completed with my team at Columbia University, 38 percent of depressive and manic-depressive patients had attempted suicide before lithium treatment. A patient with a severe mood disorder usually has a 16-percent chance of successful suicide. After lithium treatment is begun, however, the suicide rate drops drastically. Out of nine thousand depressed and manic-depressive patients followed on lithium at three large treatment centers in America, including my own Foundation and practice, only four suicides occurred over twenty years. Clearly, with correct medication and maintenance treatment, most suicides can be avoided.

In most cases antidepressants will help a suicidal person through a crisis. With adolescents, however, medications and psychiatric treatment tend to be rejected. They need an understanding physician and supportive parents to convince them to be treated.

What Family and Friends Should Do

First, be alert to the possibility of depression and suicide, especially in children and teenagers. If you notice changes in behavior, ask directly about suicidal feelings, thoughts, or plans. Usually a suicidal teenager or adult is relieved that someone is concerned enough to see hidden clues and appeals for help. Most people will not volunteer suicidal thoughts, but *will* answer honestly if asked.

Ascertain how long the person has had such feelings. How urgent is the situation? Find out if there is a *definite* plan and means available. Remember that all suicide threats and attempts should be taken seriously. Especially among adolescents, who are more impulsive than adults, a disbelieving remark or criticism ("You wouldn't be stupid enough to do that") may provide the impetus to act.

Be especially aware of the danger if there have been previous suicide attempts in the patient or the family, if the person possesses a gun, has made defiant open threats, is a reckless driver, and/or has been found sitting on the windowsill or on the roof alone. Under these circumstances, immediate hospitalization and treatment is imperative.

If a friend confides suicidal wishes, listen, don't judge. Ask questions like, "What makes you feel so low?" Many times a suicidal state has been defused by the person talking about his or her feelings. But don't take chances: Get the person to a psychiatrist immediately.

If the person seems in immediate danger, don't leave him or her alone. Call a suicide prevention center, hospital emergency room, crisis intervention center, physician, psychiatrist, or hotline. Most hotline phone numbers can be found in the Yellow Pages. In most cases a suicidal patient should be hospitalized immediately, not even allowed to go home to spend the night.

The family should be involved in the treatment process. Most suicidal situations involve a significant other with whom there has been a fight or rejection, or loss through death. It is important that a depressed, suicidal patient not be returned to the same stressful environment. A parent should consider changing the child's school, teachers, or outside activities, reducing course load, getting academic help.

A suicidal patient often does not keep follow-up appointments, so I make it a point to insist on a contract of weekly visits to me for medication and therapy—and I have my nurse call the patient to make sure that the appointment is kept.

Most suicides *can* be prevented.

EIGHT

Moods and Great Men: Abraham Lincoln, Theodore Roosevelt, and Winston Churchill

Abraham Lincoln

It is an astonishing fact that Abraham Lincoln suffered recurrent periods of mental depression during the years he practiced law in Illinois and later when he was President of the United States. His depressions are documented in his letters, in the newspapers of the period, and also in the journals and letters of those who knew him intimately. Biographers have noted that a prominent feature of Lincoln's personality was melancholy, and most of those who knew him commented on it. No one was able to determine what caused it, and few have viewed his alternating periods of achievement and depression in the light of modern biochemical theories of manic depression.

Lincoln's recurrent states of despair and exhaustion, alternating with periods of hard work and very effective functioning, were what I would consider a mild form of bipolar manic depression; or at the very least its closely related form, unipolar recurrent depression. Bipolar manic depression usually comes on in the early twenties and is characterized by a lifetime of alternating mild-to-serious highs and lows. Unipolar recurrent depression, in contrast, usually has its onset in the late thirties and early forties and is characterized by recurrent depressions, alternating with periods of normal functioning, during the remaining years of life.

It is puzzling that Abraham Lincoln's depressions have not been written about or talked about at greater length. Evidently the problem of mental disabilities in high office was of little concern to the public until Senator Thomas Eagleton's vice presidential nomination on the Democratic ticket in 1972, when his history of severe mental depressions and electroshock treatments became widely known.

Psychologists have explained Lincoln's melancholic state in classical Freudian terms, claiming that some real or imagined loss must have preceded each of his depressed periods. His depressions have also been explained as the result of a childhood fall in which he received a possible fracture of the skull and resulting brain injury. Naturally, if such an event did take place, no firm diagnosis could have been made because of the lack of modern X-ray methods and the fact that so little was known about the neurophysiology of the brain in the nineteenth century. Others have accounted for Lincoln's depressions simply as part of his unique genius, suggesting that the minds of great men defy probing, particularly when the probing is retrospective.

There is no adequate record of a history of depressions or psychiatric disturbance among Lincoln's relatives. However, we do know that Lincoln's father was dissatisfied and restless in his youth, moody and impulsive in middle age. Lincoln went through an overtalkative, wild, and possibly hypomanic period in his adolescence and early twenties, involving himself in numerous fights. On one occasion, when he was not invited to a wedding, he wrote a long-winded, inappropriate, and insulting poem to the bride and groom. On another occasion he wrote a note on "Suicide" for the *Sangamon Journal.*

Lincoln, at the age of twenty-nine, following the death of his first love, Ann Rutledge, plunged into a profound depression. He was seen wandering up and down the river through the woods, distracted and filled with indescribable grief. Fearing that he might commit suicide, his friends deprived him of knives and razors. At the time of Ann's death, according to his landlady, "the community said he was crazy, but he was not crazy, but simply very despondent for a long time."

When grief over the death of a loved one produces such a prolonged and deep depression with accompanying physical symptoms of appetite and weight loss, sleeplessness and suicidal threats, I would be concerned that it might be more than simply a reactive depression due to grief and loss. Instead, I would suspect a depression with underlying biological roots and an autonomy apart from the actual stress of the death of the loved one; in other words, the depressive phase of a preexisting manic depression. Depression might have developed even without the stressful event, which is often simply coincidental in time with manic-depressive episodes. Despite evidence that Lincoln had a hyperactive period in his adolescence and early twenties and was subject to depressive moods prior to age twenty-nine, most biographers have been content to ascribe his first deep depression to the death of Ann Rutledge. Nevertheless, there is good reason for a biochemically oriented psychiatrist to believe that Lincoln's first major depression had not only environmental but also metabolic roots. I am also influenced by the fact that it continued for many months after Ann's death, incapacitating him completely at first. Later he was able to read law, to help with the harvest, and to return to the legislature, although he continued to be dejected beyond the normal period of grief.

Eventually Lincoln consulted his physician, Dr. Anson Henry, who told him he had a nervous condition, noting his depressed state of mind, lack of energy, and his obsessive thoughts and indecisiveness. At age thirty Lincoln was described as introverted and withdrawn, yet at times energetic and ambitious. He was regarded as a fine trial lawyer and a calculating politician, but as somewhat shy, self-doubting, and diffident with women.

As I have often found with mildly depressed people and low-keyed individuals, Lincoln chose for his next love a woman whose personality was the opposite of his. Mary Todd was full of energy, impulsive, extroverted, and ambitious. A socially dominating woman, she sought out enjoyment and excitement, quite unlike Lincoln during that period.

In January 1841, when Lincoln and Mary Todd were to be

married, Lincoln failed to show up at the wedding. Friends found him at daybreak walking alone, restless, desperate, and seriously depressed. Again it was feared that he might take his own life, and he was watched day and night; knives, razors, and every other instrument that could be used for self-destruction were kept out of his reach. Lincoln's law partner and biographer, William H. Herndon, wrote that Mary Todd's sister, Mrs. Edwards, in whose home Lincoln lived, viewed Lincoln's unusual behavior as insane, and Mary also expressed this opinion to relieve her own embarrassment. Lincoln's depression at the time had the symptoms of loss of interest in his surroundings, headaches, nervous indigestion, anxiety, frustration, and fatigue.

The details of this story may be apocryphal, but Lincoln in 1841 did suffer a second, well-documented major depression; and he himself referred to it as beginning on "the fatal first of January." Despite her mortifying experience, Mary Todd's interest in Lincoln continued, and eventually ended in marriage.

Various biographers of Lincoln, including Carl Sandberg, have explained that his illness was brought on by poor food, exposure to bad weather, and overwork. R. P. Randall attributes Lincoln's depression to flu and the fact that the Edwards family thought him unsuitable for Mary Todd because of his humble origins and lack of culture. All of these "explanations" cannot account for the severity of the depressions, or for the fact that they now appear to have been recurrent and intrinsic, indicating some chemical vulnerability. Of course, retrospective analyses and diagnoses of historical personalities are always suspect. However, as a biological psychiatrist with a background of psychoanalytical training, on the strength of what I have read about Lincoln, I would diagnose his mood disorder as a mild bipolar manic depression, since historical records suggest highs between deep depressive attacks.

The acute phase of Lincoln's depressive attack in January 1841 lasted for more than a week. Lincoln was too agitated and unreasonable to be able to work, but he was never irrational and delusional about his personal relations. His inability to attend the legislative sessions, and the fears of his colleagues that he would attempt suicide, would in modern times prompt most psychiatrists to arrange for inpatient hospitalization and treatment. I would insist on hospitalization, observation for suicidal intent, antidepressant drugs, and later administration of lithium as the treatment of choice for such a condition.

Although there was an effort to keep Lincoln's condition quiet, it was a common subject of gossip in Springfield. During this period his law partner complained that he was slow and not sufficiently energetic in a particular case. Years later, after his inauguration as President, Lincoln's characteristic slowness was noted when he protected himself, no matter what the emergency, from being rushed into decision making.

He was distant and few people really got to know him; but alternatively, when he was thrown into a social situation he could become gregarious and talkative, telling stories, joking, laughing, adapting to the situation. He was extremely moody, and at times his mood would swing back in the other direction, from overtalkativeness to a reticent and secretive state.

His rival in Illinois was Stephen A. Douglas, who was described as magnetic, a man who attracted a host of friends. In contrast, Lincoln at forty-nine was a man who did not care for a following. The look of melancholy was always with him. Despite his humility, Lincoln had a sense of himself in history during the great Lincoln-Douglas debates. At the time he showed unusual nervous energy, as many of the negative comments in the Democratic newspapers relayed. His speechmaking—fifty speeches in all—in the Senate race required excessive effort, and I would be inclined to interpret this period as the end phase of a mild manic mood cycle.

After his crowning speech in the debates in Quincy, he broke down, agitated and exhausted. I suspect that this switch into a low mood marked the beginning of the depressed phase of his subtle manic-depressive cycle. His friends then took him to a hotel room, where he commented that he was so exhausted he might have to give up the race, but after a night's sleep he seemed to revive.

Douglas, his diminutive, arrogant, and ambitious rival, finally won the bitterly contested Senate election, and is credited, in fact, by some historians as having won the debate. Even though Lincoln lost this crucial Senate race he remained in good spirits; the stress of losing did not seem to precipitate the least hint of a depressive reaction. This fact helps substantiate my hypothesis that Lincoln's depressions were mostly metabolic in origin. In some instances they may have been precipitated by stress, but more often than not they seem to have occurred independent of loss and adversity, as most metabolic depressions do.

Lincoln's lack of depression after the startling defeat in the 1858 Senate election was a surprise to his friends and critics. Even though he lost, Lincoln said, "The question is not half settled. New splits and divisions will soon be upon our adversaries; and we shall [have] fun again." In fact, Lincoln made it clear that he was not giving up and would continue to fight, mapping out the strategy that eventually won for him, in 1860, the Republican nomination for the presidency.

During Lincoln's first eighteen months as President of the United States, he had many periods of uncontrollable depression characterized by many of his previous symptoms, resulting in periodic ineffectiveness and indecisiveness when leadership was much needed. The worst period came when his son Willie died in the White House, and Lincoln gave up every Thursday to sitting alone and mourning his son's loss. From all the evidence, including personal letters written during those months, from biographies and various after-the-fact psychiatric opinions, it is clear that he suffered from a major depressive moodswing.

My hypothesis, that Lincoln in reality suffered from a subtle form of bipolar manic depression, is partially supported by some critics who have claimed that there were also mild, elated states in Lincoln's personal life that compensated for his melancholic periods. However, these mild elations were at no time documented as pathological manic bursts of activity. With historical figures we cannot assemble an accurate family pedigree, as we can now do with depressed patients and their relatives. Modern psychiatrists specializing in manic depression interview all available relatives directly, searching for a family history of depression, manic depression, alcoholism, or suicide to help substantiate a diagnosis of manic depression. But the fact that Lincoln's depressions began in his early twenties is consistent with the onset of manic depression and with the findings of most modern genetic studies of this illness.

The mild highs so difficult to substantiate in historical records on Lincoln are just as elusive to document in great men today, if one is not searching between the lines. Usually it is the depressive phase, when functioning fails, which receives the attention of family, physicians, and the media. Mild mania and highly effective functioning often merge. This area of human behavior remains unexplored, and hyperperformance remains poorly defined in relation to manic-depressive moodswing. The depressed person will usually seek help, but during the mild, manic high the bipolar personality does not consider himself sick. As in the several case histories cited earlier, he or she often functions exceptionally well. Many manic-depressives may thus be highly effective, forceful, and energetic, and they are not labeled as ill except during their depressions.

Although it was generally not publicized as part of Lincoln's temperament, there were well-documented periods when he swung out of his melancholy and lethargy into states of excess energy. At one time he delivered twenty speeches in two weeks. Frequently during such times he had trouble pacing himself and wound up exhausted—typical of the hypomanic.

Lincoln's high drive despite deep depressions helps account for the leap from his impoverished life in the Illinois log-cabin days to the Presidency of the United States. This upswing side of Lincoln's personality has gone unnoticed by biographers. Although his range of ideas, lack of sleep, impulsivity, and moodiness furnish us with certain characteristics of the hypomanic personality, Lincoln does not come across as the classical manic with flair, spark, and charm who often goes too far.

Lincoln's depressions may have been much the same as those of Senator Thomas Eagleton. However, Eagleton, living in a period when modern psychiatric treatment is available, received antidepressant drugs and electroshock treatments. Lincoln did not receive these treatments because they were not available. Instead, he got calomel. Lincoln would probably have responded, I think, to maintenance lithium-carbonate therapy and periodic antidepressant-drug treatment, but the weight of public opinion would have ruled him out as a Presidential candidate in modern times.

Theodore Roosevelt

Theodore Roosevelt was the first after Lincoln to claim attention as a major charismatic figure in the White House. Unlike Lincoln's, Roosevelt's moods were predominantly high. For him life was strife. He was constantly active. His flamboyant personality was worlds apart from that of his presidential predecessors. Not since Thomas Jefferson, and not again until John F. Kennedy, was the White House so teeming with fascinating men and frenetic activity.

Roosevelt was viewed by most of his contemporaries as the most interesting man of the times, and his buoyant spirits became reflected by a national mood of mild elation and optimism. His enormous capacity for work and his constant involvement in new projects gave a lift to the spirits of millions of average men. Henry Cabot Lodge wrote that "his mere presence was so full of vitality, so charged with energy, that it was contagious, and seemed to bring out all the possible joy of living as a gift or rather as an atmosphere to those who rode or walked beside him."

Even as a boy Theodore Roosevelt was, despite his delicate health, overactive and precocious. He was always interested in nature, in the world around him. His high moods as a child were associated with overtalkativeness—a hypomanic trait that was to be present for most of his life and to worsen with time. In 1869, when he was eleven, his family moved from Manhattan to Oyster Bay, Long Island; and in 1870, when they returned to the house on Twentieth Street, they built a gymnasium in it to help his poor physique. As a result of his strenuous efforts at body building, at seventeen he began winning at the broad jump and the pole vault, and was soon an excellent boxer.

His career at Harvard was unimpressive and gave few clues to the greatness that was to come. In his freshman year he neither smoked nor drank. At Harvard it was considered poor form to be too enthusiastic, to show too much ambition or too great an interest in study, or even to walk too fast. And Roosevelt, as one of his fellow students said, "was always running." His talkativeness and nervousness made him unpopular and something of a joke. He had few friends in college and was remembered as being sometimes depressed during this period. He finished twenty-first out of a hundred in his class. He was competent, but no leader.

Interestingly enough, in view of his later male chauvinism, his senior dissertation was on equal rights for women and men: "The Practicability of Equalizing Men and Women Before the Law," in which he took up the feminist cause. But perhaps this was the influence of Alice Lee, whom Roosevelt had met in 1878 and whom he defiantly took to the Porcellian Club, which had never before been entered by a woman. Alice discouraged his eagerness, which caused him much annoyance at times. But she probably saved him from exhausting himself on many occasions.

Roosevelt's attraction to this calm girl illustrates once again the tendency of hypomanics to be attracted to and to marry people whom they can control, who do not frustrate their schemes or interrupt their goals and demands, but who often turn out to be their salvation, because of their slower, steadier pace and their more realistic judgment.

Roosevelt married Alice in the same year he graduated from Harvard. Four years later, on February 14, 1884, Alice died after giving birth to a daughter. Roosevelt's mother died twelve hours later. His grief was deep, but it did not extend beyond the normal grieving period into a prolonged depression as Lincoln's grief had after Ann Rutledge's death. Roosevelt continued his new political duties in the legislature and was married again in 1886, to Edith Kermit Carow. With her he had five children.

In 1882, as a young politician in Albany, he had been considered so excitable and impatient that his career had been in jeopardy. Nevertheless, he "rose like a rocket," in his own words, displaying traits of the hypomanic charmer—doing too much and talking too much—first in the New York State

Assembly and later as governor. During those years he had moods of mild depression and elation, but he always continued working despite them. He was not introspective, and surrendered to depression only for short periods.

In 1887, after a brief period of melancholy, he switched again into a hypomanic state. When he had first seen the American West in 1883, he had been drawn to it as an outlet for his restlessness and had started a ranch. The West exhilarated him as much as public life did. During this period he had many hobbies and pursued every subject with an insatiable thirst for knowledge and experience. He was never bored and rarely inactive physically or mentally. Most psychoanalysts would interpret such frenzied activity as a defense against depression. I would interpret it as mild manic activity, mostly chemical or metabolic in origin and not so inappropriate that treatment would be considered. In his case it was productive and in many instances creative. Creative talent, I have found, must be there on its own to begin with, and, if present in such a human dynamo, it may express itself in extraordinary ways.

The irrepressible Roosevelt soon began to personify the new American ego—all action and energy—in the national policy of foreign expansion that was to follow. Happy manics, not paranoid manic personalities, are likable and amusing. They attract a following as long as they are not crossed. If they go too high, they tend to become irrational, and people lose faith in them as leaders. Roosevelt was soon appointed a member of the U.S. Civil Service Commission. He applied his enormous capacities to corruption in the Civil Service system and became famous when newspaper headlines began to recount his violent quarrels with anyone who dared stand in his way.

In 1895 he was appointed to head the police board of New York City and, as with most hypomanic bosses, was said to be inconsiderate of the feelings of his colleagues. During his reign, there was constant friction and fighting, since a hypomanic must impose his will and he often tries to do so with complete lack of tact. The first day he was in office he charged into headquarters, got himself elected chairman, and demanded as he caught his breath, "What'll we do now?"

His police-commissioner days made him famous, since his hypomanic personality permitted him to stay awake nights walking the streets of New York City. He hoped to find a patrol officer asleep while on duty, or talking to a prostitute, or having a drink in the local bar. In the early morning Roosevelt would return to his office couch for one or two hours of sleep, and by ten he was refreshed and energetic, ready to deal with bewildered employees—victims of his nocturnal inspections.

These nights of walking and little sleep are solid diagnostic clues to Roosevelt's excess manic energy. Many manics work all night and can go without much sleep for days, weeks, or months on end. I always ask about a person's sleeping habits, which are critical in trying to pin down a diagnosis of manic depression.

His reform politics as well as his manner often made Theodore Roosevelt unpopular. In 1895 Roosevelt wrote to his friend Cabot Lodge that he needed advice on his shortcomings, since not one New York City newspaper or politician was on his side. Lodge told Roosevelt, "Talk as little as possible," but the Roosevelt loquaciousness persisted.

In the same year, Roosevelt told Lodge that the "country needs a war." This attitude offended President Charles W. Eliot of Harvard, who called it a "chip on the shoulder" attitude that was inexcusably dangerous and offensive. Roosevelt seemed unable to suppress ideas that demanded a show of arms on the part of the United States. At the possibility of a war with Spain over Cuba, Roosevelt jumped with enthusiasm stating, "I'm for it," and his manic energy may well have been a significant factor in precipitating the Spanish-American War.

Roosevelt himself was a colonel in the Spanish War. He helped organize and eventually commanded a front action cavalry regiment known as the "Rough Riders." He could hardly wait to get to Cuba, where he led the famous cavalry charge in the battle of San Juan Hill. He was idolized by his men, who would follow him anywhere. Such ability to lead and inspire is typical of other intelligent, manic leaders, many of whom can persuade others to do almost anything. The combat losses in his regiment were incredibly high as compared to those of the other five regiments, and Roosevelt's efficiency in Cuba was none too good.

By 1899 Roosevelt was governor of New York, and his energy and enthusiasm were greater than ever. To get Roosevelt out of his hair, Thomas C. Platt, the Republican boss in New York State, arranged to have him nominated for the vice presidency. Roosevelt wanted another term as governor, but with characteristic drive he began campaigning for the vice presidency. During the next few months he seemed to be in the grip of a messianic urge, commonly seen in manics, which enabled him to stage a vice presidential campaign so strenuous that even he found it a bit wearing. By mid-October his voice was giving out and he was being criticized for neglecting his duties as governor of New York.

The reward of the zealous, manic campaign was victory; the McKinley-Roosevelt ticket defeated William Jennings Bryan. In September 1901, McKinley was assassinated. When Roosevelt took over the presidency at forty-three, he was the youngest President in history.

Critics feel that Theodore Roosevelt was then as high as he could get—politically and, I would add, emotionally. Mark Hanna, the Republican chairman, referred to him as a "madman." Henry Adams wrote, "Power when wielded by abnormal energy is the most serious of facts," and all Roosevelt's friends knew that his restless and combative energy was very abnormal. His rise to the presidency was viewed by some with alarm, and people feared that this man of moods might do something impulsive, endangering the country. But for the great majority of the public, his colorfulness was so intriguing that they became more interested in his personality than in his speeches and actions.

He was at the presidential desk by 7:30 A.M., and he had visitors at breakfast, lunch, and dinner. People predicted his collapse, but cartoonists were delighted with this new, impulsive, undiplomatic figure in the White House. Often he would go too high, work himself into a rage, and distort the facts. He demonstrated that he could lose his head completely in a manic rage when he sued the *New York World* and *Indianapolis News* for criminal libel. He became so angry that he contradicted himself a number of times. In spite of his enormous prestige, his attempts to bully the court and suppress freedom of the press met defeat.

I have treated a number of manic patients who enjoy legal battles, and their forceful, demanding personalities are often well known to Washington politicians and the senior partners of powerful law firms. More often than not, their grandiose schemes are undertaken with good legal backing. Since lawyers only advise and act on points of law, they cannot diagnose a request that is motivated by a manic or depressive mood, or refer their clients to a psychiatrist, unless a very serious disturbance is evident. Even then they risk being fired.

Many people were disturbed by the motley crew Roosevelt dragged into the White House. Acting in the democratic tradition, he would often turn his back on the privileged. The White House became a circus. At luncheon he would talk incessantly with the visitors crowding his table. After lunch he would run to his office, where he saw senators, cabinet members, bureau chiefs, congressmen, and a long, steady stream of average citizens. Later in the day he would go riding, swimming, or walking—sometimes all three—before dinner. In Roosevelt's day, it was one big "powwow" at the presidential dinner table, with Theodore dominating, talking nonstop—and he didn't talk so much as shout.

His day would continue long after midnight, when he would devour current literature, Greek classics, or biology. He would study special subjects if an authority was coming to lunch the next day. Specialists were astounded by his knowledge.

He slept erratically, but after his eighteen-hour workday the little sleep he had was sound and refreshing—a sine qua non of the hypomanic state. This incredible schedule was his living pattern. A visiting Briton stated that the two most extraordinary works of nature in America were Niagara Falls and the President in the White House. Theodore Roosevelt he described as "an interesting combination of St. Vitus and St. Paul."

Some of Roosevelt's biographers insist he had no unusual endowment. But the evidence is that he possessed the amazing mental energy of the manic coupled with his own physical strength. After battling verbally with senators and congressmen, he would occasionally go a few rounds with a hired prizefighter, who would finally knock him down. Psychoanalysts might claim that a man with so much activity absorbing his life is simply defending himself against an underlying depression. Biographers have said that Roosevelt, forcing himself all the time, attempted to cram his days with more than they could hold because otherwise life would have been "intolerable."

One of Roosevelt's secretaries stated that during his governorship and presidency he wrote 150,000 letters. Like many manics I have known and treated, he was constantly occupied with telephoning, talking, and letter writing. If the estimate that he wrote eighteen million words in his lifetime is true, he produced the equivalent of forty years' work in the lifetime of a literary man. One edition of his writings, made up of books and articles, papers and speeches, totals twenty volumes, and at least 100,000 of his letters have been preserved.

In 1908 William Howard Taft, a comparative slowpoke, was selected by Roosevelt as his successor. Theodore Roosevelt was fifty years old. He didn't know how to retire. "I like my job," he said. "The burdens will be laid aside with a good deal of regret." His problem was what to do with himself and his manic energy. In the same year, when the president of Harvard resigned, Roosevelt became a contender. But an overseer, Henry Higgenson, wrote, "We need a man of judgment, and is judgment to be found coupled with such enormous energy?" The post was not offered to Roosevelt. His physical stamina was still high. In 1909, when he was fifty-one, he rode horseback over one hundred miles to shame grumblers in the Army who resisted an order requiring them to ride a certain distance. To keep busy he took off on a prolonged and dangerous trip to Africa. Many thought he would not return alive, being middle-aged, blind in one eye, and overweight. The nation was fascinated by the newspaper accounts of his experiences killing lions and searching out adventure.

He then toured Europe in an elated state and wrote back that he was having a magnificent time. He was enraptured and amused by the customs and personalities of European monarchs. He wrote in a grandiose fashion to Lodge when he was in Cairo, "I have been administering private discipline to the Pope and the Kaiser on questions of ethics and etiquette respectively." At a solemn banquet hosted by King George in honor of visiting monarchs at the time of King Edward's death, it was feared that Roosevelt might insist on wearing his Rough Rider uniform, which had accompanied him throughout Europe. His ultimate reception home from Europe drew multitudes of people, including bathing beauties, twenty-five hundred politicians, generals, and others—evidence that Roosevelt was still considered the first citizen of the world even though Taft was now in the White House.

In 1912 Roosevelt decided to try for a third term. I feel at this point in his career his moodswing was up, and severely so, as reported by some biographers and evidenced by his repetitiveness. It is possible that he was having a more overt manic attack at this time. Dr. Morton Prince, then an apostle of Freudian psychology, commented on Roosevelt's subconscious desire not to be nominated or elected—an interpretation at odds with modern biological psychiatry. I feel that his moodswing was recurring and that it ultimately played a role in his failure to be renominated.

A final estimate of Roosevelt expressed by Senator Nelson Aldrich was that he was not the greatest statesman, but was probably the greatest politician of his time. He was accused by reactionaries of every conceivable crime, while among the righteous he was felt to be insane. But it is also true that he seemed to be the happiest man who ever lived in the White House. His happiness, often merging with manic elation, no doubt affected history.

Winston Churchill

In the early 1960s I had the good fortune to meet and talk one evening with Sir Winston Churchill's only son, Randolph, the writer and journalist, who died in 1968. Randolph was then fifty, and he had a reputation for moodiness, heavy drinking, and marital instability; he was considered a relative failure, when compared to his father, in almost everything he undertook. At the time Randolph was working on a biography of his father.

This social meeting occurred during a period of my own life when I had just finished my psychiatric training and I had begun to have serious doubts about the value of psychotherapy or psychoanalysis for treating any of the recurrent depressive or manic-depressive states. I was then beginning to search for a viable therapeutic alternative for these conditions.

Randolph Churchill told me that he had been painfully depressed during major periods of his life and that he had become a chronic alcoholic partially as a result of his attempts to treat his depressions with alcohol. He talked about his father's serious and prolonged depressions. Randolph also told me his father had had periods of high energy when he was forceful, driving, tireless, and in need of very little sleep. At those times Winston seemed to be able to achieve whatever he wished, to conquer any impossible situtation, to succeed brilliantly as a writer, politician, warrior, or prime minister. My talk with Randolph Churchill provided some firsthand knowledge of the Churchill family pedigree. In retrospect, with insight into the genetics of manic depression, knowledge acquired during the past twenty-five years, I would conclude that this was indeed a family in which moodswing prevailed and had been passed down from generation to generation.

Winston Churchill was born in 1874, at the home of his grandfather, the duke of Marlborough. He was the eldest son of Randolph Churchill, who died in 1895, and Jennie Jerome, a rich and beautiful American. Randolph was a prominent and quite imaginative Tory politician who reached his height in politics in 1886, when he became chancellor of the exchequer.

Churchill's two ancestries were powerful, and either might have produced a man of stature. On his maternal side his grandfather, Leonard Jerome, was an American millionaire; and on his paternal side, the first duke of Marlborough had won a series of decisive military victories against King Louis XIV of

France at the beginning of the eighteenth century. He was known as a man who always had to win.

Like his father, Winston Churchill was intensely ambitious, but like the young Roosevelt, he somehow failed to show any early promise and was shunted off to the military. He was educated at Harrow and at eighteen he became a cadet at the Royal Military College at Sandhurst. He was soon aware of the possibilities that the world offered him, and it was obvious at an early age that he was intent on fame and fortune as well. As a young man he fought in India on the northwestern frontier and then served with the Nile expeditionary force. After writing a brilliant book about each of these war experiences, he participated in the Boer War as a correspondent and was captured and escaped. This became material for yet another book. His writings were bold and outspoken, and told the facts. Before he was twenty-five, he had already attacked the cruelty of wars, the incompetency of generals, and the frailties of government.

Winston Churchill began his political career when the British Empire was the most powerful influence in world politics. From 1906 to 1922 he moved up fast, as undersecretary for the colonies, president of the Board of Trade, and home secretary. During the First World War he was first lord of the admiralty, then minister of munitions. From 1918 to 1921 he was secretary of state both for war and for air. Then he was made secretary of state for the colonies. From 1924 to 1929 he was chancellor of the exchequer, but his aggressive energy and his increasingly critical attitude toward his colleagues weakened and isolated him, and he suffered a number of political setbacks.

At the time of the Second World War, Churchill again rose to great heights and became prime minister, leading Britain against Hitler. Churchill could not see the possibility of solutions other than his own for problems. His unwavering confidence in doing things "my way" during his energetic periods is typical of manics I have treated, as was his love of words, as evidenced by his endless talking and writing.

He was a masterly writer, and he was able to present his own version of events with an overpoweringly persuasive rhetoric. From an early age Churchill had developed knowledge of and love and respect for English prose. Speeches and articles flowed from him. The constant letter writing and talking were looked upon by his peers with amazement. I view these aspects of his hypomanic personality as hypercompetency, not surprising in a manic-depressive. Naturally his intelligence, position, and a host of other factors were also of key importance to his impressive accomplishments.

Churchill devoted himself single-mindedly to the immediate question at hand, whether it was solving the problems of the poor or how to unload a truck. He was very methodical and believed that administration should not be haphazard, that all orders should be conveyed in writing, or, if discussed orally first, they should then be written out.

Certain of his memoranda had red tags saying, "Action this day," and that probably helped produce the efficiency essential later in winning the war. Churchill's irritability hurt many people's feelings, and his Edwardian high spirits, what I would view as outright hypomanic elation, were too much for many of his political contemporaries.

His life was turbulent; his own energies made it so. He was never complacent and never still. Churchill's excitement about any new possibility that offered itself and his frequent overcommitment to the cause of the moment continued throughout his life.

People had thought that at the rate he was going, there would hardly be room for him in Parliament at age thirty, or in England at age forty, since his rapid pace could not last. At an early age he had been far ahead of his contemporaries. Around the turn of the century, like Roosevelt in America, he had been known as someone terribly colorful; there were wonderful stories about him. Stanley Baldwin, later the Tory leader between the wars, acknowledged many of Churchill's gifts, but felt that, since he lacked judgment and wisdom during his high, frenetic energy states, his opinions could not be taken too seriously. The famous critic, of course, was right; Churchill's moodswings did result in a lack of caution and balance. The same accusations had been leveled at Theodore Roosevelt.

Churchill was known as being reckless of his life and of his money, indifferent to all consequences. This lack of censorship, typical of manics, can result in disaster. David Lloyd George saw Churchill's impetuosity as being in need of supervision. Men with his temperament and mentality, said Lloyd George, need exceptionally strong brakes. But manic people refuse to have others slow them down, and Churchill's pace continued.

Churchill's contemporaries therefore distrusted him, just as Theodore Roosevelt's had. Churchill's tireless energy, they thought, would be invaluable only when controlled. Such criticism even today raises the question of how to manage manic genius, particularly when it is possessed by a leader. His future, some felt, depended on whether he could establish a reputation for prudence without losing his energy. Lord Beaverbrook saw him as a man with prolific new ideas, exploding in different directions like machine-gun bullets, but lacking caution.

Churchill was viewed as brilliant but hotheaded, impulsive—and certainly insolent and domineering. In his high periods he talked nonstop and said whatever came into his mind. He tried to do too much; not one department or one war was enough for him. Like Theodore Roosevelt, Churchill was a universal and inevitable subject for discussion at every dinner table and on every level of society. He had more ideas and presented more memos than any other cabinet member. In presenting proposals of strategy, he usually offered more than the entire general staff. Harold Nicholson called Churchill an "Anglo-American freak" who did many things at the same time—writing books, learning history, managing the War Office, and undertaking grandiose plans on all sides that had to be curtailed by his immediate team.

Such a perfect description of a hypomanic is found in most psychiatric textbooks. General Montgomery thought of his main quality as supremacy over others—"Churchill must dominate." Aneurin Bevan thought that Churchill needed to be kept in check, that he did too much and did not have colleagues around him to whom he could delegate responsibilities concerning the central direction of the war. Bevan feared that his defects could be extremely dangerous.

At times his contemporaries thought that he had lost his head completely, and called him as H. G. Wells did, the British Führer. "He has never given evidence of thinking extensively, or of having any scientific or literary capacity. Now he seems to have lost his head completely."

With his enormous capacity for work, Churchill frequently stayed up all night. He could not always wait until breakfast to read the morning papers, but would send for them during the night when they came off the press. For most manics time is crucial and not to be wasted. Despite this pattern he had a tremendous capacity to relax. While his brain was working, he rested his body. He did much reading and writing propped up in bed.

Churchill also had his depressed periods as well as his highs. His famous episodes of "Black Dog," or deep depression, are well known. All his life he fought against severe spells of melancholy. His physician, Lord Moran (Sir Charles Wilson), mentions Churchill's Black Dog in his biography. He quotes Churchill as saying:

> When I was young, for two or three years, the light faded out, I did my work barely, sat in the House of Commons, but black depression settled on me. It helped me to talk to Clemmy. I don't like standing near the edge of a platform when an express train is passing through. I like it wider between me and the train. I don't like to stand on the side of a ship and look into the water. I don't want to go out in the world, even so at all, at such moments.

These autobiographical comments on his depressive moods are invaluable in diagnosing Churchill as manic-depressive, and they emphasize the seriousness and depth of his depressed phases, as well as suggest his fear of suicide.

One politician told Moran that Churchill had always been a despairer, looking at the dark side of life. Moran states in his book that Winston made very little effort to hide his depression after the age of fifty-five, and that little seemed left for him in life. Churchill's later depression, described by Moran, in part reflected apathy—a giving up of reading, speaking very little, sitting for hours in what I would interpret as a serious depressive stupor.

Sarah Churchill, his daughter, in her book *Thread in the Tapestry*, portrays her father as follows: "Despite his eulogies, accolades and honors, Winston still had a void in his heart, in the heart of his being, which no achievement or honor could completely fulfill." Was it worth it? This is a question that occurs again and again in the lives of people who suffer from depression. A depressive exhaustion and wish for peace filled Churchill's soul even at thirty-one and thirty-two, when he wrote his novel, *Savrola*. In this book an underlying despair and the feeling of uncertainty are already evident. Before his death Churchill stated, "I have achieved a great deal but I've achieved nothing in the end," illustrating the emotional impoverishment that manic-depressives feel in the depressed phase of their illness.

Most of Winston Churchill's depressions seem to have been chemical or metabolic, occurring for no apparent reason and persiting for protracted periods. However, during the years he was struggling for power, his depressions seemed to be precipitated by, or at least coincidental with, external circumstances. In this respect, Churchill did have a succession of disappointments and political defeats. He said at one point before the Second World War, during a deep depression, "I'm finished."

During the thirties, Churchill, who had been famous for his rudeness, defiance, and high energy in what I would consider periods of mild manic elation, suddenly became as decorous as a churchwarden. The spark was still there in his eye, although it was now harnessed by some unknown force, and only partially obedient to its master. This was the depressive phase of his manic-depressive cycle. Churchill's earlier impetuosity and his tendency toward distractibility are common personality traits in manic people.

As prime minister he seemed to have his manic impulses under better control, and he spent his fabulous energy and enthusiasm leading England through the Second World War. Churchill's indefatigable high spirits during his first term as prime minister are legendary. He was minister of defense as well as prime minister. Even in his sixties and seventies he was up most of the night, exhausting secretaries, staff, and advisers, often much younger men.

Churchill's psychodynamics have intrigued psychologists and psychiatrists for years. There is very little doubt that the moody temperament was part of the Churchill inheritance. His vitality was incredible. He survived until the age of ninety; by eighty he had surmounted a heart attack, three bouts with pneumonia, two strokes, and two operations. He ate too much, drank too much, and smoked too much. Until he was seventy he rarely complained of fatigue; yet he had started life with considerable physical disadvantages, as had Theodore Roosevelt.

Jung would have described Churchill as an extroverted intuitive. In terms of classical German Kraepelinian psychiatry, Churchill would be described as cyclothymic (moody), or manic-depressive. Five of the last seven dukes of Marlborough suffered from severe melancholia, which, I feel, supports the theory that such mood disorders are hereditary and principally biochemical in origin.

Not every psychiatrist would agree with this interpretation or at least with the predominant emphasis that I place on the hereditary determinants of Churchill's major moodswings. Heredity, I feel, was significant in determining the ups and down of his moodswing and thus his political career and life-style.

According to Anthony Storr, the psychobiographer of Churchill, his aggressive courage and dominance were not rooted in the genetics of his family background but were products of his determination, deliberate decision, and iron will. Storr states that the descriptive classification of his highs and lows is not as valuable as an additional psychoanalytic study of his childhood, adolescence, and interpersonal relations. Storr claims that depressives deny themselves rest or relaxation because they cannot afford to stop. The frenetic activity is a defense against the underlying depression. If they are forced by circumstances to stop, the black cloud comes down. This was the explanation most people gave of Churchill's depressions when he left the Admiralty in 1915, when he lost his seat in Parliament in 1922, and when, in 1931, he was still excluded from the government. Depressed patients are seen by modern psychoanalysts as characteristically depending on external forces to maintain self-esteem. When something in the external world of a depressive goes wrong, it throws him into despair. This is the traditional analytic model that for half a century has been applied not only to mild and transient neurotic depressions but also, sweepingly, to all depression, including manic depression and recurrent unipolar depression.

Traditional psychoanalysts say, in accordance with the well-worn cliché, that depressives like Churchill fail to get their anger out, and therefore they are depressed. This is still the cornerstone of the psychoanalytic and psychotherapeutic treatment of most depressed patients today. Storr states that if all depressed people could be engaged constantly in fighting wicked enemies, they would never suffer depression. He feels that those who venture along the corridors of power—the extremely ambitious, highly vulnerable individuals—become exhausted in their energy, vitality, and external drive. This concept of depression invokes unconscious drives and mechanisms of defense in classical Freudian analytic terms. Today this psychoanalytic concept of depression is giving way to modern biochemical theories of elation and depression and their control with lithium.

Psychoanalyst Storr has employed the preconceived model of adult depression and applies it to Churchill's character and past history, concluding that Churchill's depression was due to early deprivation and loss of the love object, mainly his mother. This has also been the traditional explanation for Lincoln's depressive illness. I feel that the high genetic loading of depression, manic depression, and alcoholism in Churchill's family pedigree supports the diagnosis of bipolar manic depression, transmitted mainly through the genes and less so by the environment. The environment helped shape the personality of the man but did not determine the relentless course of his manic depression.

Storr admits that psychoanalytic theory sometimes fails, since it cannot explain Churchill's remarkable ability, which enabled him to conquer his depression for uninterrupted periods in his old age. Most modern chemotherapists would think that Churchill's depressions at that point remitted spontaneously, and given enough time would have recurred.

I have found that manic-depressive individuals share certain personality traits, whether they are born to aristocratic or common parents, whether they go into politics, the arts, business, or the sciences. These traits in part result from the personality of the individual trying to cope with his fluctuating energy levels. Achieving the heights of Theodore Roosevelt and Churchill is not specific to manic-depressive illness. Not all great achievers possess internal energy and drive, nor do all manic individuals possess the intellectual capacity or organizational talent of these leaders. When circumstances, intelligence, and a host of social and cultural factors work together in an individual who also has the manic-depressive chemistry, this individual, I believe, can rise to greater heights than other individuals of similar background who do not possess the internal manic drive.

Findings with the lithium-carbonate prophylaxis of manic depression tend to weaken the psychoanalytic interpretations and explanations of Churchill's manic-depressive illness. Psychoanalysis of an individual may affect his personality, but it will not basically change or prevent his manic and depressive moodswings. Despite severe environmental stresses, lithium and antidepressants tend to prevent the abnormal mood cycles. Ascribing behavior exclusively to an internal alteration of chemistry would likewise be an oversimplification on my part. In this biochemical age of psychiatry, however, it is archaic to explain away a man and his moods with the traditional psychoanalytic terminology above.

Modern biochemical, genetic, and clinical studies would lead me to diagnose Churchill as a manic-depressive. Lithium treatment probably could have controlled his moods. The stubborn bulldog would no doubt have insisted on brandy and soda instead, and history would not have been affected.

NINE

Psychiatric Intervention in Government and Politics

Now that words like *paranoid, schizophrenic, depressed,* and *manic* have become part of ordinary dinner-table conversation, we no longer appraise our leaders in the same terms that were used fifty or a hundred years ago. The front-page news we read often presents soap-opera scenarios of military, political, and economic depression and paranoia. Occasionally, there are intimations on television and in newspapers of mental breakdown on the part of distinguished Americans.

We now use new psychiatric principles to analyze the personalities and motives of people in high office. We are suspicious, and we need explanations for a man's behavior. Educators, politicians, business executives, and those who practice the new science of psychopolitics have begun to believe that psychiatry, if applied correctly, will make men better, will solve problems, and possibly help prevent another Watergate or Irangate. In this age of psychiatry it is inconceivable to many that psychiatrists, like bishops during the Crusades, do not have the answers to all problems of emotions, politics, creativity, finance, biology, and sexuality.

I recently asked a young lawyer what provision the law made for removing a judge who, let us say, became mentally ill when he was in office, who was drinking heavily and hallucinating that people were threatening to kill him.

The lawyer pondered my hypothetical case and finally suggested that the procedure of removal might have to be initiated by the judges of a higher court, who could arrange an examination by two psychiatrists, and both would have to agree the judge should be declared unfit.

Actually, there are several procedures for reviewing and retiring judges whose minds are impaired. These methods are judicial self-policing; they are also complicated and difficult, and none of them entails the opinion of a psychiatrist, even as a consultant. It is fitting that the law should have the best legal means of policing its own members, but it is also unsettling that these means should be as slow and inadequate as they are. No adequate legal procedure exists to remove a Supreme Court justice who has become ill or deranged in office. California voted in 1960 to establish a Judicial Qualifications Commission to deal with unfit judges. Of the first ten cases that resulted in retirement, three were because of severe mental impairment, instability, erratic and perverse behavior, failing memory, inability to concentrate or understand what was being said. Not a very encouraging record. However, the final opinion of the judiciary seems to be that no psychiatrist is more fit to judge a judge than a judge.

Several years ago I was asked to consult with other doctors about a patient in a severe manic state. He was a distinguished lawmaker in his late fifties, only recently retired. Because he was agitated and uncooperative, I learned most of the details of his history from his wife, a woman of incredible patience.

All by himself, he had been building a magnificent swimming pool for his country home in Virginia, working eighteen hours a day at it. He decided to make the pool public and open a concession stand at one end to help defray the mounting costs of the project. When his wife suggested that he might be going overboard, he became furious and threatened to leave her for another woman. Soon afterward, when his wife was out, he took many valuables from the house—his share, he claimed—and sold or pawned them. Complaining that his wife was a stick-in-the-mud, he decided to throw a round-the-clock party, and he invited to the house almost everyone he passed on the street. This psychotic behavior went on for weeks, and during this time he slept only two to four hours a night. He had no time to eat, and he talked continuously, planning grandiose sexual schemes "as soon as someone takes my wife off my hands."

I learned from his long-suffering wife that he had finally staged a mock robbery in their home, tearing apart the living room, spilling things out of drawers, even adding a final touch by dusting the whole mess with a bag of Betty Crocker flour. When his wife returned, she called the family doctor, who advised calling the police. The politican was hospitalized and had to be restrained—forcibly—with nurses around the clock.

The hospital I was called to was a small, private, out-of-the-way facility that was barely capable of handling his case of manic psychosis. On my arrival and introduction to the patient it was quite clear that his stay had been less than enjoyable, as far as he was concerned. He claimed he was in "the Black Hole of Calcutta," and that the hospital was full of filth, rats, and insects. He proclaimed loudly that he was being kept there against his will and without proper authorization. Using a dinner fork as a hacksaw, he had tried to file his way out of the window, but was foiled by an alert guard. Not to be deterred, he enlisted the aid of a twelve-year-old fellow patient and tried to escape from the hospital in a laundry hamper. They were both caught by two attendants who had come on duty early that day.

On the day of my visit, the poor fellow became momentarily cooperative, but I could see that he was trying to please me and convince me he was perfectly sane. He talked nonstop and showed a manic flight of ideas, confusion, and lack of judgment and insight. He said he felt fine, "never felt so good in my life," and it was everyone else who was just too "dead on his feet" to keep up with him.

He seemed typical of the chronic, successful hypomanic—the individual who succeeds in many things because of an unusual endowment of energy and enthusiasm that on occasion goes over the top. On questioning him further, I found that he had been born and raised in a large southwestern city, the youngest son of doting parents. His father was something of a hustler who saw to it that his son lacked nothing. An uncle and aunt on his mother's side were alcoholics, and his mother, near the end of her life, was hospitalized for depression. This is often the genetic pattern of manic-depressive families. In high school the patient had been captain of two teams, valedictorian, and president of his class, although he had few close friends. In college, a prestigious private school, he did just as well. He established an erratic, intense study pattern—two days of studying around the clock, followed by a binge in which he would stay out all night drinking and chasing women and then sleep through classes the next day. He was in the top of his class in graduate school and the youngest to receive his Ph.D. in international diplomacy. He was a distinguished politician by the time he was twenty-eight, when he had already written two books in his field.

The sex life of my patient as a young man had been frenetic. He was, he said, inexperienced until he was twenty-one, after which time he "acquired a taste for it," and became an insatiable sex-seeker. No doubt he was overstating it, but he reported having had hundreds of girl friends, and claimed he had made at least ten of them pregnant. He got abortions for all ten, he said. He described his attitude toward sex as "wholesome and healthy," and summed it up as "the natural desire of men to impregnate as many of the opposite sex as possible while capable."

When I saw this patient for the first time, I was impressed by his incisive manner of speaking, despite the fact that he was in an elated, manic state. He was gray at the temples and in excellent physical shape. He had a spark in his eye and a wild, manic grin on his face. Although he was loquacious and intense, his attention span was brief, and he avoided direct questions. He became suspicious of the interview as it progressed and made it clear that he would rather be somewhere else. He became increasingly arrogant and overbearing and tried to turn the tables so that he was interviewing me. During the interview he paced up and down, picked things up, and put them down. He seemed unable to control his excessive talking or his activity, and he insisted his drinking was no problem.

He told me that his first encounter with psychiatry had been in 1945, when he had had an eight-month period of psychotherapy and finally electroshock therapy for a severe depression. The electroshock treatments had had excellent results and no one had known of his illness. He had continued his job in politics, but by the time he was through therapy, he said, "the psychiatrist was on the couch and I was treating him." He had another series of electroshock treatments when it became necessary in 1950.

Ten years later, he and his wife were in the middle of a trip through Europe when he began feeling manic once again. One night, after an automobile collision that could have killed them both, he was arrested for arguing with the Spanish police. The American embassy intervened on his behalf, and he was allowed to return to the United States. He refused to see a psychiatrist or submit to treatment.

This manic attack was not over, however. He invested in two fly-by-night companies and bought a thirty-room house, which he planned to renovate in his spare time. He became involved in altercations with local officials over zoning laws because he wanted to convert the house into a "retirement" hotel for a select group of politicians and their occasional girl friends. His wife, at the end of her tether, left him for four months. He became so abusive to workmen and city officials after failing to "pull strings" that he had to abandon plans for his project. He sold the house at a tremendous loss, and the deduction he claimed on his income-tax return was so staggering that he was investigated by the Internal Revenue Service. Eventually this manic attack subsided by itself.

Because his wife was independently wealthy, he decided to retire. The following year, while taking a trip around the world, he began experiencing another manic episode in Tokyo. As he was driving a car at top speed toward Fujiyama, which he was intent on climbing, he was involved in another collision. Although he was not injured in the accident, his wife took him to the American Hospital in Tokyo for sedation, hoping that the episode would pass by itself. Upon awakening, he became so angry at his doctor, who he thought had tricked him, that he punched his way out of the hospital. He ran into the street in a hospital gown. Later he reported to me, "I fought off twenty policemen with my bare hands and two fountain pens." A large blanket was thrown over him, and the patient was subdued, sedated, and sent back to the United States to recover.

According to his wife, who was a reliable witness, the politician had had several previous depressions and three manic episodes during the past fifteen years and had recently resumed a pattern of heavy drinking. Between manic and depressive attacks he was sober, extremely adroit, and certainly possessed of all his faculties. He had run several businesses lucratively, and had managed his political office.

Following the consultation a complete physical exam, blood chemistries, and an EKG, I placed him on twelve hundred milligrams of lithium carbonate daily, and for the last several years he has been in excellent condition, free of his manic and depressed states.

The case of the politician illustrates several interesting features of mania. As an alcoholic manic, he became angry, argumentative, and suspicious and he refused treatment until backed up against the wall. Happy manics, on the other hand, are usually euphoric and cooperative. When milder forms of mania are further complicated by drinking, they appear as argumentativeness, chronic irritability, or flouting of authority. This behavior is usually accepted by others as evidence of a troublesome, difficult temperament complicated by drinking. It is not suspected that the mania may be due to an underlying mood disorder and a chemical imbalance in the brain.

In my patient's state of extreme manic excitement, his judgment was severely impaired. He spent excessively, got involved in grandiose schemes to make money, undertook large projects, and tangled with legal authority with great relish. He also drank excessively. Having "political friends" enabled him to fend off the ordinary restraining legal forces of society during his earlier, milder attacks. Thus he resisted any treatment for years.

How can society protect itself against the impaired judgments of severely manic politicians, judges, financial advisers, or doctors, particularly when it appears that many successful professional people seem to have a tendency to be hypomanic? There is usually no deterioration in total personality, judgment, or reality perception between attacks. Such cases may slowly cross the line from normality into a state of mild elation that gradually may become more intense. Severely elated and depressed states, such as those experienced by this patient, are obvious to family and society, and eventually the patient is just packed away. However, milder forms of elation go unrecognized for years. In the case of the manic politician, what protection is there when charisma and intelligence in a highly capable and powerful person become suddenly transformed into a type of mild insanity?

Democratic institutions in general tend to agree that the mental stability of a man in political office is judged best by his peers. James Forrestal, while secretary of defense, suffered crushing depressions. For a long time his associates preferred to see this as fatigue; they were convinced he was mentally ill only when he became extremely depressed, unreasonable, argumentative, and suspicious of everyone. Even then it was nearly impossible to get psychiatric attention for him because of the stigma attached to it by various military and government groups. Forrestal's case illustrates the difficulties of diagnosing and treating a mood disorder in a VIP. When he got treatment it was too little and too late; he jumped out of a window at the Bethesda Naval Hospital in Maryland and destroyed himself.

In this way the country lost a man many consider our most brilliant secretary of defense. The Forrestal history also makes us aware of how long a person with severe emotional impairment can continue to make decisions in a strategic governmental post. Forrestal is not an exceptional case, however. Many hard-driving politicians suffer from emotional disorders. The strains of campaigning and office holding would try the strength of Hercules. Politicians tend to be superachievers who drive themselves hard to succeed, and this effort often takes its toll. The tragedy is compounded by the fact that it is not easy to arrange psychiatric treatment for men in their positions.

Who knows how many prominent Americans hospitalized for "pneumonia" or "fatigue" are really hushed-up psychiatric patients? Who knows how many important decisions have been and are now being made under mental conditions less than ideal?

To some degree we are all aware of this difficulty, examples of which are Senator Eagleton's admission of a history of psychiatric disability and the pathological behavior of the Nixon administration. Contemplating the Watergate affair, one can only guess at the amount of depression, paranoia, and acute emotional turmoil experienced by President Nixon and his top political advisers. Suicide must have been at least one of the options considered as the stress mounted and the cover-up unfolded. This kind of depression induced by stress and relieved by removal of the stress is reactive, not metabolic; however, suicide may become the final solution in both instances.

In the film *Doctor Strangelove,* the commander of a Strategic Air Command base, thinking everyone is after his precious body fluids, saves the country by destroying the world. We all laugh nervously, but the possibility is there, especially in this age of "high security," when no left hand really knows what the right hand is doing.

What protection is there? The military, unlike the rest of the government, has thorough psychiatric screening procedures, at least for the lower echelons, by which psychiatric disability can be diagnosed and treated routinely. The regular armed services procedures are common enough knowledge. The Strategic Air Command has, besides regular security clearance, a psychiatric screening that disqualifies anyone with a history of mental illness. Aside from the dubiousness of these tests, one other thing is worthy of note: the higher up you get in the ranks, the less these criteria apply and the harder it is to enforce them. A military commander, because of the way the organization is structured, is virtually impossible to remove if he develops an emotional impairment.

Captain Queeg in *The Caine Mutiny* is no imaginary fantasy—in many forms he has inflicted himself on his subordinates in the past, and he will continue to do so. An American commander once held a post even though his subordinates had tried to have him disqualified for overt paranoid behavior. Even the American ambassador, requesting that the man leave his post because he was in danger of precipitating a war, could not get the man relieved of command—because the commander controlled all channels of communication. When large numbers of subordinates united with the ambassador in protest to the Surgeon General, the latter was skeptical. Through a bureaucratic mistake, a huge amount of correspondence on the matter was returned through regular channels, which meant that literally hundreds of people read these confidential reports. When the commander finally saw them, he took reprisals. The confusion was so great that no action was taken to judge whether or not he was actually sick.

Should we therefore require psychiatric testing for presidential candidates and other high officials? This idea has been debated for some time. Many people agree with it, some laugh at it, some say it sounds fascistic; others say there is simply no way to do it, because it is impossible to be objective in a psychiatric examination. Who is to say what the disqualifications should be? If we include any previous history of psychiatric illness, then many of our best and brightest politicians and government employees would be lost to us. If this were a criterion, Abraham Lincoln, by today's standards, would be disqualified hands down. George Washington himself was said to have been severely depressed when he was at Yorktown during the Revolution. How many of our greatest leaders have been at some time in their lives emotionally impaired?

Shall we base our test—our "Wassermann" for candidates—on the basis of an interview? Too subjective, for it depends on the psychiatrist. Or use a Rorschach? Again, subjective, and not much believed in anymore. Should we use the MMPI (Minnesota Multiphasic Personality Inventory), which many feel is the closest to objectivity? But even it is considered by most psychiatric researchers as an unreliable criterion for screening in or out psychiatric illness. Full-blown schizophrenics have been known to achieve normal scores on this test. Besides, who is to say what the standards for a "normal" leader must be? If such a testing procedure were ever instituted, the psychiatrist would be dictating to the politician—hardly a state of affairs anyone would relish.

Should our testing give the candidate or official a clean bill of mental health, what is to prevent him from having a nervous breakdown his second week in office? A clearance is not much insurance against the future, most psychiatrists will admit. The idea that a "panel of experts" should be able to intervene in such cases—an idea propounded by the Group of Advancement of Psychiatry, of the Committee of Governmental Agencies— presumes that "qualified psychiatrists" would have the last word in dictating what goes on in political affairs even if these experts were purely on a consultant basis. The fallacies in this position are numerous. Probably the greatest argument against it is the strictly practical one that even among themselves psychiatrists cannot agree on their diagnoses or on which of their colleagues is "qualified."

The rate of agreement of psychiatrists on the diagnoses of major mental illness is about 50 to 70 percent, which is not very convincing. Although significant disagreement may be a good sign of controversy within the profession, it indicates a poor risk in relying on an expert consultant. Furthermore, psychiatrists themselves come in all shapes, sizes, and persuasions. They may require that you lie on a couch and freely associate about your oedipal fantasies, or they may leave you to cool your heels in an orgone box, or they may have you salivate when they ring bells, or they may simply tell you to take a pill. Which of them is to set the standards for the range of permissible deviation for an attorney general?

In its extreme form, of course, psychiatric intervention in government and politics is presented convincingly in a grim, harshly ironic fantasy, Aldous Huxley's *Brave New World,* in which human embryos are developed in bottles and controlled by a few devious scientists of the mind who use the universal drug, "soma." In George Orwell's satirical novel *1984*, what is now called behavioral therapy ("Big Brother is watching you") is used to control the minds of entire populations. Basically, psychiatric interference has these connotations to all of us; it conjures up totalitarianism armed with an invisible potent weapon: knowledge of how the mind works. We are uncomfortable when we think of the "reeducation" that has been said to go on in countries like China. We begin to cherish our deviations and hangups as symptoms of our precious liberty and individuality.

And the idea of a psychiatric review board or a resident psychiatrist in the White House, or Senate, or House of Representatives—a man or men with the power to hospitalize anyone—reminds us of the convenient system many totalitarian countries have devised for "hospitalizing" troublesome individuals. A number of foreign dissidents have been buried for life in mental institutions, chemically straitjacketed on hidden wards, put on tranquilizers and comfortably out of the way, at least according to reports and hearsay.

Nevertheless, a large number of citizens believe that we need some kind of psychiatric balancing arm in the government. Everyone, particularly since the Watergate crisis, can cite cases where a politician would have benefited from psychiatric contact. When Drew Pearson alleged that Nixon had seen a psychiatrist, many people assumed the man was unfit for office. But who could honestly deny that a national leader in a position of constant strain would in all probability benefit at one time or other from some association with a psychiatrist of his own choosing? Any man who presumes to know how to run this nation and does not take advantage of the existing knowledge as to how men's minds function and what psychiatry is all about is probably closed-minded after all and not really presidential material.

Nixon, while he was hidden behind barriers of secrecy in the White House, became a popular target for speculation. On his television appearances during Watergate he appeared remarkably lacking in overt depression, despite his nervousness at times. Although it is impossible to judge from the limited clues one gets while viewing behavior on television, facial expressions are nevertheless of value to psychiatrists when diagnosing depression. Most of the depressed patients who have walked into my office and clinic over the past fifteen years, numbering in the thousands, have not had the ability to smile, twinkle, and joke as did Richard Nixon throughout the entire Watergate ordeal. Psychoanalysts would say that Nixon denied or covered up his depression and might have avoided the physical deterioration and depression that came later if he had not suppressed the truth and his own feelings of despair.

Not to succumb to a reactive depression under such adversity could indicate a certain mental strength. Of course, it might also make a person more subject to unpredictable future mental breakdown, since depression under such stress is a normal reaction.

This brings up another objection to psychiatric screenings of politicians, generals, and business leaders. In certain new schools of psychiatry, notably the existential, avant-garde group of R. D. Laing, it is popular to say that traditional psychotherapy is based on a dangerous fallacy. It attempts to make the maladjusted person conform to a system that may be familial, social, or ethical. Often, however, says Laing, this system itself is "insane," in the sense that it is arbitrary, contradictory, and destructive. Who, then, is really crazy? the Laingian psychiatrists ask. Is it the mother who makes her child schizophrenic, or the schizophrenic child? The business world that kills off its executives from joyless overwork, or the executive who has a nervous breakdown? The nation that goes to war, or the psychotic boy who won't be drafted as a soldier?

According to Ralph Nader, "General Motors is insane." They are dirtying the world, killing people with their products, making money only to make more money. If a person does such things, he is called emotionally disturbed. But the executives of a large corporation are said to function rationally within an irrational system. They are sane but their sanity is at the service of an irrational milieu. Therefore, are they crazy? Or are the effects of their "sane" behavior crazy?

The same paradigm applies to Nixon's administration. The Watergate plumbers were not paranoid. They were quite in touch with the realities of snooping and bugging. But the system they served had developed into a structure or model of functioning analogous to what in an individual we would diagnose as severe mental impairment. Therefore a larger issue arises: It will do no good to police the sanity of individuals while it is still possible to have the insanity of institutions run unchecked, as it did in Washington.

Dr. Arnold Hutchnecker, in his book *Psychopolitics,* discusses the effects that the psychological makeup of leaders has on the political life of the nation. The President's subconscious wishes, according to Hutchnecker's view, may cause a war or annex a territory; or maybe he will buy battleships because he likes long, phallic shapes (i.e., is a phallic narcissist). Such a view, making the individual supreme, is myopic in the extreme. Hutchnecker says, for example, that Lincoln brought on the bloody Civil War because he was depressed. This singular explanation ignores the fact that the Civil War may have been inevitable from the time the Founding Fathers disagreed about the legality of slavery at the Constitutional Convention. All Lincoln inherited were the last-minute preparations and the obligation to conduct the war as best he could. His depressed mood during the first eighteen months he was President may have prolonged the war and cost many lives. Most critics would question even this interpretation.

The opposite view to psychopolitics is practical and strictly political, suggesting that institutions and historical processes have a life and logic of their own, and more or less override the psychological makeup of their leaders. Arthur Schlesinger, for example, believes that government is perfectly capable of policing and screening itself by political means, primarily impeachment.

In subtle ways psychiatry is beginning to dominate the study of economics and politics. Psychiatry has also found its way into the roots of education and marketing, and even into religion in the form of pastoral counseling. And, of course, psychological considerations affect marriage, child rearing, dieting, and, last but not least, the new field of thanatology (how to face and experience death).

What used to be for our forefathers the greater glory of God is now paraded around for ego strength. Psychiatry has become our religion, whether we know it or not. We are saturated with it; we believe in it. But what is it exactly?

Alice and Norman are getting a divorce.
Standard Reply No. 1: They should see a marriage counselor.
Standard Reply No. 2: He/she should go into therapy.

Martha's in a group. Tom's a child-guidance counselor (one who strengthens egos for second-graders). Their kids get therapy to soften the pangs of sibling rivalry.

If Frank drinks, he starts psychoanalysis at the insistence of his wife. He still drinks.

If your stomach aches, it's psychosomatic. If you diet, you have a strong death wish.

To put it another way, we have so many psychiatric reasons for every conceivable type of conscious or unconscious behavior that the explanations fail to have any real meaning and instead become the subject of jokes and cartoons. There is so much serious division among psychiatrists themselves regarding theory and practice that it is questionable whether they could agree on any set of standards for suitable behavior for politicians and public officials. If psychiatry is a science, it has not for the most part conducted itself in a scientific manner to date. At least, this seems to be true of the psychological schools, which, although in operation for decades, have not yet devoted much time or money to prove conclusively whether their techniques are effective.

Schlesinger says that psychiatry is in the same position economics was in before the first stock-market crash. "Economics was a pseudo science before the Depression. That catastrophe created a need for a real science of economics." Analogously, Schlesinger says, "we are headed for a psychiatric disaster in our government that may be the beginning of a true science of the mind." The numerous psychotherapies that have been passing for science are not. Thus, how can a group of experts, so seriously divided among themselves, decide what constitutes questionable or suitable behavior for another expert? How can they provide consistent rational evaluations, if this "suitable behavior" in their own body of knowledge is based on shifting and uncertain postulates, which most critics of psychiatry feel do not qualify as scientific knowledge?

One final argument against psychiatric intervention in government is the argument I feel most strongly about. It is simply that the traditional psychiatric approach to human behavior has always focused on psychopathology, the abnormal or "sick" aspects of the mind and the individual's functioning. The basic psychiatric approach has tended to ignore healthy areas of the mind's functioning, such as the adaptive aspects of being a maverick—the willingness to create, to be different, and to try new ideas and methods. Psychiatry sees behavior in terms of Freud's psychopathology of everyday life, which has become a subtle brainwash affecting our actions and behavior. Everyone's behavior can be described by clichés. Certainly the fallacy of this type of psychiatric thinking is best demonstrated by certain extraordinary individuals who have been called psychologically sick. Erik Erikson did such a job on Martin Luther, who had a thing about dirt and sin. St. Paul had a thing about sex. One is rather relieved that Jesus and Buddha, because of the exigencies of time and space, are safely beyond the analytic pale. In the arts the greatest geniuses have also been labeled as simple victims of their pathology. Leonardo da Vinci was undone by as respectable a critic as Freud. Bach was compulsive. D. H. Lawrence only wanted to be a woman. So an excessive drive to do and create, viewed this way, is seen in traditional psychiatry as energy resulting from neurotic or psychotic conflict, except by a few psychoanalysts such as Kubie. Many others in the profession have seen creativity as compensation for destructive urges or as sublimated sexual drive.

Guilt, conflict, and a host of other negative terms have comprised the essence of the psychiatric experience for many. These tenuous theories have managed to hang on solidly, unquestioned for years. A substantial number of prominent psychiatrists have not dared to challenge that the theories have, in effect, become cults. They will only admit it privately.

If religion and art are forms of sickness, the drive to excel in the affairs of politics and of the world is no better. The analytic psychiatrist generally sees all forms of intense and fierce competition as something negative—perhaps compensation, perhaps sibling rivalry, perhaps a deep-seated sense of failure. If a man has the unstoppable drive and ambition to get himself elected President or appointed prime minister, he must be compensating for the coldness of his father or the indifference of his mother. Or else he is driven to get elected because he admires his father, or because he has no strong feelings about his father either way.

Although the argument becomes absurd, it still affects us too often with the quiet suspicion that anyone who runs for office or excels in any way is driven by something he wants to hide or overcome. Why would any sane man want to become president? Or, today, why would any sane man want to be head of anything? This is what psychiatry often snidely and obliquely asks us. It is the same beautiful and perfect reasoning that some psychiatrists use to intimidate competitive women with Freud's interpretation of penis envy. Why does the woman want to write a book? PE. Why does she want a job? PE. Why does she want to have a baby? PE, naturally. There is no aspiration or accomplishment of women that has not been attributed to PE.

Perhaps one reason analytic psychiatry has persuaded a whole culture to follow this approach is that it constitutes a respectable form of sour grapes: pity the poor millionaire, he is a driven man, i.e., Citizen Kane. At odds with this traditional psychiatric view is my own conviction that mental illness, when it is painful, self-destructive, and harmful to others, should be recognized as such and treated. Other forms of so-called mental illness often constitute simply what is normal for the culture and should be left alone. The mild moodswings, for example, are not always maladaptive, but, on the contrary, beneficial—at least part of the time. If businessmen and creative artists can benefit from their highs, what about the hypomanic politician?

If the idea of adaptive hypomania is true for politicians as well, it would mean that we would have to take another hard look at the Eagleton affair and our ideas of what constitutes "fitness" and "unfitness" for office. Perhaps there are just as many highly successful manic-depressives in government as there are in business, the arts, and the military. The percentage of hypomanic personalities in politics is at least the same as that of hypomanics in other walks of life. Hypomanic politicians are the tireless campaigners, charismatic leaders, indefatigable organizers. They are particularly suited to the life-style of the Senate or the House of Representatives. In fact, anyone who has the drive and stamina to survive in American electoral politics has to be a little manic. One peripheral Kennedy adviser said of Robert Kennedy's New York campaign headquarters, "They are all high down there, all the time. Now I know why people go into politics." For the superpolitician this degree of excitement may serve as a clue to his biochemical energy that demands release and his need for frenetic activity. Deny one of these individuals his campaigns, his filibusters, his wheeling-and-dealing committee work, and he may go into a manic rage. Is it possible to imagine Theodore Roosevelt sitting still? He could not, in fact. When he left politics he had to go on safaris and tours of state through Europe, cowpunch, even organize his own small army to fight the First World War. Roosevelt is an extreme example of the hypomanic politician victimized by his own need for activity.

The hyperactive politicians, senators, and congressmen are the men who leave a trail of exhausted staff members behind them— the most devoted of whom have to throw in the towel. Hypomanics like these can be deceptively calm and collected. The cool exterior of the successful Ivy League executive may be only the outward expression of an inner frenetic behavior pattern. We see only the excessively efficient and overly productive individual whose tireless energy is modestly conceded.

A good example of a controlled hypomanic in American public life is Ralph Nader. He has been known to give twenty speeches a week, in ten different states. No two speeches are alike. Between lectures his life is "almost an unbroken succession of plane rides, car rides, hurried half meals at widely irregular intervals, three- to four-and-a-half-hour nights in a hotel or motel room with press conferences on the run." Nader is tremendously hard on his staff. "You cannot collapse," he says. "You must pick up and not flake out." And, "You go off on a trip for a week with some twenty-five-year-old lawyer, and when you come back he *wants the weekend off,*" he has said, with obvious disapproval. The telltale sign of hypomania is Nader's need for very little sleep. Outwardly, Ralph Nader does not usually appear nervous or hyperactive. Instead, he is quite charming and rational, more logical than most of us.

One cannot say that such a person's judgment is not accurate. In fact, it is probably more acute than most people's, since the hypomanic individual is able to perceive the defects in others most rapidly and get to the core of the matter. He is able to convince people of what he believes. People will follow the hypomanic because of his energy and enthusiasm. They are attracted by his vitality. He thinks big and he is generally able to seduce others into relinquishing their conservative scruples. Sometimes this can be a disaster, but sometimes it is an inestimable advantage. John Brown, the American abolitionist, was able to attract a large following precisely because of the grandiosity of his ideas. General George S. Patton was able to execute brilliant military feats while he was impetuous and manic. Theodore Roosevelt helped inspire the country to shed its plodding, self-involved isolationism and conservatism for a manic policy of aggression and expansion.

Psychopathology in a leader does not necessarily mean impaired effectiveness. Arnold Hutchnecker says, "I refute the idea that a neurotic man cannot be a great leader." This kind of thinking is laudably tolerant. "Some of my best friends see psychiatrists" is a common attitude toward mental health today. For all its well-meaningness, this position underlines the simplistic way psychiatry has taught us to look at mental functioning: Whoever is extraordinary "may be abnormal," and whoever seems to be lacking in conventional behavior needs psychiatric treatment. Deviations seen this way must be hidden.

This kind of egalitarianism ultimately will get us, as a nation, into trouble. Or at least we may become a nation of mediocre people, a nation where the exceptional people are forced to hide their exceptionalness and appear as "nonmanics," for instance.

Manic depression in its milder forms is a two-edged sword. The hypercompetency and adaptation in creative and productive hypomanics are of inestimable value. If one becomes too manic, loses judgment, and exhibits psychotic symptoms, the biological disadvantage becomes obvious. If a manic swings into depression, loses his fire and sparkle, his plans and ambition, and even his desire to live, the other edge of the sword is exposed. These Jekyll-and-Hyde transformations can become painful, frightening, and disruptive to all, since one cannot rely on the consistency of mood changes. What happens when the congressman who was a ball of fire during his first term in office is too depressed to introduce a single bill during his second term? His ups and downs may not be clear to his peers. If he is a manic-depressive, his moods are sure to affect his performance. The chronic hypomanic who does not have depression, as Ralph Nader appears to be on the surface, is less common. Most nonstop hypomanics in public life have valleys of depression and periods of inactivity: hospitalization for "fatigue," mysterious vacations sandwiched in between campaigns, and busy periods in the House are the only clues.

The problem can be stated simply. Many people in high office have a tendency toward moodswings, since their manic energy has helped get them there in the first place. Once they are in office their emotional makeup and mood often shift cyclically. At some point, although not necessarily so, their judgment may become impaired, and in times of extreme depression and extreme mania the distortions in judgment may be severe. Political decision-making is certainly affected, positively or negatively, by the politician's mood. There is a stronger possibility, moreover, that a person with manic depression or simply unipolar recurrent depression is more severely impaired in his decision-making than the person with only mild to moderate moodswings. For a person in a position of power, particularly political power, this can be dangerous. The social responsibility of the politician and his relative freedom to do what he wants, coupled with his extraordinary power to force his will, makes hypomania in high office a potentially dangerous situation, as well as an asset.

How reliable exactly is the judgment of a person with a mood disorder? Simply because of the possibility that he may at times have impaired judgment, should he be disqualified from public life in spite of frequent periods of hypercompetency and outstanding performance? Questions like these became critical in light of the Eagleton affair. The discovery that the vice presidential nominee had a history of mental illness caused such a furor that the other issues of the campaign, such as the Vietnam War and Nixon's economic policies, were temporarily buried in an avalanche of recriminations and counterrecriminations. The entire country was forced to examine its attitude toward emotional disability. The final result, many felt, during this enlightened, post-Freudian age was discouraging and disappointing. Some claimed it showed that we had regressed, since Lincoln's time, to the attitude of the Middle Ages toward mental illness. Everyone had something to say. Eagleton's sudden exposure made us nervous, in spite of the fact that all of us knew other men like him who were equally respected and had achieved success in their professional lives.

Thomas Eagleton was more or less the Wunderkind of Missouri politics in the late fifties and sixties. He became circuit attorney in 1956. In 1960, at the age of thirty-one, he became attorney general. He became lieutenant governor in 1964 and then senator in 1967. He was never out of office again, but proceeded right up the ladder. His record in the Senate was brilliant; he came out for all the right issues: strongly for consumer protection, against the supersonic transport, against the war before anyone else, against pollution. One couldn't have asked for a better politician. In his home state it was said that even if you didn't agree with his politics (and it was a conservative state, so many people didn't), you still voted for him because he was such a good man. His enthusiasm and good spirits won him popularity. "Moving with unusual speed" as a freshman senator, he introduced a lot of bills and brought attention to himself as an "assertive legislator" and a man who was going somewhere fast.

It was said that the whole time that he was in office he never stopped campaigning. His well-known penchant for being the first one into the office (usually by 8:00 A.M.) won him the grudging admiration of his staff. When he was chosen by George McGovern as his running mate, he seemed almost too perfect.

Soon after the nomination, Eagleton announced at a press conference that he had been hospitalized three times for "nervous exhaustion and fatigue." The first episode had been in December 1960. He had spent the month after the campaign in Barnes Hospital, recovering from "nervous exhaustion." He had had shock therapy for the first time, which had remitted the depression. The second time, he had gone to the Mayo Clinic for the week after Christmas 1964. He had just been elected lieutenant governor. He had received no shock therapy, just simple rest treatment for an undefined stomach ailment. In 1966, not an election year, he had gone to the Mayo Clinic for three weeks, from September to October. "I was depressed," he said. He had had electroshock treatments, which were successful. "As a young man, I drove myself too hard," Eagleton said. When asked if he had at any time lost his ability to make rational decisions, he said no, and he added that he had come away with the discovery that "I'd better learn to pace myself." Since that time, he said, he had been okay.

Eagleton's disclosure landed on the American public like a bomb. Many prominent people were polled to see if they thought Eagleton's record was any the worse for his psychiatric history. Members of Congress and politicians from Missouri said that his history of treament was well known in his home state and among some associates on Capitol Hill. "I have never seen anything to warrant a question" about Eagleton's health, said Senator Abraham Ribicoff. Mike Mansfield, the Senate Democratic leader, said he would have been routinely advised by the Capitol physician if any senator had a serious medical problem, but that to the best of his knowledge Mr. Eagleton had been in "excellent physical and mental health" during his four years in the Senate. Several associates supported Eagleton's assertion that he had been a hard-driving, high-energy type of campaigner, and one Democratic staff member familiar with Eagleton's activities on a pollution subcommittee said: "Probably sixty percent of the members of the U.S. Senate seem unbalanced to me. But of all the people who ever impressed me as sane and sensible, Thomas Eagleton would rank highest."

The national debate that followed underscored two important points in the American attitude toward psychiatric disability: First, mistrust of a leader with a psychiatric record—no matter what kind of record. Second, the old and hard-to-eradicate idea that any kind of consultation for an emotional problem was, in Eagleton's words, "something that's dirty, filthy, corrupt, illegal, sinister." And, he added, "electroshock is simply something you don't go around talking about at cocktail parties." This second point is painfully obvious. We may be enlightened enough to make cocktail gossip out of our sessions with the analyst; but severe depression and hospitalization for a problem of the mind is still very much something that most people, if they answer honestly, would rather cover up. The idea of a psychiatric hospital often conjures up drooling maniacs and violent, hallucinating patients—psychotics who cannot control their sexual and aggressive impulses. It still calls forth images out of the last century: gibbering characters out of *Marat/Sade,* or some unfortunate hooked up to Frankenstein's electroshock machine. President Johnson can show his gall-bladder scar on nationwide television. The fact that President Eisenhower moved his bowels at one point was respectfully reported by *The New York Times.* But Eagleton's psychiatric stay at the Mayo Clinic in the national mind was a "dirty," ugly thing.

Our bodies fail us, and it's all right. Our minds fail us, and it's unprintable. That is the real social stigma, and not just for politicians. Anyone who has a psychiatric hospital record is probably going to endure a lot of subtle patronization for the rest of his life, no matter how charming his nervous breakdown, no matter how famous he is.

Eagleton's responses—first, that he had nothing to hide, and second, that he would doggedly refuse to quit the ticket—were inevitable. Given the American people's double standard in this matter, it was just as inevitable that he would be removed from the ticket eventually by McGovern. Like the American people, Senator McGovern said he did not mind the disclosure and he did not mistrust Eagleton, but he asked him to leave the ticket anyway for what looked like precisely those reasons. Mail from constituents was interesting. To McGovern, it ran five to one in favor of keeping Eagleton on the ticket. To Eagleton, after he appeared on "Face the Nation," mail ran ten to one in favor of his staying on the ticket. Whether a history of mental disability was a liability in high office actually became the paramount campaign issue.

Opinions in the press were divided between the necessity of an enlightened position on mental illness, shock treatments, and hospitalization and the same deep distrust of the ex-mental patient. The tremendous uncertainty about Eagleton remained, even though he had proved himself a first-rate official and politician in every office he had held. If Eagleton had been an ex-convict, he might have suffered less disgrace. If he had been a reformed alcoholic, AA could have had him canonized as the first ex-alcoholic on the national ballot. But Eagleton was an ex-mental patient who had suffered from depression. His colleagues could testify until they were blue in the face that he had always behaved "normally." His record was flawlessly "sane," and, in fact, superior to the records of hundreds of political dull plodders. We might *say* we don't hold it against a man to have sought help for psychiatric illness. The fact is, Eagleton was crucified because of it. The electorate today in America has a conservative instinct when mental disability is an issue. Maybe this is all for the best. The fact is that the political arena is filled with people like Eagleton, but their histories are not fully known and disclosed.

At least the Eagleton affair, even though it showed America its ambivalence in a not very flattering light, also emphasized the way we need to examine our attitude toward the mental health of our leaders. As soon as Eagleton's disclosure was made, sketches of him began to emphasize his "unstable" aspects. One reporter noted Eagleton to be an "intense man," who often seemed "as tightly wound as a spring." "His gestures," said the reporter, "are short and choppy and his hands sometimes shake." He perspires profusely ("Eagleton sweats on Christmas Eve," he himself said), and he smokes two packs a day, the reporter noted suspiciously. Eagleton was presented as a borderline psychotic whose every quirk and habit were interpreted as a symptom of insanity. We could simply not permit him to be a leader, because the idea that a leader might be fallible was intolerable to us.

We in America have had our consciousness raised by the Eagleton affair, particularly when we now realize that Forrestal, Lincoln, Theodore Roosevelt, and Churchill were other politicians who had similar moodswings. Perhaps we will have to begin revamping our ideas about the kinds of leaders we will tolerate. We may find that hypomanic, hypercompetent people with alternating low moods are woven through the strongest portion of the fabric of our society and our institutions, and that they in fact hold up that wavering fabric, without our knowledge, a good part of the time. If my hypothesis is true, the benefits of mental illness will soon for the first time receive the same attention in psychiatry as pathology of the mind has over the centuries. People with moodswings may even be sought after for positions of leadership.

TEN

Does Psychotherapy Work?

It is most difficult for the layperson who is seeking help for depression to choose the type of treatment that will give the quickest and most lasting results with the minimal expenditure of time and money. Of the patients who have come to our Foundation clinic or have seen me in private practice, approximately 90 percent have had past experiences with other forms of psychiatric treatment—particularly some form of psychotherapy. Many have also had multiple and often nonspecific drug therapies, or electroshock therapy. When it comes to choosing among analysts, psychotherapists, psychopharmacologists (who may also be lithium specialists), there is truly an embarrassment of riches.

Most depressed patients I have seen want relief of their symptoms so that they can function effectively. They do not want a total exploration and reconstruction of their personalities. Many of my patients have had traditional psychotherapy for years, or at least short attempts at classical analysis that have helped with general problems in living but which have failed to alter their depressions. Certainly most have had one or more of the so-called analytically oriented forms of psychotherapy with poor results at preventing future highs and lows.

Classical psychoanalytic therapy is the most esoteric form of psychological therapy. It usually takes the longest and is the most expensive. The patient goes to a psychiatrist (M.D.) or psychologist (Ph.D.) who has trained four to eight years after his doctorate in the application of psychoanalytic techniques. The analyst has also undergone his own analysis for four to eight years and has usually graduated from an approved analytic-training institute. Classical psychoanalytic therapy requires the patient to lie down on a couch, following which the analyst and patient engage in an uncovering of the patient's unconscious. This is accomplished through free association (in which the patient says everything that comes to mind) and through the analysis of his or her dreams. The patient's feelings, fantasies, facts, and distortions are viewed in the context of his or her current life, past experiences with significant people, and relationship to the analyst. The patient is encouraged to develop a particular relationship with the doctor, the so-called transference neurosis, in which he or she transfers to the therapist feelings about important figures of the patient's past. In this way he or she reenacts the traumas, guilts, loves, and fears of infancy and current life in the doctor-patient relationship. The analyst indirectly helps correct the frequent distortions. This is thought to help the patient to achieve a greater sense of maturity and to adapt to current problems of living.

Besides classical psychoanalysis, which requires four to five sessions a week on the couch, there is a gamut of sitting-up, psychoanalytically oriented psychotherapies, almost as many forms as there are psychiatrists practicing them. Most therapies require a visit to the psychiatrist two to three times a week. Compared to the emphasis on the past in classical analysis, there is a greater focus in psychotherapy on the here and now; although the therapist usually employs the same principles and is most of the time a passive participant, saying very little.

A host of specialized schools have developed as offshoots of the early Freudian technique. With so many to choose from, psychiatrists combine a number of theories, methods, and techniques they feel comfortable with and that work well with their specific personalities. Within the psychological therapies the various techniques are generally distributed along a spectrum labeled "expressive" at one end and "supportive" at the other. Expressive therapy is most often associated with psychoanalysis and with the more formal kinds of psychotherapy, which concentrate on transference. Supportive therapy, on the other hand, requires a therapist who interferes more and guides the patient into specific areas. The supportive therapist may ignore the patient's childhood altogether, which a Freudian therapist would never do, and may concentrate on day-to-day responses and feelings. The supportive psychotherapist may suggest, interpret, persuade, and give advice, which the psychoanalytic therapist almost never does. For the depressed patient modern psychiatry represents a veritable treatment supermarket, if you add the chemical and behavioral approaches.

It is important to understand that there are four major classes of depressive states. The first two are primary and physical in origin: bipolar manic depression and unipolar recurrent depression. The second two are secondary and psychological in origin: reactive to stress and secondary to a neurosis. Treatment of primary chemical depressions (i.e., those that are physically caused by biochemical imbalances) with antidepressant drugs and lithium requires precise diagnosis. They must be distinguished from secondary depressions following stress or caused by neurosis. Of course there are other secondary depressions following other psychiatric illnesses, alcoholism, schizophrenia, etc.

Reactive depressions due to stress are normal and they can occur in anyone. The most common example is the reaction to death in the family, and it may be accompanied by the same symptoms seen in chemical depressions—depressed mood, anxiety, guilt feelings, and appetite and sleep changes. A grief reaction usually goes away within several months. Other stress depressions are commonly seen in people who have lost jobs, suffered financial loss, developed severe medical illnesses, or encountered sexual or marital problems. These specific stresses in the environment are usually obvious. Most reactive depressions either disappear with the removal of the stress or get better on their own as time passes.

In depression secondary to neurosis, psychological difficulties have been with the person for years. The dominant symptoms (of which depressed mood is only one) include anxiety attacks, phobias, obsessional thoughts, and general stunting of maturity.

Both in stress depressions and in neuroses with secondary depressed mood, drugs and time help enormously, with recovery from symptoms. But drugs and time are less likely to be the whole answer; psychological or behavioral therapy may be required for social and marital readjustment.

Does psychotherapy or psychoanalysis work specifically for bipolar manic depression, recurrent unipolar depression, depression secondary to stress, or secondary to neurosis? The question is critical if you should happen to be depressed and are seeking some form of help, if you are considering investing time and money in psychotherapy, or if you are already doing so. It is important for you to know what sort of depression you are suffering from, and what your chances are of improving your depression in a lithium program (with or without antidepressants), in psychotherapy, in analysis, or in a combination of these treatments. Is it possible that in one of these therapies you might become, instead of better, worse? Or would you get better anyway on your own without any form of drug or psychotherapeutic intervention? If you decide to choose a psychotherapist or to take lithium and antidepressants, how should you go about it?

My own experience has taught me that most depressed patients are not aware of the various psychological and drug-intervention techniques. They have little idea of what is offered, the time or cost required, or the results to be expected from specific treatments, once the form of depression they are suffering from is correctly diagnosed. The patient may be convinced of the necessity of exploring his or her depressed feelings, to discover whether the depression is the result of some unconscious conflict, or of some unreconciled event that has caused him or her to feel loss, disappointment, or frustration. I maintain, however, that this psychological approach is of value only with a small proportion of depressed patients—those suffering from a specific stress with which they want help, or cases in which there is a primary neurosis with secondary depressive symptoms that are first relieved with antidepressant drugs.

Usually a person can identify a specific loss, traumatic event, or stress that is associated with a reactive depression. However, at times the patient cannot find any reason to explain how bad he or she feels. The patient has no idea whether the depression is from psychological conflicts, or from a biochemical imbalance that simply appears from out of the blue. The person may not be able to make an educated choice of therapy that will work best for him or her because the patient has no way of distinguishing which type of depression he or she is suffering from and may be too ill to want to find out.

Most psychiatrists agree that certain treatments are effective for some depressions while other treatments are harmful or, at the very least, ineffective. Sometimes the wrong choice of therapy or therapist can result in a real disaster. The wrong therapy can be a waste of time, money, and effort. Sometimes it can become, no matter how skillfully applied, a frustrating treatment in which the patient actually becomes worse.

Psychoanalysis, even under normal conditions, is an anxiety-producing experience. Generally, one does not undertake analysis unless there is a fair degree of stability, judgment, and psychological aptitude. If a person who is potentially psychotic undertakes an analysis, he or she may form a negative transference with the analyst that can develop into a transference psychosis instead of the usual transference neurosis. Psychoanalysts are the first to agree that analysis is not for everyone, and that analysis must be undertaken only by patients with potentially strong egos, sufficient time and money, and high motivation to change their self-defeating personality traits. Psychoanalysis is inappropriate if applied to borderline psychotics, schizophrenics, or people with deep depressions or manic elations.

I also consider any of the previously mentioned psychotherapies inappropriate when applied to recurrent depressions and manic depressions, *before* an actual drug stabilization is achieved with lithium, antidepressants, or both. Only when patients' symptoms are alleviated can they make a rational decision as to whether or not they still want to investigate their personality and their problems in psychotherapy. In my experience most manic-depressives and recurrent depressives who have been stabilized and maintained in a normal mood do not want psychological therapy. Usually they don't need it, but, of course, problems in readjustment after the depressions cannot be completely eliminated with lithium or other drugs. These may be based on marital difficulties resulting from years of uncontrollable depressive or manic behavior. Some patients may require help in finding a residence or job. There are also work conflicts experienced by patients stabilized on lithium or antidepressants. If such problems persist after drug treatment, many of these patients may benefit from supportive psychotherapy, behavioral modification, or group or marital counseling. Some people stabilized on medications may continue to have problems that are due to a preexisting neurosis in addition to their chemically responsive moodswing. These patients, surprisingly few in my own experience, should be referred to a psychotherapist who is best equipped to help with primary neurotic conditions.

If the estimate of twenty million depressed people in American is correct, there may be as many as eight to ten million Americans suffering from manic depression and unipolar recurrent depression. I am convinced that neither psychoanalysis nor psychoanalytically oriented psychotherapy prevents these primary depressive disorders, which are physical in origin. With respect to the remaining secondary depressives who seek help, does psychotherapy work?

Let's first assume that the diagnosis is correct and the prospective patient with a depressed mood secondary to a neurosis or stress is not a typical candidate for lithium, but with antidepressant drugs the depressive symptoms have substantially improved. What scientific evidence do we have that additional talking therapy works in preventing future psychologically caused depressions?

Over the last three decades, there has been a great controversy in the field of psychiatry. There have been publications in scientific journals that "prove" that psychotherapy does or doesn't work, or that psychoanalysis works best for neurotics or it doesn't, or that borderline schizophrenics and neurotic depressives do better with one kind of treatment or another. Almost all of these studies have failed, since they have come up against difficulties inherent in measuring human behavior. Therefore, the specific effects of psychotherapy to date have not been established scientifically to the research psychiatrist's satisfaction. In addition, most analysts and psychotherapists have shown little interest in validating scientifically what they do.

No well-controlled published investigation has been carried out with depressed patients on the question, Does psychoanalytically oriented psychotherapy work? Yet this form of therapy continues to be applied on a large scale to all four major classes of depressed patients seeking treatment.

In 1972 an impressive study was completed by analysts of the Menninger Clinic who evaluated the effects of psychoanalysis on neurosis in general. They concluded that patients who began treatment with considerable ego strength (personality integration) and good social relationships did better than those who came to psychoanalysis with low ego strength. This conclusion has been interpreted by skeptical critics to mean the obvious: The more normal you are when you begin treatment, the better you do. No conclusions regarding the effects on depressed mood can be made from this eighteen-year study.

Another basically similar study of the effects of psychoanalysis—one of the first attempts to measure results—showed that 60 percent of those who undertook analysis at the Chicago Institute were cured. On close scrutiny, however, the results included only those who had completed their analyses, which cuts the success rate in half if one includes all patients who dropped out.

Most of the information in these two studies was based on subjective ratings done by social workers, the psychotherapists, or patients themselves. The investigators failed to use minimum criteria, which most of today's researchers insist on for evaluating any type of treatment—for example, random assignment* of patients to the treatment group or a control group; also, patients of the same age, sex, and diagnosis in both groups. Furthermore, the control group should not receive the therapy to be evaluated, and both the control group and the treatment group must be given a blind evaluation† by objective raters for mood, specific behaviors, and general level of functioning.

---

*Assignment determined by chance, i.e., the flip of a coin.

†Evaluation by raters who do not know which treatment the patient has received.

It is difficult to establish a control group of patients who do not receive the primary treatment and yet who are willing to be evaluated periodically by a scientific team. There are also too many variables in human nature to satisfy all the critics that the scientific method has really been carried out satisfactorily in a "Does psychotherapy work?" experiment.

Several other studies that have been performed with acknowledged limitations have shown a number of interesting and contradictory facts. For instance, the same percentage of cures in the group receiving psychotherapy has been found among the untreated patients of the control groups.

Jerome Frank, an authority in this area, has suggested that simply having an explanation for one's distress may have a salutary effect on many neurotic patients.

> Statistical studies of psychotherapy consistently report that about two thirds of neurotic patients . . . are improved immediately after treatment, regardless of the type of psychotherapy they have received, and the same improvement rate has been found for patients who have not received any treatment that was deliberately psychotherapeutic.

Other critics of psychological treatments argue that the simple passage of time is often beneficial to neurosis, which may disappear spontaneously with or without formal treatment. In this respect, it is extremely important to point out that if recurrent depression or manic depression is being treated inappropriately with psychological methods, the depression almost always remits spontaneously if enough time passes. Since the usual duration of chemical depressions is anywhere from one to six months, if a psychological treatment is applied during this time, the efforts of the psychiatrist may not bring about actual termination of the depression, which will end anyway.

"The neuroses," one critic has said, "are 'cured' by Christian Science, osteopathy, chiropractic, nux vomica, bromides, benzedrine sulfate, change of scene, a blow on the head, and psychoanalysis, which probably means that none of these has yet established its real worth in the matter. . . . Moreover, since many neuroses are self-limited, anyone who spends two years with a patient gets credit for the operation of nature."

One group of doctors has gone even further and concluded that psychotherapy may be harmful as often as helpful: Its average effect, according to them, was comparable to receiving no help. This is the extreme position of C. B. Truax and R. R. Carkhuff, who maintain that there are so-called deterioration effects in psychotherapy and analysis. Deterioration effects are negative results from therapy, such as increased depression and anxiety, and a decreased ability to function. Such effects are what I call *psychotherapy toxicity.*

Another study found that two groups of inpatients benefited from it, while long-term psychotics actually deteriorated from it. Surprisingly, the long-term psychotic controls who received no treatment showed improvement during the same period. This would simply mean that those who did not receive psychotherapeutic treatment in an inpatient hospital setting and were classified as psychotic did better than those who did receive the treatment.

In contrast to these negative studies, one well-controlled study showed that brief supportive psychotherapy was effective in improving the level of social adaptation of depressives to their environment once the acute depression had been successfully treated with antidepressant drugs. In this study done by psychiatrist Gerald Klerman psychotherapy was not shown to have a major impact on preventing relapse or improving symptoms in patients recovering from depression. Instead, acute depressive symptoms of outpatients remitted rapidly with drugs. However, psychotherapy appeared to improve later social adjustment to problems in living. Psychotherapy in this study was performed by social workers twice weekly and dealt with reality-oriented problems of readjustments to life after the depressive episode.

The question of whether psychotherapy works, with or without the aid of drugs, or whether one type of treatment is more effective than another is more than academic for the prospective patient. In all other branches of medicine, patients are advised that there are three possible outcomes of treatment: They may get better, they may stay the same, and they may get worse; and they are usually given the likelihood of all three possible outcomes, expressed in percentages. Yet those who go into analysis or psychotherapy are generally led to assume only that they will improve. A patient should know that authorities in the field are still very much at odds with one another as to intensive psychotherapy's effectiveness in all forms of neurotic illness, certainly including neurosis with depressed mood. Therefore, it might be more fair to say to a prospective patient that psychological approaches to depression are still being warmly debated within the profession. Furthermore, no well-designed study on major depression exists that clearly shows whether intensive psychotherapy works or not.

Psychiatrists can also inform depressed patients that there have been well-designed outpatient drug studies with antidepressant agents, using placebo (imitation of an active medicine) control groups. These have shown that substantial rates of spontaneous cure occur in several months without drugs (say, 30 to 40 percent). However, most carefully conducted antidepressant-drug trials with all forms of depression show that up to 75 percent improve substantially within two to six weeks of drug treatment. In other words, drugs *are* helpful and rapid for neurosis with depression as well as for recurrent unipolar and bipolar manic depression, in which they are clearly the therapy of choice.

Patients are entitled to know these facts when they are depressed and are looking for treatment and guidance. Patients want relief from their depressive symptoms. I have found that they are not primarily interested in becoming more "mature" from a psychological approach. They want rapid relief from pain, not deep insight or personality growth.

During the past two decades of the drug revolution in psychiatry, psychoanalysis has become less practical for most individuals. Assuming that it is sometimes effective and that the patient really wants to devote four or five hours a week to explorative therapy, he or she is still confronted with the serious problems of cost and time. These practical drawbacks to long-term analysis, plus the advent of drug and behavioral therapies, have made analysis less in demand and less fashionable. Nevertheless, the basic analytic principles and techniques continue to be overapplied by psychiatrists to all forms of depression, in which they employ psychoanalytically oriented psychotherapies—even on a watered-down, once-a-week scale. At most scientific meetings where the pros and cons of analytic therapies are debated, scientific skeptics still criticize analysis and psychotherapy and continue to call for scientific demonstration of results. The physician who is skeptical of psychological therapies, because of his scientific training and a need for proof, is told that he is "resisting" or has unconscious conflicts about this mode of treatment. This is the position of the psychoanalytically oriented psychiatrist toward the psychopharmacologist, who insists on rigorous controls when evaluating any form of therapy. Analysts, beginning with Freud, have maintained that no one can understand analysis or psychotherapy who has not been thoroughly analyzed. "The teachings of psychoanalysis are based upon an incalculable number of observations and experiences," said Frued, "and no one who has not repeated those observations upon himself or upon others is in a position to arrive at an independent judgment." Perhaps, then, my own training and analysis with two of America's most outstanding men qualify me to offer a personal opinion.

I was trained first as a psychoanalyst and later as a researcher who evaluates whether treatment works. One of my most important criticisms of the psychological treatments is that they have not been modified that much since they originated with Freud. Even more important, as I have indicated, none of the primary advocates of these methods has clearly shown that they are effective. The burden of proof is on them. This is not to say that the methods may not be effective in certain instances. But after half a century they have simply not been clearly shown to work.

I am not alone in this opinion, which is shared by many colleagues. For example, Dr. F. C. Redlich, dean emeritus of the Yale School of Medicine, has said, "Almost everything we know about psychoanalysis today was Freud's single-handed and single-minded work," while the psychoanalytic world remains a "rigidly dogmatic and defensive guild, not plugged into major intellectual currents of the day."

My own opinion has been formed during more than twenty-five years of experience with inpatient borderline psychotics and outpatient neurotics and psychotics. During this period I have used psychoanalysis on a small number, and psychoanalytically oriented psychotherapy and drug therapy on over ten thousand patients. Of these, 80 percent have been outpatients and perhaps 80 percent of these outpatients have been either manic-depressives or recurrent depressives treated with lithium and antidepressants. Reactive depressions due to stress and primary neurosis with secondary depressed mood, along with all other psychiatric diagnoses, make up the remaining group.

It is my impression that the great majority of people seek psychiatric help initially because they are depressed, anxious, or both. Depression and anxiety are the target symptoms motivating most people to go for help. Others who seek treatment may do so simply from an awareness that there is something wrong with their patterns of living, from a feeling that they are not getting enough out of life, or living up to their potential. People in this latter group may suffer from what psychiatrists call a personality or character neurosis. They do not necessarily have overt symptoms of depression or anxiety, or other symptoms that are obvious. Some have obvious marital and sexual problems, phobias, and psychosomatic illness. Usually these latter patients require psychological therapy.

Physicians who can readily diagnose patients with chemical or psychologically caused depressions may nevertheless overlook patients with masked depressions. Few suspect depression when the patient has numerous somatic complaints for which no medical cause can be found. After repeated medical examinations these people are often labeled hypochondriacs or, simply, anxious neurotics. The physician may prescribe a tranquilizer to calm them down or something else to pep them up. He is exasperated by their constant telephone calls, their demands, and the fact they do not seem to get well.

In the case of the psychiatrist who does not recognize an underlying masked chemical depression the focus of treatment may be on a specific conflict secondary to the depression that the patient is experiencing in his marriage or sexual life. A long course of psychoanalytically oriented therapy may be prescribed;

meanwhile the physical origin of the depressive illness is neglected and thus receives no drug treatment. Phobias, obsessions, and panic attacks can also be outward expressions of an underlying depression. Some adolescent acting-out behavior, alcoholism, criminality, psychopathy, and some sexual promiscuity can represent masked symptoms of an underlying chemically treatable manic or depressive illness, and drugs should be tried first before embarking on an extensive analysis of the personality.

In 1960, shortly after I had finished my own training in general psychiatry and was embarking on a five-year training program in psychoanalysis, I spent half my week in psychotherapy practice, seeing a variety of patients on a two- or three- to four-times-a-week basis. This approach was basically Freudian. It required making the unconscious conscious, focusing on dreams, and utilizing myself in a neutral or passive role with my patients. This approach was used principally with outpatients, many of whom were neurotic, and most of whom were depressed and anxious over problems of living. Although many patients who were in psychoanalytically oriented psychotherapy tended to improve, I was never sure whether the improvement was due to true insights from treatment or whether it was due to the simple passage of time and spontaneous remission. At times I attributed it to a subtle kind of persuasion that took place. This happened, I thought, when a helpless patient came to seek change with an authority who he believed had the answer. The improvement seemed independent of the actual psychotherapeutic technique I was employing.

When patients came for treatment of depression, I would sit with them for two, four, even ten months, attempting to dig out the causes of the depressed mood. During my early psychoanalytic practice, I believed that most depressions were reactions to real or unconscious loss. The procedure was to look for the loss. I believed, according to traditional Freudian doctrine, that the patient was depressed because of repressed anger at someone, or because he had experienced an early but long-forgotten loss in life. From my training, I felt that this loss must now be repeating itself in adult life either in a real or imagined sense—

with the boss or a loved one, or in a competitive situation in which the patient had met defeat. He was not aware of the anger over the loss. The therapy consisted of getting him to see this and express it.

Therapy focused heavily on dreams, and the patient was taught this theoretical model: If you can really get your anger out and get mad at this person, the depression will simply go away.

Over weeks and months I would work with a patient, helping him to analyze his behavior and discover the reason for his depression. Generally speaking, for most moderate to severe depressives very little happened. For primary neurotics, in whom fleeting depression was only one of many symptoms, patients became involved and embarked on a prolonged course of psychotherapy that was often successful after several years. With more seriously depressed patients who were unable to talk, there were often prolonged periods of silence from week to week and month to month.

These sessions I interpreted traditionally—"the patient is blocked, and simply has to attend the treatment until the block is resolved." I viewed the block as a conflict between us in which the patient would have to discover repressed negative feelings toward me that would have to come out to relieve the depression. Thereafter, I thought, the patient would be able to start talking again. Many depressed patients eventually did improve after months or years. Some would suddenly improve for no apparent reason at all, whereupon I would wonder if some insight or breakthrough had really been achieved from my technique in applying psychotherapy.

A number of patients discontinued psychotherapy with the complaint that the talking approach did not work; they were not improving fast enough, or they could not spend years discussing their problems to get out of their depression. Other desperate and helpless patients accepted any approach I recommended.

The patients in serious depressions responded very little. Later, after I saw depressed patients respond rapidly to antidepressant drugs, it was apparent that depressed patients should not be pressed to deliver unconscious problems or dreams. In fact, they often felt worse when pushed to do so.

Mildly depressed patients, also in abnormal chemical states, would cooperate and discuss the areas of inquiry: what really was wrong between him and his wife, for instance; or him and his boss. Something would be wrong, since there is usually something wrong in most people's marital and job relationships. This is true particularly if they are unable to cope owing to the underlying chemical depression.

The only diagnostic type of depression in which patients clearly seemed to gain insight and improve from psychotherapy was the reactive depression, when a life stress, a real loss, or a competitive defeat with a peer was apparent. But these depressions, I later recognized, also tended to improve spontaneously in one to two months, and many were helped with drugs initially. Getting the patient to talk about the conflict appeared to have a cathartic effect. In the deep, chemical types of depression, regardless of the questioning, silence, or techniques applied, the depression continued on its relentless course, only to eventually remit spontaneously or swing into a high.

In the early 1960s, I began to concentrate my efforts more on patients with depressive complaints. During this period the antidepressants were becoming available for general psychiatric use. I was reluctant to use drugs, as were most psychiatrists trained in psychoanalytic techniques. A key principle of most psychotherapists is that pills are no cures to problems in living. In most instances this is correct. However, when interpersonal conflicts are secondary to a primary chemical depression, so that the person can't cope, the conflicts are not cured by a psychotherapeutic approach until the primary depression is first treated with antidepressants. If the conflicts remain after the primary depression is treated, then the patient can try the psychotherapeutic approach. This became apparent after treating a number of depressed patients exclusively with psychotherapy during my early training period, when I felt a reluctance to use antidepressants.

I spent months with patients who were dreaming, gaining insights, or expressing anger they had never expressed, and who were still depressed. With these patients I finally gave in and used drugs. Much to my surprise, these depressions were usually alleviated within two to six weeks. The effect of these new medications was tremendously gratifying, since quick relief of symptoms with or without insight was most important for patients seeking treatment. Their rapport with me was also important in bringing this about, and an explanation of their depressions in medical terms was reassuring.

The antidepressants or psychic energizers were discovered in 1956, when researcher Dr. Nathan Kline at Rockland State Hospital noted the mood-elevating properties of Iproniazid, a drug developed to treat tuberculosis. When it was given to tubercular patients the drug produced increasing mental alertness and a mild sense of elation. Kline pioneered the use of the drug by giving it to depressed patients with positive results. Thus Iproniazid or Marsilid became the first of a class of drugs called the monoamine oxidase inhibitors, which are standard antidepressants in use today. Another antidepressant, the popular drug Tofranil (imipramine) was developed earlier the same year by Dr. Roland Kuhn and his associates in Switzerland while they were seeking a more effective antipsychotic agent. When it was first tested in psychotic patients in 1956, investigators found that the drug was ineffective in treating schizophrenia, but noticed that the depressed schizophrenic became less depressed. These two remarkable discoveries and Cade's earlier discovery of lithium for manic depression revolutionized the treatment of moodswing.

My first results with lithium in treating and preventing depression were extremely gratifying. They were unlike the slow progress of analysis and psychotherapy, which often ended in failure and defeat. The dramatic difference convinced me to work exclusively with lithium, other new drugs under development, and manic depression.

As an analyst in training in the early 1960s I was faced with the fact that if I wanted to conduct a strictly psychoanalytic practice and see each patient for a fifty-minute hour five times a week I could at most have eight patients who were in a full analysis at any given time. If the average analysis lasted three years, I could see only eight new patients every three years. If I intended to practice classical analysis exclusively the next thirty years, I could treat a total of only eighty patients within my lifetime. In analytic training courses it was made clear that if one wanted to be an analyst full-time, a lifetime practice of one hundred to two hundred patients, including dropouts, was to be expected. The patients suitable for psychoanalysis would be limited. They would be people whose character was originally rather strong to begin with. They would have to want to achieve a fuller potential in life from a careful and lengthy analysis of their personality.

The third revolution in psychiatry has changed things. Most depressed people can improve dramatically in three to eight visits to a chemotherapist. In terms of time and cost, the difference is highly significant. A patient will spend $50 to $150 a visit to go to a clinic or private psychiatrist who specializes in drugs. It will cost him at least $350 to $750 to alleviate and probably cure his depression in less than two months. On the other hand, a patient who begins treatment with a psychotherapist is probably embarking on years of expensive therapy, running into thousands of dollars. As I have noted, most depressed patients once relieved of their symptoms by psychopharmacology don't usually request further psychotherapeutic exploration. The 30 percent of depressives who wish to continue with a formal exploration of their patterns of living are certainly entitled to do so, and I refer them to psychologists in my private practice or Foundation clinic for psychotherapy or behavioral therapy.

Unfortunately, chemical depressions usually recur two months to two years later if the antidepressant is stopped. To remain free of depression one must continue on a maintenance treatment. For manic-depressive patients permanent maintenance treatment means lithium. For recurrent depressives, whose depressions come frequently enough to cut into a substantial part of their years, being kept free of depression requires either lithium alone or lithium with an antidepressant drug. In some instances an antidepressant alone may be sufficient.

The number of required visits to the psychiatrist for maintenance (prophylactic) lithium treatment is usually only 8 to 12 a year. In contrast, 50 to 150 visits are involved in a psychotherapeutic approach.

The modern propensity of most psychologists and many psychiatrists to disregard the underlying chemical depression and focus on the "neurotic" depressive symptoms goes back to the founder of psychoanalysis. Freud's most famous patient, the Wolf Man, was psychoanalyzed. Out of this analysis one of the foundations of psychoanalytic theory developed. Here I and others believe a basic error in diagnosis was made. The patient was an aristocratic Russian émigré nicknamed the Wolf Man because he had a phobia about wolves. Freud, a master of his own method and technique, administered his analysis at the height of his powers. His interpretations of the Wolf Man's incredibly complex conscious and unconscious material has won and must continue to win every reader's admiration. Freud himself emphasized that the Wolf Man analysis was a keystone of his analytic thinking.

The Wolf Man was recorded as having passed through the primal scene, in which he witnessed his parents having intercourse. Subsequently he developed castration anxieties. He was later seduced by a servant and developed an obsessive neurosis toward sexual problems. The symptomatology included a wolf phobia, religious obsessions, psychosomatic diarrhea, and paranoid delusions. For Freud and his disciples it was important to believe that the Wolf Man was a cured case, although he continued to suffer recurrent depressions, thought to be treatable by psychoanalysis, during a protracted period of his life.

The Wolf Man is the only Freudian analysand to have written his memories in great detail. In his autobiography, *The Wolf Man,* several facts stand out. First, he was not by any means cured by his analysis with Freud. In fact, if anything, he may have become worse from it, going on to develop an obsession about losing his nose. Also the Wolf Man's depressions appeared to alternate with periods of elation and hyperactivity, which had little to do with what was going on in his environment. After 1945 he had periodic depressions every few years, alternating with elevated mood states.

In the Wolf Man's family tree the following is significant: His father committed suicide, and had been diagnosed as manic-depressive and hospitalized for depression several times. Emil Kraepelin, the famous German psychiatrist, diagnosed the father as a case of manic-depressive madness. The Wolf Man's sister was a suicide in her early twenties. His maternal grandfather alternated between being quiet, withdrawn, and stingy and being a cheerful, gregarious, generous person, whose optimism and blind confidence knew no bounds. His paternal grandmother attempted suicide in a postpartum depression, and his paternal grandfather was alcoholic. This genetic pattern is typical for a manic-depressive family.

The Wolf Man today would certainly be diagnosed as manic-depressive with multiple neurotic symptoms. It is doubtful that Freud was aware of this, because he focused exclusively on the psychodynamic origin of the Wolf Man's depressions. In contrast, Kraepelin, a biological psychiatrist and Freud's rival, would have diagnosed the Wolf Man as manic-depressive, as he diagnosed the father. The medically oriented Kraepelin was, of course, most concerned with the descriptive aspects of behavior and the organic or biochemical etiologies that even at the turn of the century he presumed were underlying depression and manic depression. The modern psychopharmacologist follows in this tradition.

It is valid to assume that the Wolf Man's personality was thoroughly investigated by Freud with analytic techniques. The patient may have gained insights into his unconscious motivations, and possibly he lived a more complete life as a result of his analysis with Freud. Freud may have finished treating him on a spontaneous hypomanic upswing and thought he had brought about improvement. I would nevertheless consider Freud's failure to recognize manic depression and his exclusive focus on the Wolf Man's personality to be a serious error. No treatment for manic depression existed at the time, and psychoanalytic theories were justified since they were new. Despite this, the obvious core manic-depressive illness was not diagnosed by Freud or recognized by him in his treatment of this famous patient.

Intensive psychotherapy and the analytic approach to emotional problems have lost their impact in America. Psychotherapeutic and analytic techniques are not meeting the mental-health needs of the nation. We are losing psychoanalysis as a dominant treatment in our society. Formal analysis has decreased over the last twenty-five years, and according to a recent survey, psychoanalysts "are barely keeping their hand in psychoanalytic practice." Since the sixties other therapies, especially chemical, behavioral, self-help, and group, have proliferated. There has also been an increase in self-treatments with alcohol and drugs for anxiety states and depression. Psychoanalysis has failed us as a treatment procedure useful on a large scale with positive results that can be scientifically demonstrated.

More than a decade ago, the president of the American Psychiatric Association, Alfred Freedman, predicted that "modalities other than psychoanalysis may be confidently expected to dominate the future of psychiatric care in this country." He said that quicker modes of treatment for more people were needed. He stated that the reason he felt the decline of psychoanalysis was inevitable was because of the forthcoming health care in the United States. One or more forms of national health insurance are nearly upon us. Thus in the current and future marketplace psychoanalysis will decline, since the economics of treatment are such that only wealthy members of the society can afford the time and money required.

Do psychoanalysis and psychotherapy work for any form of depression? They probably work for some neurotic patients in whom depression is first relieved by antidepressants. Subsequent psychotherapy may aid the patient in social readjustment to problems of living. However, for most people who feel recurrently depressed, the origin of the moodswing is physical, metabolic, and chemical, and psychotherapy is not usually the right primary treatment. Often the patient does not want it. He is not resisting exploration of his unconscious, but he seems instinctively to appreciate that it is not the problems in his past that are causing the depression.

I have used short-term behavioral or cognitive therapy with approximately a third of my patients who have come out of their depression with medication and who also have problems in living, problems with alcohol, or drugs, work, marriage, or school. In my practice three behavioral or cognitive psychologists carry out this treatment by focusing on the here and now, a specific phobia, compulsion, or behavioral disorder, secondary to the primary depressive illness.

ELEVEN

Misdiagnosis of Depression and Manic Depression in America

Even a decade and a half ago, the chemical revolution in psychiatry raised the question of correct psychiatric diagnosis. The results of studies performed then were shocking. Correct diagnosis of mental illness is critical for predicting its course and applying new and specific treatments. Precision in diagnosis and classification helps determine which illnesses will receive support from government and private agencies. Obviously, the diagnostic accuracy of hospital admission statistics will also affect the planning of community mental-health care in America.

Several innovative studies carried out by a team of psychiatrists in the United States, England, and Wales showed that there has been, on the part of American psychiatrists, a surprisingly strong tendency to overdiagnose schizophrenia, and a bias against diagnosing depression and manic-depressive disorders. In the last fifteen years, this has begun to correct itself. But in this international diagnostic project, headed by Dr. Joseph Zubin, former professor of psychology at Columbia University, many cases that would have been called schizophrenic in the United States were considered depressive and manic-depressive in Great Britain. But schizophrenia and manic depression are two entirely different classes of major psychiatric illness, and the failure of many psychiatrists to arrive at the correct diagnosis is scandalous and has widespread consequences.

As early as 1957 Michael Shepherd, professor of psychiatry at the Maudsley Hospital in London, observed that in the psychiatric-hospital admission statistics of the United States "not only does schizophrenia rank as the leading diagnostic label, but . . . manic-depressive disorder assumes a relatively minor place." Morton Kramer, of the National Institute of Mental Health, in 1961 compiled statistics from America, England, and Wales and showed that the hospital first-admission rate for schizophrenia in the United States was about 33 percent higher than in England and Wales. The first-admission rate for manic-depressive illness in the United States was nine times lower than in England and Wales. In addition, the hospital first-admission rate of the elderly for psychosis with cerebral arteriosclerosis was about ten times higher in the United States than that in England and Wales. The psychiatric researchers asked the following questions: Were these differences, in fact, real? Or were these differences primarily a reflection of differences in diagnostic styles or training of American and British psychiatrists?

Among young adults admitted to hospitals abroad, British psychiatrists diagnosed as manic-depressive many of the same patients whom American psychiatrists were diagnosing as schizophrenic. Likewise, in the age group of sixty-five and over, when the British psychiatrists diagnosed patients as manic-depressive, the Americans diagnosed them as psychotic with cerebral arteriosclerosis. In either case, manic-depressive illness was being called something else in the American mental hospitals by American psychiatrists—principally schizophrenia in the younger age group and cerebral arteriosclerosis in the older age group.

A further study, headed by British psychiatrist John Cooper, examined the high rates of admission for schizophrenia in American hospitals and the low rates of admission for manic depression. The most important finding was that the difference between the hospital diagnoses (from two representative hospitals in London and New York) was mainly due to differences in the diagnostic criteria used in the two hospitals, and only partly due to genuine differences in the symptoms of the patients. When uniform diagnostic criteria were employed (by an independent research-project team interviewing patients in the two hospitals), the diagnostic distributions of patients entering the New York hospital and the London hospital were almost identical.

In fact, a high proportion of all American patients with research-project diagnoses of depression, mania, neurosis, personality disorder, and other illnesses were all thrown into the schizophrenia wastebasket by the New York hospital psychiatrists. It is, therefore, fair to say that, excluding alcoholism and organic psychoses, schizophrenia was virtually the only type of mental illness recognized with any frequency by the American hospital psychiatrists in the 1950s and 1960s.

From these studies it appears that American psychiatrists used the term *schizophrenia* so indiscriminately that nothing more precise was really being said when this diagnosis was made than that the patient is "crazy." "Craziness" also occurs in severe manic states and deep depressions as well as in schizophrenia. And such specific types of craziness as mania and depression are now treatable with an excellent prognosis.

The concept of schizophrenia held by the New York psychiatrists was so much broader than that held by London psychiatrists that it embraced much of what British psychiatrists regarded as depressive illness, most neurotic illness, personality disorder, and almost everything that would be regarded in London as mania and manic depression. The contrast between the two concepts of American and British psychiatrists at that time is seen in the following diagram from the monograph written by John Cooper and the two sections of the team:

Why are American psychiatrists so apt to label so many depressive and manic-depressive disorders as schizophrenia? The research team has suggested that the diagnostic habits of the staff of a psychiatric hospital are principally determined by models and opinions of half a dozen of its senior psychiatrists, who often fail to adapt to change demanded by new research findings. In many cases even a single individual through either his or her authority or powers of persuasion may "exert a dominant and idiosyncratic influence" on the teaching of the younger staff.

Eugen Bleuler, the well-known Swiss psychiatrist, taught in the early twentieth century that the diagnosis of manic depres-

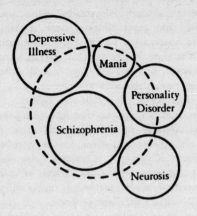

--------British Concepts

----New York Concept of Schizophrenia

The difference between the New York and British concepts of schizophrenia. (J. E. Cooper et al., *Psychiatric Diagnosis in New York and London.* Oxford University Press, 1972)

sion could be made only after excluding schizophrenia, and this has remained as a widely held view among American psychiatrists, and thus diminishes the likelihood of their making the diagnosis of manic depression or recurrent unipolar depression. The U.S. research section of the team in New York, headed by Barry Gurland, suggested that the domain of schizophrenia mapped out by the German biological psychiatrist Emil Kraepelin at the turn of the century was enlarged by Bleuler's psychological definition and the later work of the psychoanalytic schools. So-called borderline states were added and were given names that were reminiscent of schizophrenia, such as "schizophreniform" and "schizoaffective psychoses." Adolf Meyer, who was an influential psychiatrist in America for more than fifty years, emphasized that schizophrenia was a reaction and that it could have a good outcome. Early and vaguely disguised states of schizophrenia attracted attention and culminated in the concept of "pseudoneurotic schizophrenia," which referred at first to illnesses of patients who appeared to be neurotic but who didn't respond to the usual forms of psychoanalytic or psychotherapeutic treatment. Therefore, it was thought, they had to be schizophrenic and more ill than they appeared.

The concept of schizophrenia in the United States evolved as a very different concept from that in Europe. The broadness developed to the point at which schizophrenic generally meant "being out of touch with reality" or "being psychotic." Even more imprecisely, it began to be used by some psychoanalytically oriented psychiatrists to mean "failing to respond to psychotherapy," or "odd," or "severely introverted" or "not adapting to the usual expectations of society." The American concept of schizophrenia in its broadest meaning was best illustrated by the noted psychiatric leader Nolan D. C. Lewis's comment in the 1950s, "A trace of schizophrenia in anyone is schizophrenia." This definition thus strayed far from the original Kraepelin concept, in which schizophrenia was thought to be a biological illness that usually came on in the late teens and early twenties, characterized by severe and protected withdrawal, extreme ambivalence, and confusion in thought processes, often with secondary signs of hallucinations and delusions, usually going on to progressive deterioration and becoming chronic. Recurrent unipolar depressives and manic-depressives do not follow this pattern.

It might be said that the lack of agreement between British and American psychiatrists in diagnosing (or labeling) manic depression and schizophrenia then and now is based on conflicting sets of instructions handed down by leading teachers of young psychiatrists-in-training on both sides of the Atlantic. Over fifty years ago, Sir Aubrey Lewis, the influential British psychiatrist, noted the general tendency to underdiagnose recurrent depression and manic depression in favor of schizophrenia in America. He held that many schizophrenic symptoms were present in mild or subordinate forms in the manic and depressed states. His instructions, requiring careful description of the symptoms and their outcome, for diagnosing these mood disorders influenced a generation of young British psychiatrists in the tradition of Kraepelin. Meanwhile, in America, Adolf Meyer was introducing social science and psychoanalysis into the mainstream of psychiatric teaching. Meyer advocated that depressions be viewed as psychodynamic reaction types. Thus, in keeping with the psychoanalytic concept of depression stated in Freud's book *Mourning and Melancholia,* a new approach to depression and manic depression with a conflicting set of instructions was adopted by the most influential teachers and psychiatric centers in America. The instructions in American centers utilized the psychoanalytical model that all depression is basically a reaction to loss in a psychologically predisposed person and that mania is simply a denial of depression. This concept of depression applies only to bereavement and depressions secondary to a specific loss. From the case histories in this book it is evident that this concept does not apply to unipolar recurrent depression and manic depression, which are primarily chemical and hereditary in nature. When used to explain all depressions, the old concept is overinclusive and does not stand up today with the genetic and biological advances that have been made in understanding moodswings and their lithium stabilization. The early disagreements between the British and American schools in the concept of depression were real fifty years ago, and they have persisted until the present day, as the U.S./U.K. international diagnostic project clearly demonstrates.

Outright abuses of the concept of schizophrenia occurred in America for decades, resulting in an enormous error in mental-hospital statistics. These statistics reveal a steady decrease in the admission diagnosis of manic-depressive disorders from 1932 to 1950 with a corresponding increase in the diagnosis of schizophrenia over the same years, and the popularization throughout the fifties and sixties of schizophrenia in books and movies to the point of romanticizing it.

Until the early sixties the distinction between mania and schizophrenia was only of predictive value, for both illnesses were generally treated with electroshock, insulin coma, or phenothiazine tranquilizers. With lithium carbonate, legally available in America since 1970, most manic-depressives can be stabilized and remain out of hospitals, free of electroshock therapy and usually free of drugs other than lithium. Overdiagnosing schizophrenia, when the diagnosis should have been manic depression, is now of serious consequence. A finding by statistician Joseph Fleiss at the New York State Psychiatric Institute showed a tendency among American psychiatrists to associate the diagnosis of schizophrenia with young psychiatric patients and the diagnosis of depression and manic depression with older patients. This tendency prevailed even when the symptoms were similar. It also seemed to prevail in London, and it reflected a clear bias or misunderstanding of the diagnostic rules in both cities. If the American and British hospital statistics were representative of psychiatrists' diagnoses in general, it can be inferred that differences between U. S. and U. K. statistics of the incidence of depression, manic depression, schizophrenia, and cerebral arteriosclerosis were due to the different diagnostic fashions and training in the two countries. The gap in diagnostic fashion has fortunately closed considerably over the last decade and a half.

From the case histories and research findings I have described, it is easy to conclude that if you are diagnosed as manic-depressive and are in the depressed phase, you should receive antidepressants and lithium. Antidepressant drugs (tricyclic and monoamine oxidase inhibitors) have been shown to be so effective that 85 percent of depressions appear to be substantially improved within two to six weeks of initiating treatment. Lithium carbonate then takes over and stabilizes the patient so that future attacks are usually prevented or attenuated.

Depression and manic depression today constitute the single most frequently encountered mental-health problem in America. Millions suffer from forms of these illnesses that would respond to lithium and antidepressant drugs. The fact that they are not receiving these treatments calls for major change. From the conclusions of the U. S./U. K. study, that depression and manic depression are severely underestimated in America, the estimated number of patients needing these treatments is overwhelming and can only be guessed at.

A manic-depressive patient incorrectly diagnosed as schizophrenic may be sent to a long-stay unit in a hospital, given a poor prognosis, and often treated with long-term tranquilizers or electroshock treatments, or neglected for months or years. This same patient, correctly diagnosed as unipolar-depressive or manic-depressive, may not need to be hospitalized unless acutely manic or severely depressed and suicidal. Even then he would be kept in the short-stay unit, with the promise of an early discharge. He would be given a good prognosis and would receive prophylactic lithium carbonate after treatment of his acute depression with antidepressants. He would be followed in an outpatient lithium-clinic facility or by a private psychiatrist skilled in administering lithium and other psychopharmacologic agents. With the estimated millions of patients in the United States complaining of depressive and manic symptoms, it is easy to see how the incorrect treatment of manic-depressive and depressive patients as schizophrenics can lead to the loss of virtually billions of dollars of manpower. This toll does not include the years of unnecessary human anguish and suffering and the loss of creativity, for which no cost estimate can be made.

Though the diagnosis and treatment of moodswing in America was neglected in past training of young psychiatrists, considerable progress in disseminating information has been made in the last decade and a half. There are relatively few training programs in state and private psychiatric hospitals which still retain the dominant overinclusive concept of schizophrenia.

Up to the early 1980s, the education of physicians and the public to the modern concept of mood disorders seriously lagged behind the new chemical treatments available. People who could have been leading useful lives continued to live with the anguish of intermittent psychosis, hospitalization, financial ruin, divorce, and thoughts of suicide.

Fortunately diagnosis of mood disorder and the use of lithium has made it possible for hundreds of thousands of patients and their families to enjoy a normal existence.

TWELVE

When Is Hospitalization Necessary?

At three-thirty in the morning I notified the emergency ward at our private hospital in mid-Manhattan that a woman was being brought in by ambulance, under camisole restraint, in a highly excited and angry state. She arrived an hour and a half later and was seen by the psychiatric resident on call who tried to take a history from the patient and her husband.

"What is your name, please," the doctor asked.

"Screw you, it's none of your business. Furthermore, you don't even look like a doctor. You're too young. Where the hell is my new doctor—Dr. Phoebe, or however you pronounce it."

"My wife's name is Sandra White," said the distraught husband. "She is forty-eight and we live at 101 Forthington Drive, White Plains."

"Doc," Sandra interrupted, "why don't you go back to sleep? It's way past your bedtime."

Both the young resident, who had gotten out of bed at five in the morning, and the patient's husband, who had had practically no sleep for the past five nights, were exhausted; the patient, however, was obviously alert and looking for a fight.

"Perhaps," said the doctor, slightly annoyed, "you can at least tell me what the trouble is and why you've been brought in at this time of morning in a straitjacket."

"The reason I'm here," she answered, "is that this fool of a husband of mine is trying to lock me up. Since he's a lawyer, he knows all the tricks. But no one is going to hospitalize me, unless it's over my dead body. Get this thing off me and go take a history on him. He's the sick one. I swear I'll take my own life and his too. I know a lot of lawyers smarter than my husband, and they'll sue him and you, the hospital, and any other doctor that dares touch me. Fuck you all!"

Leaving the patient in a room of the emergency ward with two strong attendants, the young resident said, "Let's go into the adjoining room and you can tell me about your wife."

In the next room the husband sat down and began to explain:

"Well, she had her first breakdown in 1967, after the delivery of our first child who is now twenty. On returning home, Sandra didn't want to eat or take care of the child. She began to feel that the child wasn't really hers, and that her child was still inside her and the doctors were refusing to take it out. This thought became more and more disturbing to her, to the point where she became frankly delusional. She began to lie in bed all day and in three or four weeks lost ten pounds. I had to hire additional help, and soon afterwards at work I received a call from her nurse, stating that she had taken an overdose of sleeping pills. I rushed home and took her to the hospital, where they pumped out her stomach. She was given electroshock treatments after transfer to a psychiatric hospital with a diagnosis of postpartum psychosis, probably schizophrenic."

The husband continued: "Within several weeks after receiving eight shock treatments, she recovered and suddenly switched into a state of overactivity, talkativeness, and an angry high mood. She had all the answers. Sandra blamed me for the fact that she was in the hospital. She was rediagnosed paranoid schizophrenic, and because of her agitation and lack of sleep, she was given electroshock treatments again. After fifteen shock treatments, she was discharged, looking fairly normal but somewhat vague, with a loss of memory from the electroshock.

"Of course," he went on, "her memory damage wore off within several months, and she appeared well. She took up her usual occupations around the house.

"During the next ten years, she had an attack regularly every two to three years; then every year; lately she has had two attacks a year. They have resulted in twelve hospitalizations, over two hundred shock treatments, and years of drugs and intensive psychotherapy. No treatment has prevented new attacks. This recent one seems to be the worst so far; her anger and suspiciousness now seem to be more pronounced. She plans to sue me and anyone else responsible for bringing her here. She's also threatening suicide."

For the next several hours the psychiatric resident and her husband tried everything they could think of to convince the patient to enter voluntarily. Reasoning, persuasion, and careful explanation led nowhere and her belligerent frame of mind persisted. Ultimately, she agreed to enter voluntarily after she broke down crying and admitted that she no longer even wanted to live.

Sandra was seen by me for the first time at nine the same morning. The referral had come in the middle of the night from a colleague who had been a friend of Sandra's husband for many years. Usually the time it takes to admit a patient after arrival at the emergency ward is anywhere from one-half to six hours, depending on the cooperativeness of the patient, the availability of a bed, and the routine paperwork. In Sandra's case it took two hours.

I arranged for Sandra to be admitted to a small private psychiatric hospital close to my office, where I knew excellent clinical care was available.

Sandra was assigned by the resident to an intensive care unit because she expressed suicial threats as well as threats to kill her husband and the nurse who brought her to her room. Her thinking was delusional. She believed the KGB was eavesdropping on her through the radios and TV. Between periods of euphoria and expansiveness, when she said she talked to the Virgin Mary, she had outbursts of violent anger and combativeness. When I first saw her that morning, she had already been visited by the internist and the psychiatric resident, who had given her a brief mental status exam and started her on an antipsychotic drug. The resident had entered her history on her chart and written preliminary orders for her care.

I spent about fifteen minutes talking with Sandra, trying in vain to make contact with her through her agitated and delusional state. Having failed, I turned to her husband and her sister who had accompanied him on this visit to the hospital. Both furnished me with much valuable information about her general health and psychiatric history.

Her husband told me that she had been repeatedly diagnosed as having recurrent schizophrenic breakdowns. But he said that between attacks she was an intelligent, capable woman with a normal emotional range. It was only when she cycled into deep depressions or psychotic manic states that she would become paranoid and delusional. The fact that Sandra showed no evidence of schizophrenic thinking between episodes led me to believe that she had been misdiagnosed. I made a mental note to administer a SADS test (Schedule for Affective Disorders and Schizophrenia) later that week when she was coherent. The SADS test is a modern research questionnaire filled out by the psychologist after interviewing the patient, relatives, and medical staff to get a comprehensive picture of the patient's past and present behavior and mental status.

Sandra's family history consisted of an uncle who had had depressions and been treated for alcoholism, a sister who had had mild outpatient depressions over the years for which she was currently being treated by a psychiatrist, and a distant cousin who had committed suicide. The genetic family pedigree that I quickly sketched out on Sandra's chart was consistent with a manic-depressive illness rather than a diagnosis of schizophrenia. Manic depression, in the acute manic episode, was my working diagnosis.

I wrote orders requesting that Sandra receive a neuroendocrine workup later in the week, to measure the activity of her thyroid and adrenals. The adrenal function test called the DST (Dexamethasone Suppression Test) measures morning and afternoon levels of blood cortisol. (For further explanation, see Chapter 15, p. 236.) It indicates whether a biological depression is present, and it is the first biological test in psychiatry to help separate biologically caused depression from one due to environmental events such as loss or stress.

Sandra's internist had already ordered an electrocardiogram

(EKG) and I requested that a neurologist perform an electro-encephalogram (EEG) because she had had two discrete fainting spells several months earlier.

I believed Sandra to be suffering from a biological depression, and I began treatment immediately. I placed her on a gradual buildup to six hundred milligrams of Mellaril, an antipsychotic drug to calm her agitation, and Cogentin, a drug to reduce any tremors caused by the Mellaril. After the lithium took effect, in about ten days, I would stop all medications except the lithium.

In the beginning Sandra would receive lithium in small doses of three hundred milligrams twice daily, but I wouldn't begin them until I saw the results of her EKG and blood chemistries. Lithium is safe only if a patient has normal kidney and thyroid function, and a normal physical exam. I also needed to be sure there were no other major medical problems, including cardio-vascular disease or diabetes, before I could begin her lithium treatment. The blood chemistries (called SMA 12) returned twenty-four hours later revealed that her physical health was completely normal.

By her third day in the hospital Sandra had calmed down considerably. She complained of slight stiffness in her limbs, which was due to the Mellaril, and I increased the Cogentin from two to four milligrams a day. The lithium had been doubled on her second day to twelve hundred milligrams. Lithium would be the mainstay of her treatment, but before the lithium reached the appropriate blood levels, it would take two or three weeks, and meanwhile she would also need the antipsy-chotic medication. I left an order that her daily lithium blood levels be tested ten to twelve hours after the last dose of the night before.

Over the next ten days the nursing staff and Sandra's family corroborated what I observed each morning: Sandra was gradu-ally improving and was behaving more like her normal self. Her belligerence and delusional ideas decreased dramatically by the tenth day on lithium. By day twelve she was well enough to be transferred to an open ward.

The open ward accepts patients when the nursing staff, the patient, and family, as well as the psychiatrist, all feel that the patient is in a much improved clinical state with no suicidal thoughts or plans. At first the open-ward patient does not have permission to leave the ward or floor of the hospital. After a period of consistently improved behavior, the patient's privileges are agreed upon in daily ward meetings with the medical and nursing staff. Following a period of limited privileges when the patient has to check in and out with the head nurse comes a time when the patient is allowed day and weekend passes and finally open privileges prior to discharge.

The average highly disturbed manic-depressive patient, such as Sandra, requires about three to six weeks of hospitalization. In the hospital these patients should show marked clinical improvement in their mood, become stabilized in their drug therapy, and have the desire and ability to return home with outpatient follow-up treatment. If patients require more than a month of inpatient treatment, they may be patients for whom the first trial drugs are insufficiently long or not high enough in dosage, or they may have medical problems, or else be experiencing schizophrenic-type symptoms in conjunction with manic-depressive illness. These latter patients are called "schizoaffective." They usually do not improve as rapidly as typical manic-depressives, even those who are psychotic in the acute phase.

The schizoaffective patient, according to the definition of the American Psychiatric Association, often hears continuous voices from a third party commenting on what the patient is saying or doing; has the feeling that people are reading his or her mind and inserting thoughts in it, or that private thoughts are being broadcast out into the world. Some of these schizophrenic-type symptoms may appear in severe manic-depressive psychosis, as they did with Sandra. But Sandra had periods of normal functioning and mood in between psychotic episodes, while the schizoaffective shows a course of chronic illness with decreased normal functioning between episodes, as well as during episodes. I feel that the patient is to be diagnosed as manic-depressive if there continue to be normal periods between psychotic episodes. If the patient has a schizoaffective disorder, even when he or she is stabilized on lithium, an antipsychotic drug usually must be used along with it. Fortunately, Sandra needed only lithium on a permanent basis.

In my years of practice I have seen thousands of manic and depressed patients, and I have always felt that hospital treatment should be avoided unless the patient is so highly disturbed or suicidal that the family can no longer cope. As was true with Sandra, a patient with a depressive disorder who has been in an outpatient maintenance program of lithium and/or antidepressants rarely has a relapse. Today, Sandra is maintained by a monthly office visit when I check her medication levels and side effects, and she has never again experienced her destructive moodswings. She continues to lead a normal, full life.

THIRTEEN

Depression Treated at the Office

Hypomanic people are often the ones who turn you on whether you know it or not. It may be the supersalesman who is peddling new lingerie or the fast talker selling you a new car. It may be the garrulous guest on the talk show who keeps you up late or the nightclub comedian. Some of these people eventually get out of control and require treatment.

The manic patient who is not seriously ill does not need to be hospitalized, but he must be protected from his own poor judgment in the early months of outpatient lithium stabilization. During this period he is often happy, and his charm and cleverness are backed up by his highly logical and persuasive ways. He is so convincing and persuasive, in fact, that he may get into a lot of trouble. His social, sexual, and financial judgments are not always good.

Of course, at other times he is not so charming—when he becomes irritable, angry, and paranoid. He may even become violent.

A patient of mine, whom I will call William Smythe, is a tall, thin, highly successful businessman in his late thirties, married, and the father of three children. For twelve years he suffered recurrent manic elations and deep depressions that seriously curtailed his personal and business life. Twice during the highs, however, he invested wisely in stocks that virtually tripled his wealth. This young man's expansive highs finally reached psychotic proportions. On one occasion, because of his expansiveness while buying "hot tip" stocks, he suffered a severe financial loss. Then he began to act in an incredibly grandiose way that attracted strangers and landed a small article in *The New York Times*. When he came to me as a new patient, he told me the following story of his most extravagant moodswing.

"One fine day a few years ago, I proceeded out of the blue sky to hire a white horse and carriage driven by a young man in a white uniform, and to pick up a young couple, just engaged, to ride through Central Park. Then we proceeded down Fifth Avenue to Tiffany's, where I offered to buy my new friends a diamond engagement ring. Somewhat taken aback, they laughed enthusiastically but decided to refuse. So we went on to a branch bank where I withdrew fifty thousand dollars in silver dollars and twenty-, fifty-, and one-hundred-dollar bills. We continued down the avenue to the Empire State Building, watching the businessmen interrupt their sidewalk negotiations to scramble for the money that the three of us were throwing by the fistful from each side of the carriage. Office girls, yuppies, and even well-dressed matrons ran and stopped to grab whatever they could. After an elevator ride to the top of the Empire State Building, during which we distributed candy to all the kids, we proceeded to the Four Seasons restaurant. Our entourage by then included a motley assortment of fortune seekers. After a few well-placed twenty- and fifty-dollar tips, word spread throughout the restaurant that I was the eccentric millionaire who had thrown away money a year or two previously in New York and who had made all the papers as a result of it.

"My newly acquainted, just-engaged friend was not wearing a tie and jacket, so I gave him five hundred dollars to run and get one while I made passes at his fiancée. In the meantime he rushed to the nearest pay phone to invite a Jesus-looking, guitar-playing friend to join us for dinner. After five minutes of listening to his friend's tale of woe, I promptly wrote out a check for a thousand dollars to buy him the finest guitar needed to make his career flourish. We finished a full-course dinner with three wines and champagne and were settling down for dessert when suddenly the table was ringed by about twenty newsmen. After a number of questions, one of them suggested that our remaining money be piled in the center of the table so that they could take photographs. We complied and photos were taken. Suddenly our loot transformed the photographers into hungry vultures who picked the table clean in three seconds flat and abruptly vanished. Fortunately, the Four Seasons accepted a check, after much identification (I guess they had no choice). Afterward, I wrote several more checks for people who had gathered about us for their favorite charities—no one ever said, 'Please give me some money to spend on my greedy self'—and a thousand-dollar tip to the employees in the kitchen. We departed, to meditate in a friend's apartment.

"NBC mentioned my spree on a late-news brief that evening, which was beamed around the globe via satellite. The next day an article also appeared in *The New York Times,* and the *Daily News* carried a photo of me and my two friends with all the reporters and photographers gathered about the table piled with money.

"It was a quick way to go through fifty thousand dollars in a complete manic fantasy, or better still, a manic reality. Years afterwards, even today, I am still analyzing and rationalizing, trying to figure out what triggered that behavior. I had had manic attacks before, but never had I given away money. My well-to-do mother was horrified. Besides knowing that I had lost my mind, she was afraid I would be assassinated or kidnapped by someone wanting money. My bank couldn't believe that anyone would give away money, except, of course, through normal channels; they were afraid of becoming known as 'the bank for people who literally throw money away.' My lawyer thought that all my creditors would foreclose before sunset, if they hadn't already, and my friends, I think, were amused to read an article in the *Times* about someone they knew. My friends seemed most interested in reserving a prominent spot for themselves during the next money avalanche. No one offered me the least amount to throw away the next time. Hundreds of letters arrived the next week, the most amusing being a request by a retiring British couple for funds to take a trip they had dreamed of for a lifetime.

"Besides the financial loss (I didn't even attempt to justify deducting all or part of it from my income tax) I was left with the decay of manic elation, which began to turn grayer and grayer into black depression. It's hard to experience and appreciate average, ordinary reality—whatever that is—from the hindsight of a manic high.

"I was hospitalized, of course, for that episode, and I did eventually come out of it after getting all kinds of drugs that were slow to work. They gave so many unpleasant side effects that the cure was worse than the treatment.

"Now that I am in a normal mood state, the money spree seems most bizarre. Of course, I was high, and I unwittingly went through a most marvelous emotional experience. I was on top of the world and enjoying every incredible minute. I know that Fifth Avenue has never looked or felt the same for me as on that autumn day, with its view from the white horse and carriage and the golden-haired couple. I jokingly say that my next goal, if I ever become manic like that again, is to make the cover of *Time*."

When patients like William Smythe are up, they are happy, optimistic, and amusing but they may exercise disastrous judgment. On the other hand, when they are being interviewed in the depressed phase, the whole mood of the consulting room changes to one of sadness and despair. I become equally concerned for the patient who is suffering anguish of a different quality from that of the severely ill manic, the depressed patient who may at that moment feel so low that he is considering taking his life.

Beth, an attractive, articulate, thirty-four-year-old housewife, recounted her experience in the depressive phase of a manic-depressive illness. She had lived a normal, energetic life until her late twenties, having had three children over a five-year period. At twenty-eight she began to experience recurrent depressions interspersed with states of mild and pleasurable manic elation. The feelings she described to me are typical of her depressions.

"While watching a TV program," she said, "alone in the living room this last Monday, I was suddenly overwhelmed by tears. Why? I looked around me. What could be a house filled with laughter and beauty was so meaningless to me; suddenly I felt so empty because Jim and all of my children were trapped and ensnared by me. I felt my stupidity and ineptness so overwhelmingly that I ruined everything that was good. I felt so sorry for Jim, who suddenly had lost that indestructibleness and who seemed tired and beaten. He believed in me, so it was devastating to me, the disappointment that I brought to him. I feel up and then so down. I don't seem to be able to cope. With other women I feel so empty and stupid and incapable, not smart enough. When I think about it or it crops up in even some insignificant way, I get frightened and scared for my family. I want to be like other people. Why do I have to be the way I am? Nothing, but nothing, is ever less than a struggle. Every event is hampered by my inability and gets to be an impossible hurdle. I feel this awful sadness, and there doesn't seem to be an end. I ask God on my bended knees to protect my family and watch over them while I flounder. I feel things could be so different, full of life and joy, but everything is joyless and a struggle for me.

"Is there no help available, no doctor, no priest, or anyone else who can help me?

"I can't bear it. I can't stand the humiliating fact that I'm the only woman in the world who can't take care of her family, take her place as a real wife and mother, and be respected in her community. When I speak to my young son Billy, I know I can't let him down, but I feel so ill-equipped to take care of him; that's what frightens me. I don't know what to do or where to turn; the whole thing is too overwhelming. Maybe I should end it all. Maybe they'd be better off if I did; I can't be of any use to them this way. I must be a laughingstock. It's more than I can do to go out and meet people and have the fact pointed up to me so clearly.

"Furthermore, I just don't see that any new psychiatrist could do anything about this. None of the previous ones whom I've talked endlessly with have helped me. There is no pill in the world that is suddenly going to make me capable and alive again."

* * *

Both these patients are suffering from the same mood disorder. Both were treated in my private practice in New York City. At my office their manic depression could, it was hoped, be brought under control. Both patients have been free of their mania and depression for the past six years while seeing me or my associate and my nursing team and receiving lithium carbonate treatment. Beth also sees my associate psychologist for behavioral therapy and help with her problem of overweight.

Patients like William and Beth are often maintained on lithium in conjunction with antidepressants. They remain essentially well, requiring only periodic monthly follow-ups for lithium blood levels and changes in mood or side effects that might indicate too little or too much of the drug. A patient with recurrent depression or manic depression is seen monthly for a short period of time and remains free of highs and lows 85 percent of the time without hospitalizations. Patients have now been coming to the practice for over twenty years. Their lives and the lives of their families have dramatically improved since they were placed on lithium chemotherapy.

When William first came to see me, the first priority was for me to take a careful history and arrive at an initial diagnosis. The diagnostic interview that I use is my own version of the latest clinical research diagnostic instrument. It was approved of by the American Psychiatric Association and describes the symptoms of every presently known psychiatric disorder, including depression and manic depression.

At the initial interview, which eliminated other possible conditions, William was diagnosed as bipolar manic-depressive (he had been hospitalized for both manic and depressive states). His lows on three occasions had reached such serious levels that, during the first depression, hospitalization had been required. During the initial consultation I recorded all key information on data-collection forms that allow for later computer scanning by my nursing team.

The family history was normal on his father's side but filled with depression on his mother's side, a clinical genetic marker in manic-depressive disease. His maternal grandfather had manic depression; one aunt had committed suicide; his older sister was alcoholic.

Because of the family history, the repeated highs and lows, and otherwise normal functioning between episodes, during which time he ran his life quite energetically and capable, William was an excellent candidate for lithium.

He was slowly placed on twelve hundred milligrams daily. He entered my private practice in a normal interval phase in which he was neither high nor low, so that no other medication was required. A complete physical exam preceded initiation of the drug, including a cardiogram, complete blood biochemistries (SMA 12),* urinalysis, and baseline psychometric testing along with research studies. He was also given the Dexamethasone Suppression Test (DST) to determine the amount of plasma cortisol in his blood. If a patient is depressed, the amount of cortisol in the blood is much higher than for a nondepressive. While this test is not 100 percent reliable, it is still extremely useful in major depression. (For fuller details of it, see Chapter 15.)

William was asked to come back weekly for three weeks to be checked for blood lithium levels, observations of mood and behavior, side effects, and to volunteer as much information as possible about his family tree. Thereafter he was scheduled for monthly visits with me and my clinical research nursing staff. He was warned of lithium's side effects if too much was taken. (These side effects include hand tremor, nausea, excessive urination, and diarrhea.) He was told to stop the drug if any of these appeared. He was told that diuretics (drugs used in medicine to produce urinary excretion of excess fluid and salt) and low-fluid and low-salt diets should be avoided while on lithium. William's family was likewise fully informed.

This chemical approach to depression is an extremely efficient way to give top-quality care to a large number of patients. Whereas a practicing psychotherapist might see a limited number of patients weekly, with this system one psychopharmacolo-

---

*A blood test that gives results on twelve routine blood chemistries. These include blood sugar, liver enzymes, etc.

gist and the nursing personnel handle ten to twelve patients in four to five hours in complete safety. A nurse draws blood from patients so that I can monitor the levels of lithium and antidepressant medications right in my office. The patient comes to my office, with relatives or a friend whenever possible. The initial diagnostic consultation may take up to an hour but in subsequent visits the patient is seen for less time and questioned and scored on rating scales with regard to his or her clinical course, sleep pattern, mood, lithium dosage, side effects, and any adjunctive medications taken during the month since his last visit. Two psychiatric research nurses collect personal and family background information, along with current mood and behavioral data. (See Fievr-Dunner Manic-Depressive Mood Scale on p. 203.)

If a patient has become depressed or manic, or is experiencing side effects, the nurse usually detects it first at the office visit if the patient or the family hasn't already called in. Thereafter, my associate or I will corroborate these findings during the visit and a change in treatment will be made immediately. The patient is required to return to the office again that week or the following week.

In addition to the medication program, I have an active psychotherapy program of group and individual counseling. These therapies include behavioral modification and cognitive* therapy, which help to restructure counterproductive thought and behavioral patterns. These therapies are active, short-term interventions.

Such delivery of health services has been referred to in general medicine as a health-maintenance organization, whether in the private or low-cost sector. This represents one of the first illustrations of a specialty clinic in modern psychiatry that could expand the services of community mental-health centers if incorporated into their present structures.

Located in the same building as my private office is the Foundation for Depression and Manic Depression which in 1976

---

*Form of psychotherapy in which therapist tries to undo patient's negative view of self, world and future.

Fieve-Dunner Manic-Depressive Mood Scale*

(To be filled out independently by nurse and patients)

100 Medical emergency. Wildly manic and psychotic; can't stop talking; incoherent, overactive, belligerent, or elated. Not sleeping at all. At times delusional; hallucinating. May be either violent or paranoid.

90 Extreme elation so that patient can't rate self; in need of more medication and control. Completely uncooperative.

80 Severe elation. Should be admitted, or if in hospital usually wants to sign out of ward. Sleeping very little; hostile when crossed; loss of control. Needs medication.

70 Moderate elation. Overactivity and talkativeness; irritable and annoyed. Needs only four to six hours' sleep. Socially inappropriate; wants to control. Outpatient treatment has been advised by doctors.

60 Mildly elevated mood and many ideas for new projects; occasionally mildly obtrusive. If creative, the energy is highly useful. Hyperperceptive. Feels wonderful, on top of the world. Increased sexual drive; wants to spend money and travel. Treatment may be contraindicated or not needed.

50 Mood is within normal range (45–55).

40 Mildly depressed mood, but noticeable lack of energy; chronic lack of optimism and pleasure. Feels slowed down. Treatment may not be desired, although it may be indicated. Decreased interest in sex. Decreased motivation.

30 Moderate depression. Loss of energy; disinterested in others; early weight, sleep, and appetite disturbance; able to function with effort but prefers, if possible, to stay in bed during day; doesn't want to go to work, but may force oneself; feels life is not worthwhile. Little sexual interest. Outpatient treatment advised by doctors.

20 Severe depression. Takes care of daily routine but needs prodding and reminding; loss or gain of weight; sleep disorder is serious. Volunteers suicidal feelings; very withdrawn, may be paranoid.

10 Extreme depression. Actively suicidal, totally withdrawn or extremely agitated. Difficulty rating self on mood scale.

0 Medical emergency. Unable to eat or take medication; can't follow ward routine; delusional, suicidal. Stuporous. Stares into space; very little response on questioning. May require tube feeding.

Nurses' and Psychiatrists' Rating Scale

Patients' Self-Rating Scale

Inpatient

Outpatient treatment

Inpatient

*Ronald R. Fieve, M.D., and David Dunner, M.D.

was established to help the then hundreds (now thousands) of depressed and manic-depressed patients who needed low-cost treatment. Many were originally discharged from the acute services of metropolitan New York hospitals. Many more had been Medicaid or Medicare patients of psychiatrists or physicians who had had little success in controlling these patients' moods with conventional talking therapy or drug therapy.

Our low-cost Foundation clinic is decidedly not psychoanalytic in its philosophy. However, nursing staff and psychiatrists manning the Foundation encourage patients to seek some type of psychotherapy or counseling through the Foundation when needed. Most patients have previously been in some form of psychotherapy with two or more psychiatrists. In some instances these psychotherapeutic sessions have gone on continually or periodically for a total of twelve to fourteen years. Most of the patients have expressed considerable disappointment with the failure of their previous psychotherapy alone to cure their mood cycles or to prevent future ones. However, several patients did feel that they learned more about their general problems of living than they would have had they not had their years of psychotherapy.

Many patients and their families regard lithium as a wonder drug and have great expectations for its curative potential. The feeling is reinforced in the waiting room, where patients hear numerous lithium success stories from other patients. It is reassuring for new patients to learn that there is a biochemical basis for an illness they thought for years resulted from unconscious conflicts in their personalities, deeply rooted since childhood, and probably from sexual, aggressive, or guilty feelings towards parents or siblings. These feelings had been engendered, they thought, during the first few years of life, leaving scars on their personalities that led to depressive or manic moodswings decades later.

Their learning of the biochemical cause of their illness seems to result in a marked diminution of guilt in patients and families about behavior during attacks. They are now taught that their behavior cannot be changed simply by "bucking up" or by "digging deeper and longer" into the unconscious. These patients are educated in the concept that lithium is a perpetual preventive much like insulin.

From its inception, this treatment approach proved to be an extremely successful, quick, and inexpensive method of treating manic-depressive disease. Costs are approximately 5 to 10 percent of prelithium treatment. Note: A cost-analysis estimate reveals that to care for a manic-depressive or depressive patient in a clinic setting costs approximately 20 to 30 percent of his or her previous care, with hospitalization, other drugs, and oftentimes ill-advised electroshock therapy. For a private patient, lithium maintenance costs are approximately 10 to 20 percent of previous financial outlay.

With a limited amount of time and psychiatrist-hours, close to five thousand Medicaid patient visits per year can be handled by the low-cost Foundation clinic with relative ease. The effectiveness of this system is demonstrated by the minimal hospitalization rate and lack of suicides in ten years, although the overall mortality due to suicide in manic-depressive illness runs to about 15 percent, making this group an extremely high-risk population for suicide among psychiatric patients.

The traditional emphasis on the patient, the psychiatrist, and the fifty-minute hour two to five times per week has been changed to patient, psychiatrist, nurses' rating team, and the brief fifteen-minute monthly visit, with supportive short-term psychotherapy if needed.

I have received thousands of grateful letters from patients describing their personal feelings and reaction to lithium and how their lives have changed. One patient wrote the following in a letter:

My lows began fifteen years ago, when I started to be afraid of things in my business that had never bothered me before. I was afraid to be criticized by my superiors. I was afraid to get up in the morning to face my store. I was afraid to go to sleep. I couldn't sleep nights. I couldn't taste my food. I would go to work and then turn around and go home. The store felt like a dungeon to me. My hands would shake. I wanted to be a laborer with no responsibilities. I wanted to quit. I was just a mess and I couldn't get out of it; my married life was bad. But one odd thing during all these years, I never thought of suicide, not even the slightest. I had eight years of psychotherapy with four different psychiatrists. My lows kept recurring as I talked my heart out. Finally I had shock treatments but my lows came back a year later.

After being on lithium for five years it was like a new world in front of me. I enjoyed my work so much. I looked forward to the mornings so I could be at my store. I made decisions fast and right. I stood my ground with my superiors, and I gained their respect. I would reprimand an employee without feeling guilty. I became very strong in my convictions. I had a sense of humor which I never had before. I'm enjoying each day to the fullest. My marriage came to life again. When I look back at the fears I had in business, I just can't believe that I lived through them.

As new patients call my office, they are screened by a telephone interview by my nurses, and then come for an initial diagnostic evaluation with me or an associate. They are asked to provide or schedule a physical exam. Background data, including previous hospitalizations and outpatient treatments, are recorded. In addition, a detailed family pedigree is drawn up by the geneticist who sees the patient and family during initial visits. Modular data-collection forms for computer storage and retrieval require the following information:

Module I	Biographical Data
Module II	Medical and Psychiatric History
Module III	Family History
Module IV	Sequential Data During Treatment

When I see the patient at subsequent monthly visits, mood ratings, side effects, lithium dosage, and other medications are recorded. Monthly weight, blood pressure, and menstrual periods are noted, as well as life events and stresses that might be related to the precipitation of a manic or depressive episode.

Whether or not stresses in life actually precipitate depressions or highs is still a much debated problem in psychiatric research. Studies have tended to conclude that life events are not directly related to the precipitation of depression or mania, as most psychiatrists have traditionally thought. However, further research is needed. Any creative or productive events, alcohol or drug consumption, and gambling sprees are recorded. All data including nurse's mood ratings are tabulated and stored for computer analysis.

People with manic depression or depression alone, if actively suicidal, are admitted first to the Depression Ward at our private hospital or have nurses around the clock at home. (Of course, patients who feel suicidal during any subsequent visit are strongly encouraged to be admitted to the hospital for protection.) Depressed patients are treated initially with antidepressant drugs and simultaneously placed on lithium for prophylaxis.

A typically depressed patient, Judith Mayer, was a forty-one-year-old married woman complaining of her fifth recurrent depression. She helped the nurse fill out the modular data forms, a depression questionnaire, had her family pedigree drawn, and gave the following information to me:

"When depressed this past month I have felt bewildered, sad, physically tired, and completely lacking in physical desire and total energy, to the point that I could not talk to anyone; I just wanted to sleep. I was not interested in anything and could not understand what was happening to me. I could barely do my work and at times had to quit completely. Although sad, I never seemed able to cry. Everything seemed unreal. As you know, I'm an artist, and my choreography demands inspiration, imagination, and creativeness. During my depressed periods I am completely noncreative and nonfunctioning. My sleep is impaired, and I wake early in the morning; I tend to want to sleep all day instead. My eating increased and I went from one hundred and twelve to one hundred and twenty pounds in two months of depression. I felt that life was not worth living during previous depressions but not this time. In the past I have made two attempts on my life: once with sleeping pills and another time by trying to hang myself on the bedpost. Fortunately neither worked."

My treatment approach at the time of Judith's visit after her first evaluation and diagnosis was to place her on an antidepressant* and lithium. To begin lithium and/or these antidepressant drugs, there must be no evidence of heart or kidney disease and the patient must be in good medical health. Once her preliminary medical workup was cleared I began her antidepressant three times daily along with nine hundred milligrams of lithium. She was further instructed on the common side effects of both drugs. If any side effects occurred, she was told, she should call me immediately for instructions. She was warned of possible toxicity.

I tell patients that during the first phase of lithium treatment and stabilization and during any acute manic or depressive phase, they will have to return weekly for periodic lithium-blood-level monitoring. Below the recommended level, highs and lows tend to recur, and above this level early toxicity may begin. Patients are cautioned on the need to continue normal food, fluid, and salt intake to maintain the electrolyte and lithium balance. The nurses hand out several articles on the history of lithium and its side effects, as well as material that explains chemical depressions and the side effects of the medications. This information is helpful to patients and their families, who need to understand the medical approach that I use.

In the event the collaborative research program that I direct at Columbia University, New York State Psychiatric Institute, and the Foundation for Depression and Manic Depression yields one or more biological markers, future laboratory tests may be developed to help in the diagnosis of different subtypes of mood disorder—tests of similar value to blood sugar levels, which help diagnose diabetes, and liver enzymes, which aid in diagnosing liver and heart disease. Eventually diagnostic screening tests may also predict specific responses to antidepressant treatment.

The discovery of an altered biological marker in manic depres-

---

*Standard and safe widely used antidepressants include the tricyclics, such as amitriptyline, the MAO inhibitors, such as phenelzine, and the newer, second-generation drugs, such as trazodone. (See Chapter 15).

sion, with a specific mode of genetic transmission, would constitute one of the major breakthroughs in psychiatry in the twentieth
century—and make it possible to do far more early diagnostic
and preventative work in the office.

FOURTEEN

The Lithium Breakthrough

The ways man has responded to moodswing over the centuries make up psychiatry's history. For several thousand years the most enlightened civilizations resorted to euthanasia, imprisonment, chains, and forceful restraints; the list of treatments took such forms as exotic potions, bloodletting, and electric eels applied to the skull. Then came more modern methods: insulin coma, lobotomy, electroconvulsive shock treatments, psychoanalysis, and psychotherapy, and most recently the vast array of newly synthesized tranquilizers and antidepressants. But not until the advent of lithium did any form of treatment succeed for long in bringing moodswing under control.

Today, lithium controls and prevents recurrence of the chronic and debilitating moodswings typical of manic-depressives. Lithium also is clearly effective in preventing recurrent depressions, even when manic episodes are not present.

In the early Greek and Roman tent hospitals some eighteen hundred years ago, the physician Soranus of Ephesus prescribed mineral-water therapy for manic insanity and melancholia. In fact, he advocated in his writings the use of specific alkaline springs for a number of physical and mental illnesses. The tradition persisted for centuries. Today many of these alkaline springs developed by the Romans in southern and western Europe are known to contain high quantities of lithium.

It was not until 1817, however, that the lightest of the 1A group of alkaline metals in the chemists' periodic table of elements was discovered by the young Swedish chemistry stu-

211

dent Johan Arfvedson. He named it lithium because it was found in stone (*lithos* in Greek). Lithium was soon found to be one of the most reactive of all the basic elements, and although it was never found free in nature, its occurrence could be noted in the mineral rocks, natural brines, mineral waters, and in some plant, animal and human tissues. The specific presence of lithium in the mineral waters of European and American spas that were used for drinking and bathing was widely advertised during the nineteenth and early twentieth centuries. The name Lithia was often given to these springs, which are thought to promote physical and mental health. Toward the turn of the century, Presidents Cleveland and McKinley both paid a visit to the widely known mineral springs spa at Lithia Springs, Georgia, for a "cure." Even today, despite the fact that the large hotel burned down and the spa changed hands several times, Lithia Springs Bottling Company continues to bottle up to five thousand gallons of lithium mineral water every day, and distributes it throughout the United States and Europe. Letters continue to come in praising the high-content lithium water, claiming many total and miraculous cures for mental and physical disorders. Because of the publicity given to lithium's therapeutic and preventive effects on mood disorders, the sale of Lithia Springs mineral water has soared over the past decade. Many patients and non-patients alike swear by it.

In some instances the nineteenth-century promoters exaggerated the amount of lithium in the springs to attract a larger clientele. In the 1840s it had been discovered that lithium salts, when combined with uric acid, were able to dissolve kidney stones and to treat gout and rheumatism, as well as other physical and mental diseases. The use of lithium for the treatment of these disorders was largely discontinued when newer and more effective therapies were developed.

Some enthusiasts still believe, however, that mineral springs are capable of curing a wide variety of medical and psychiatric ills. In fact, in some countries—West Germany, for example—the cost of spa treatment is today recoverable from health insurance. In Eastern Europe and the Soviet Union there are large state-owned facilities; numerous spas in Western Europe, the United States and Japan are still active enterprises. Carefully specified courses of mineral-water treatment are offered in each of these establishments for one or more chronic disorders, particularly for nervous conditions given a variety of names, including neurasthenia, neuralgia, and "nervous breakdowns"—meaningless terms that over the centuries have included all forms of depressive disorders.

Early in this century lithium bromide was used for epilepsy, and it was also considered an excellent sleeping medication. In the late 1940s in the United States lithium chloride became a popular salt substitute for patients on sodium-free diets. It was sold under such names as Westal, Foodsal, and Saltisal. Among the patients using lithium as a food seasoning were some with heart and kidney disease, conditions for which, it is now known, lithium is particularly dangerous. When at least three deaths and many serious poisonings attributed to lithium were reported in 1949, American drug manufacturers swiftly removed lithium from the market.

In the industrial field the use of lithium and its compounds proceeded much more rapidly. Scientists found a number of ways to take advantage of its unique attributes. Because of its light weight and ability to maintain integrity in a wide temperature range, it found its way into nuclear technology. Its peculiar atomic structure was exploited in the fission-fusion reaction of thermonuclear explosion, and it became an essential compound in the hydrogen bomb. Industry was also quick to capitalize on the versatile and reactive properties of this basic element in other ways. Since lithium attracts water, it was soon used in dehumidifiers and purifiers in air-circulation systems. Lithium stearate was also added to lubricants to make them efficient over a wide temperature range.

The discovery of the therapeutic effects of lithium against mania in 1949 was entirely serendipitous. The Australian psychiatrist John F. Cade suspected urea as the toxic substance causing manic states, and he found it in patients' urine. To test this hypothesis he needed to inject uric acid into guinea pigs, so he used lithium, which was able to form the most soluble salt, lithium urate. When he injected lithium urate (and later lithium carbonate) into guinea pigs, however, they became very lethargic instead of excited. After he had administered lithium carbonate to ten manic subjects with dramatically positive results, he reported his first findings. Lithium, he claimed, restored manic patients to normal mood states, and on maintenance doses several of his more chronic and hopeless patients became well enough to leave the hospital.

The publication of these remarkable findings stimulated the interest of many clinicians, and it was not long before trials with lithium salts were under way in Australia, France, Italy, England, and Denmark. In 1954 the first double-blind trial was conducted in Denmark by Mogens Schou. Ratings of improvement in manic behavior were made by doctors who did not know which patients received lithium and which received an inert placebo.

In the United States neither Cade's 1949 report nor Schou's impressive work published in 1954 aroused any research interest in lithium. Because lithium first appeared in Australia at the same time as the American cardiac deaths resulting from its misuse, the American medical profession remained frightened of its toxic and potentially lethal effects. Instead, American psychiatrists began to show exclusive interest in the newly synthesized psychoactive drugs—tranquilizers and the antidepressants, and antianxiety, stimulant and hypnotic drugs that appeared in rapid succession in the 1950s. Furthermore, lithium, being a natural element, could not be patented, and the American pharmaceutical industry could not see any commercial potential in the drug.

In 1958 the Danish reports prompted Schou's former professor, Dr. Heinrich Waelsch, and Dr. Lawrence C. Kolb, then director of the New York State Psychiatric Institute, to encourage me to begin systematic clinical research trials in the United States. I performed these initial trials in the acute ward of the New York State Psychiatric Institute with psychiatrist Shervert Frazier, later director of the National Institute of Mental Health. In 1960 Dr. Samuel Gershon, an Australian psychiatrist who had just arrived in America, reviewed lithium's unique action and encouraged American doctors to try the drug. During the early 1960s word of lithium's dramatic action spread westward. An uncontrollably manic Texas professor, simultaneously writing ten books and forty research papers, was sent to New York for lithium treatment. He responded astonishingly well to the lithium that my colleagues Lawrence Kolb and Ralph Wharton, and I, gave him. He was sent back to Texas "cured" on lithium, much to the amazement of the Texas psychiatrists who had been unable to subdue his frenetic, psychotic high for the better part of a year. They were so amazed at his rapid recovery that experiments in Galveston were then begun.

The Texas study and the New York State Psychiatric Institute's study were presented simultaneously at the American Psychiatric Association's meeting in May 1965. This was lithium's debut in the psychiatric profession in the United States as a treatment for mania.

In the late 1960s interest in lithium increased among American psychiatric researchers and it was suggested that legal limitations on the use of the drug be formally reviewed. At the same time, marketing of lithium was still illegal in the United States. To use it experimentally in the hospital we had to make up capsules in the pharmacy and obtain an investigational drug number from the Food and Drug Administration.

In response to this interest, the American Psychiatric Association created in 1969 a lithium task force, which I was a member of, and which assisted the FDA in the preparing of a package insert describing the drug. In 1970, upon recommendation of the task force, the FDA again approved lithium as a standard prescription drug. This time, however, its marketing was much more cautiously managed. Lithium was approved exclusively for the treatment of acute mania with insistence on careful blood monitoring and rigid controls. A year later, approval for the maintenance use of lithium in manic-depressive illness was recommended.

But the claim of being able to manage and control manic-depressive conditions with lithium provoked a serious international controversy among European and American psychiatrists and researchers in the late 1960s and throughout the 1970s. Did it really work? Did it work better than other standard antidepressant and antianxiety drugs?

The potent antipsychotic tranquilizers and antidepressant compounds synthesized and marketed in the late 1950s relieved the symptoms of psychosis, anxiety, and depression, but did not specifically get at the core of the illness. Lithium, in contrast, biochemically assaults and controls the illness itself—and is the first drug to do so. Since 1949 many hundreds of thousands of men and women all over the world with severe mood disorders, have been successfully stabilized on lithium salts. Since its reintroduction in the United States in 1970, the drug has been given to hundreds of new patients daily. Few experiences in psychiatry are as dramatic as watching lithium carbonate utterly transform a manic-depressive personality in one to two weeks. And while tranquilizers and psychic energizers in large doses have many unpleasant side effects, lithium at optimum dosage has virtually none. Few patients object to taking lithium, especially people who have resigned themselves to living out their lives in institutions, or in paralyzing depressions between bouts of mania.

Lithium's acceptance as a specific treatment and maintenance medication for manic depression marked the first time in the history of psychiatry that a simple, naturally occurring salt controlled a major mental disorder. This idea was a threat to psychiatry's traditional and costly ways of treating mood disorders. Its acceptance could equal the impact of insulin or digitalis on the medical field!

To begin with, stabilization of a major mental illness with a naturally occurring chemical salt strengthened the hypothesis of a genetically inherited biochemical defect as the primary cause of moodswing. Major mood disorders are estimated to affect at least 3 to 4 percent of the general population, and the introduction of lithium treatment would require many physicians to change their psychological orientation and conceptual understanding of these conditions. Practically speaking, psychiatrists could start treating the patient with lithium carbonate and antidepressants instead of the hitherto employed psychotherapy, psychoanalysis, electroshock treatments, and often inappropriate or short-lived pharmacotherapy.

Psychotherapy, with its emphasis on the one-to-one, fifty-minute dialogue, would have to assume a less important role in most cases of moodswing, and no role in many. Electroshock and hospitalization would rarely be needed. Lithium might prove to be an embarrassingly inexpensive, yet effective way to treat the major mood disorders. One might even postulate that the world economic market for treating moodswing was now being threatened by a simple and inexpensive salt that could not be marketed with any great profit to anyone.

When lithium came upon the scene in the early 1970s psychiatry was already going through a transition from psychological to biochemical treatments in America. Many physicians feel that the fact that it is specific for manic depression is proof positive of the biochemical nature of this mental disorder, and suggests that many others may also be biochemical in origin.

In the decade and a half since this book was first written, an entirely new attitude has developed concerning traditional psychotherapy and analysis. As I predicted, they have changed radically and in some respects have become obsolete. This does not mean that human contact between patient and therapist is any less important. It simply means that pure "talking therapy," as I named it, need not be done by a medically trained psychiatrist or psychoanalyst. The fifty-minute hour is no longer a sacred time frame in which to make contact with the patient. Instead, therapists of diverse styles and orientations have become popular, and most medically trained psychiatrists have changed their approach from talking alone to drugs alone or drugs and psychotherapy. Traditional psychoanalysis is still being taught and trainees still graduate, but training is less popular nowadays. Bright young psychiatric residents who used to go into psychoanalytic training now often go into research or careers in clinical pharmacology instead.

Nowadays most psychiatrists will admit that the traditionally taught psychotherapeutic techniques have been notoriously unsuccessful as a primary treatment for the major mind disorders: manic depression, unipolar depression, and schizophrenia.

Undoubtedly, modified psychological approaches will be the wave of the future for neuroses. Drug therapy enhanced by behavioral modification techniques has been successful in treating many specific symptoms such as phobias and obsessions. The term *neurotic depression* is an imprecise phrase that is rapidly disappearing among American psychiatrists. In its place the *Diagnostic and Statistical Manual of Mental Disorders III Revised* of the American Psychiatric Association uses the term *dysthymia* to define minor depression. Depressions are now diagnosed specifically as either recurrent major depression (unipolar, meaning no highs), recurrent manic depression (bipolar, meaning highs and lows), or else as recurrent dysthymia (also unipolar, but less severe). Dysthymia is milder than major depression but more chronic.

Dysthymia afflicts about half of the twenty million Americans currently suffering from some form of depression. The symptoms are: chronic disturbance of mood; loss of pleasure in usual activities and pastime; feeling sad or down in the dumps. Sleep is disturbed—either by insomnia or oversleeping—and the patient feels tired most of the time. There is a sense of inadequacy and loss of self-esteem, an inability to respond with pleasure to praise or rewards. These patients are pessimistic about the future, and may feel sorry for themselves, or be tearful. Dysthymia may last many years in adults, and may even be lifelong It usually begins early in adulthood, and the onset may be gradual, over several years. Social function and job performance are mildly but consistently impaired. The person is often likely to become a substance abuser. These people can get by in life without seeking professional treatment but the price is high.

In my practice, I tend to see the more severe cases. Of the thousands of depressed patients I have treated over the past twenty years, fewer than a third are actually suffering from the milder, recurrent dysthymic disorder. Two thirds of these depression patients have a major depression, which may involve suicidal thoughts, hospitalization, severe impairment of social function, and even hallucinations and delusions. These major depressions can be treated with antidepressants and/or lithium.

Many patients' so-called neurotic life-styles improve rapdily with chemical relief from their dysthymic depressions. But there are yet some patients who do not improve with medication, most often those who have personality disorders underlying the depression: maladaptive, inflexible lifelong traits that chronically impair the person's work performance and emotional bonding. Personality disorders are grouped into three clusters: (1) the paranoid and schizoid types, (2) the histrionic, narcissistic, antisocial, and borderline types, and (3) the avoidant, dependent, and passive-aggressive types. In my opinion, one third to one half of all depressed patients have a long-standing personality disorder underlying their depression. They benefit from psychotherapy or behavior therapy along with drug treatment, or instead of it in some cases.

Another type of depression, called reactive depression, occurs in response to a loss or stress: The death of a loved one, retirement, or too much raipd change may precipitate a depression. A reactive depression is usually self-limiting and will disappear after four or six months, but it will often disappear sooner with the new medications available.

Surprisingly, recent studies of the neuroses indicate that phobias, obsessive-compulsive disorders and anxiety states also may often have genetic biological components, and can be relieved by medications. What is usually considered "neurotic personality" may be biological and passed down through the genes in a much more subtle manner than is presently understood.

One potential use of lithium may be in certain forms of alcoholism. Researchers at Rockland State Hospital in New York State in a joint project with the Veterans Administration

Hospital in Maine, gave daily doses of lithium to half of seventy patients with severe episodic drinking problems. The remainder of the group received a placebo. After about two years drinkers on lithium had significantly fewer severe binges. Although they did not necessarily give up drinking, the lithium-treated alcoholics required only half as much hospitalization for their alcoholism and accompanying detoxification. It is possible that lithium curtails successive drinking sprees in some people who drink to combat periodic depression and who have dual diagnoses; it is also possible that lithium works directly on the aberrant biochemistry of the alcoholic and his metabolism of alcohol. However, a lithium research group in Denmark was unable to produce similar results using a different experimental design.

It has been suggested that lithium may be effective in the long-term reduction of aggressive behavior. Twenty-seven recurrent violent prisoners in a medical facility that is part of the California Department of Corrections were chosen for a lithium study on the basis of their extremely violent, provocative, angry behavior. Taking an average of eighteen hundred milligrams of lithium carbonate daily for ten months, fifteen of the twenty-two remaining prisoners had fewer disciplinary actions for violent behavior; four had the same number as before; and three had more. The psychiatric staff at the hospital observed that "fourteen of the prisoners improved substantially on lithium carbonate, and twenty-one improved to some extent." Dr. Joseph Tupin, head of the University of California team that made the study suggested that "lithium might be effective in the long-term reduction of aggressive behavior— the characteristics of the positive responders suggesting that a careful search for brain damage is now indicated in these individuals who exhibit recurrent angry and violent behavior."

Siamese fighting fish become less aggressive when lithium is present in their tissues in higher-than-normal concentrations. The same is true of aggressive rats and other animals.

Given these provocative findings, it is fascinating to speculate about the social changes that future applications of lithium research might bring about. Prisons and reform schools may have a number of unfortunates whose only real crime is a defect of metabolism, an inability to function normally due to a basic problem in brain chemistry. The idea that lithium might be a physiologically essential mineral like sodium or potassium, or a trace element like copper, is intriguing.

The possibility that lithium might be essential to mental health received widespread attention some years ago when Dr. Earl Dawson and colleagues at the University of Texas in Galveston compared mental-hospital admissions and local lithium concentrations in the drinking water in twenty-seven Texas counties over a two-year period. They concluded that the higher the concentration of lithium, the lower the number of mental-hospital admissions. El Paso has one of the highest lithium levels in the drinking water throughout the country. The percentage of the total population admitted to mental hospitals in El Paso is about one seventh of the percentage in Dallas, where the lithium level is among the lowest. Dawson went on to show a correlation between homicides, armed robbery, and violent crimes with lithium levels in drinking water. When the report was released, a great debate began. The press, including *Time* magazine, referred to lithium as the "Texas tranquilizer." There were headlines like MENTAL HEALTH THE WATER WAY, SALT KEEPS YOU SANE, and LITHIUM PUT IN DRINKING WATER MAY CURE MENTAL ILLNESS, despite the fact that the study did not rigorously investigate population composition, or the presence of other chemical substances in the water and soil, or whether state hospitalization rates accurately reflected community mental health.

As yet we do not know if lithium is essential for normal biological processes. Some researchers have suggested, in my opinion prematurely, that lithium may one day be added to water supplies in the same fashion that fluoride has been added to water to prevent tooth decay. At a symposium on water quality control in Washington, D.C., I took the position that lithium should not, on the basis of the present evidence, be added to the water supplies now and that it probably never should be, since the overall evidence is lacking that such an infinitesimal amount of lithium in drinking water could have any effect on moodswings. Nevertheless, the fascinating possibilities exist.

There is a very real danger in assuming that lithium is a panacea for mental illness. It is not. Bipolar manic depression and unipolar recurrent depression are the only diagnostic categories for which lithium has been shown to have a long-term preventive effect. It is relatively ineffective in schizophrenia or anxiety states and it cannot be used indiscriminately or without close and periodic supervision. Lithium, if not prescribed properly, can be *toxic* and potentially *lethal*. Its use must be carefully monitored by taking regular blood-level readings.

Beginning in the late 1950s several published studies indicated that cardiovascular death rates are lower in communities with hard water. As water hardness decreases, death rates go up. Researchers have also noted shifting arteriosclerotic death rates over the years in communities where the degree of water hardness has changed—death rates go down as water hardness increases. While first reports linked the findings to concentrations of calcium, potassium, or magnesium in the water, more recent reports by Antonie Voors and her team in North Carolina have drawn attention to the fact that lithium concentration increases as water hardness increases. Voors speculated that lithium may affect some factors that contribute to heart disease. These factors traditionally have included hypertension, diabetes, high cholesterol and triglycerides in the blood, smoking, stress, and type A behavior—a psychiatric term denoting the hypomaniclike behavior of the driven, overactive, overconscientious, and successful individual. But as interesting as this possibility is, it is hard to separate the effects of lithium from the effects of other minerals on these factors that contribute to heart disease. Furthermore, the amount of lithium in mineral waters is microscopic, a thousand times smaller than the therapeutic dose needed for manic depression—too small, many researchers think, to have any effect.

Lithium carbonate appears to have some future value for women suffering from recurrent menstrual depression. Women usually experience some change in emotional response during the menstrual cycle, and for most women the distress is something that they are able to tolerate. But for a special group of women who suffer from premenstrual syndrome (PMS), the emotional upheaval of the menstrual cycle is associated with severe depression, crying spells, headaches, insomnia, and irritable, angry outbursts. Researchers think that PMS, because of its periodic recurrent nature, might respond to lithium. In the 1960s Drs. Samuel Gershon and Ivan Sletten at the University of Missouri Medical School tried lithium on women who had suffered from severe PMS for years, and the results were encouraging. I've treated many women patients with lithium who had the depression and physical malaise typical of severe premenstrual tension. In most cases, the women reported they felt much relieved by lithium treatment. More controlled scientific studies are needed to confirm that lithium can be more widely used than it now is to alleviate the moodswing of PMS patients.

Lithium is being used experimentally for some kinds of cancer in which the white blood count is low. Lithium normally raises the white count slightly, so physicians have reasoned that it might help the victims of certain forms of leukemia in which white blood corpuscles are not produced sufficiently. In such leukemias the body is unable to fight off infection, which usually proves fatal. Although results have not yet been made known, there is the possibility that lithium's ability to raise the white count in such patients might at least buy them additional time.

One of the most exciting experimental uses of lithium has been with children and adolescents who are said to be suffering from "emotionally unstable behavioral disorders." Emotionally unstable children are not diagnosed as "depressed" or "manic" because their symptoms take forms other than those we recognize in adults. When a child is depressed, for instance, he or she usually complains of physical ills: stomachaches, headaches, dizziness. These children may suffer from bedwetting, have trouble concentrating in school, and are often phobic. Bursts of aggressiveness and frenetic activity may alternate with periods of sluggish passivity in a way that resembles the periodic fluctuations of adult moodswing. Sometimes antidepressants help these children. In adolescents a similar underlying mood disorder is often called "behavioral disorder" or "character disorder." These troubled young people may be drug takers; they are moody, defiant, and rebellious. Psychiatrists at Hillside Hospital in New York studied these adolescent patients and described them as "giddy, pleasure-seeking and impulsive for a few days; then they became withdrawn, morose, sullen, threatening suicide at times." There were rapid moodswings from elation to depression in a matter of hours or days. They were not suffering from manic depression as we know it in adults. They did not generally respond well to antidepressants. They disliked the traditional tranquilizers because of the zombielike effect. However, when they were given lithium, the results were remarkable. Their moods seemed to even out, and there were no appreciable side effects to change their feelings. The controlled study as well as an uncontrolled group studied at our Foundation showed that the lithium group did dramatically better than the control group of emotionally unstable adolescents.

Teenagers are being treated more often with lithium, and the results are promising. Eight adolescents with manic depression were given lithium at the Institute of Philadelphia Hospital by Dr. Harvey Horowitz. This is a landmark study because all eight psychotic teenagers were admitted to the hospital and diagnosed as schizophrenic. They were given the antipsychotic drugs usually reserved for schizophrenia: Thorazine, Prolixin, and Haldol. All of these patients failed to respond; they were reevaluated and rediagnosed as manic-depressives. When they were treated with lithium they improved rapidly.

Psychosis in adolescence is particularly difficult to diagnose. It can be precipitated by many stress factors, such as taking drugs, the breakup of a relationship, confusion about emerging sexuality, or pressures at school or from parents. The psychotic episode in adolescence is often bizarre, with depressive mood and behavior that often mimics schizophrenia. Psychiatrists often misdiagnose it as an acute schizophrenic reaction. In an adult, a longitudinal history, which may span dozens of years, helps in making the diagnosis. For a teenager the family history becomes critical in making a diagnosis. In the case of many teenagers first diagnosed as schizophrenic, there may be a parent or near relative who is depressed, manic-depressed, or alcoholic, which helps considerably in making the correct diagnosis of mood disorder.

Most psychiatrists still acknowledge a lack of empirical research data on mood disorders in adolescents. Dr. Javad Kashani at the University of Missouri studied 150 adolescents and found major depression in almost 5 percent, and less severe dysthymia in 3 percent. This is almost the same incidence of depression as occurs in adults. In adolescents the second most common psychological disturbance is anxiety disorder. Kashani's research indicated that adolescent depressions are likely to lead to adult forms of depression or manic depression.

The youngest child with a "behavioral disorder" to have been given lithium was a six-year-old patient of Dr. Anna-Lisa Annell of the University of Sweden. Dr. Annell gave lithium to adolescents and was encouraged by the results to try it on sixty children. She reported that it calmed manic symptoms in half the children it was given to. "It's so definite when it works," she said, "you can practically name the day you'll see the change—usually four days after optimum blood concentrations are reached. If a child is depressed, lithium seems to act against the somatic symptoms but not against the uneasiness and discomfort the child feels. Some children still get depressed, though not as depressed as they used to, but they still feel discomfort and irritableness. If we see this, we add antidepressants to the lithium and the results are often quite excellent." Dr. Annell believes that many of the lithium responders are suffering from the early equivalent of adult manic depression, which opens up a whole new area in child psychiatry. Dr. Eva Frommer of St. Thomas Hospital in London has had comparable results. She gave lithium to emotionally disturbed children whose overactive behavior suggested hypomania and others whose terrible outbursts of temper alternated with depressive, sullen moods. "Several children have found this drug combination so helpful in controlling themselves that they insisted on continuing with it until they felt well again."

Are there substances similar to lithium that we don't yet know about? The alkali metal elements run in a series of increasing atomic numbers and decreasing chemical activity, from lithium to sodium, potassium, rubidium, cesium, and francium (a heavy, unstable element produced in a cyclotron). We know the body normally needs sodium and potassium. Does it need lithium in small quantities, or other, similar elements?

For a number of years at the New York State Psychiatric Institute my research team has been investigating the possible antidepressant properties of rubidium chloride in withdrawn, chronically depressed patients. Unlike lithium, rubidium had a great deal known about it before it was experimentally applied to humans. It was first used on humans by a Russian physician, S. Botkin, Jr., in the 1880s, who studied under the great psychologist Ivan Pavlov. Although the drug was given initially to cardiac patients, Botkin observed that it was sometimes associated with a sense of well-being. In the late 1880s rubidium was used in small amounts throughout a number of medical clinics in Europe for cardiac and syphilitic problems, but because better treatment replaced it, it gradually fell into disuse.

But rubidium is lithium's sister element. It belongs to the same group of alkali metals as lithium, sodium, and potassium. In fact, it is often extracted from the same mineral sources. Since lithium has proven so effective in manic episodes and as a prophylactic for certain types of depression, I speculated that rubidium might play a similar therapeutic or prophylactic role that is complementary to that of lithium.

Initial rubidium studies were undertaken by Dr. Herbert Meltzer and myself at the New York State Psychiatric Institute in the 1970s. Rhesus monkeys were given rubidium in their orange juice. Lithium, we knew, made monkeys calmer. Rubidium, much to our surprise, made them overactive and aggressive. Intrigued, we made brain-wave tracings on these rubidium-fed monkeys and found that the tracings had changed drastically toward the higher frequencies. In contrast, lithium caused the brain waves to become much slower. We have found that rubidium's behavioral, electroencephalographic and biochemical properties markedly contrast with those of lithium. Rubidium produces what can be described as an "opposite" effect to that of lithium.

A 1988 study by Dr. Hygop Akiskal at the University of Tennessee in conjunction with researchers at the University of Pisa has confirmed our original positive rubidium findings in depression. Because rubidium has a long half-life of sixty days (meaning it does not come out of the body completely during that time), the Food and Drug Administration has been rightfully cautious about permitting further studies in the United States. Dr. Guy Chouinard in Canada gave rubidium to schizophrenic patients and found they needed much less antipsychotic medication. Half a dozen major university research teams in Italy have found that rubidium works in severe or chronic depression. But because rubidium, like lithium, is a simple, nonpatentable salt, drug companies have shown little interest in testing or marketing it. Yet rubidium is only the latest addition to the exciting, expanding field of trace metals in modern psychiatry. In time, not only rubidium and lithium but other trace metals may be used to treat mental illnesses in ways we are only beginning to understand.

FIFTEEN

How to Obtain the Latest Antidepressant Drug

Many of the patients who come to see me have failed to get relief from their depression, while going to other experts and clinics. Some have taken up to ten medications that have not worked. About 30 percent of all depressed patients who take antidepressant medication do not improve from it. This may be because of the individual's particular psychological resistance or biological makeup, or because the drug has too many side effects that make the patient uncomfortable. Or the patient may have a medical problem such as heart disease that makes some antidepressants unsafe. These patients have gone from psychiatrist to psychiatrist, clinic to clinic, and sometimes from expert to expert.

The earliest antidepressants were the monoamine oxidase inhibitors (MAOI) and the tricyclics (TCA). The MAO inhibitors block an enzyme, monoamine oxidase, which leads to the breakdown of neurotransmitters, or brain hormones. The MAO inhibitors were discovered by accident in the 1950s, when the antituberculosis drug Iproniazid made TB patients feel euphoric. Within a few years it came into use as an antidepressant in psychiatry.

But the MAO inhibitors worked mostly for atypical or what used to be called "neurotic" depressions, where the patient complains of weight gain rather than weight loss, of oversleeping rather than the insomnia that is found in typical endogenous, biochemical depressions. And the MAO inhibitors also had the serious drawback of the so-called "cheese" effect: Taken with certain foods containing the amino acid tyramine the inhibitors could cause serious cardiovascular problems—the taboo foods being aged cheese and wines, chicken liver, chocolate, bananas, and over-the-counter medicines.

The second most important early antidepressant of the 1950s was the tricyclic antihistamine imipramine. It was called tricyclic because of the three chemical rings in its structure. It appeared to alleviate depression by affecting the amount of serotonin (5HT) and norepinephrine (NE) at the nerve synapses in the brain. The latter are two hormones that act as chemical transmitters in the brain.

But the tricyclic antidepressants ran the risk of cardiovascular problems, and were often fatal if a patient overdosed—a serious consideration with depressed patients. Minor, uncomfortable side effects were frequently dry mouth, constipation, blurred vision, weight gain, and lowered blood pressure.

In the early 1980s the second-generation antidepressants were developed by pharmaceutical company researchers to help avoid some of the side effects of the early medications. Physicians wanted a drug that began to work faster than the two to three weeks required by the older antidepressants. Some of the new antidepressants that became available in the early 1980s in the United States were amoxapine, trazodone, maprotiline and, in 1988, fluoxetine, one of the few antidepressants that may be associated with weight loss. Other antidepressant compounds that became available in Europe are mianserin, fluvoxamine, clomipramine, viloxazine, bupropion, dothiepin, and amineptine. These drugs have no faster onset than their predecessors in relieving depression but have fewer side effects. Even so, a quarter to a third of depressed patients still don't respond to them. Most of these European drugs are being studied in the United States for eventual marketing.

The tricyclic antidepressant drugs that are most commonly used in the United States are imipramine and amitryptyline which have the same basic single amine chemical structure. Other tricyclic antidepressants work mostly by blocking serotonin uptake. These drugs—desipramine, nortryptyline, and protryptyline—whose chemical structure is made up primarily of secondary amines are more potent than their single amine relatives.

Clinical and population studies have shown that patients in the upper socioeconomic classes who are suffering from a gradual onset biological depression respond better to amitryptyline and imipramine. If I prescribe one of the tricyclics to a depressed patient and don't get results in four to eight weeks I will switch to a second tricyclic and if this does not markedly improve the depression I will gradually discontinue the drug. I will allow ten days to elapse for safety reasons, and then I will begin a monoamine oxidase inhibitor such as phenelzine, tranylcypromine, or isocarboxazid. The patient must realize that choosing the right drug and bringing it to the right dosage is an art performed by the psychiatrist, who bases the dosage on previous clinical experience and scientific studies as well as by monitoring the blood level of the drug. It is tailored and individualized to each patient according to the patient's history, symptoms, past experience with medication, family history of response to medications, and clinical studies. A common error of most general practitioners trying to treat depressed patients is that of giving too little medication for too short a time, because they are fearful of using the drug in full therapeutic dosage.

Before giving a drug, I tell the patient about his or her chances of recovery. Symptoms such as weight loss, late insomnia (early morning awakening), loss of appetite, and slowed physical responses mean that a good response to the antidepressant is likely. Those patients who have many neurotic symptoms, hypochondria, hysterical traits, severe personality conflicts, or a great deal of hostility don't respond as well. Oddly enough, if a patient has medication side effects such as dry mouth, blurred vision, lowered blood pressure, constipation, and initial slowness in urination, that patient is likely to get a better antidepressant effect from the drug.

As I treat patients I obtain antidepressant blood levels in our laboratory initially every one or two weeks and then monthly to monitor the quantity getting to the brain, especially if the patient isn't responding to the drug. Blood levels also tell me if the patient is taking the prescribed amount of medication, overdosing, or reaching too high a level because of his own metabolism. Elderly patients in particular need to be closely monitored, in much the same way I monitor lithium, for maximum safety.

There are always new antidepressant and antianxiety compounds under development in our Foundation for Depression's clinical testing program, drugs that will, we hope, be more specific than previous ones as to the brain chemicals they effect. Although depressions may appear to be identical to the observer, there are probably many biochemical subtypes, each of which responds to different antidepressants, suggesting that different brain hormones are responsible. Many of these new drugs are still without a name and just bear research numbers from pharmaceutical laboratories. Some of them have already been given to humans, others have been tested only in animal studies at the pharmaceutical company. During the period of 1975 to 1985, seventeen new antidepressants were introduced worldwide. Sixty other antidepressant compounds were being tested.

Many people with "hopeless" depressions find their way to my office in New York City where I have successfully treated thousands of so-called treatment-refractory mood disorders. I began to treat one of these patients after she wrote me the following letter:

Dear Dr. Fieve,

I have seen six psychiatrists over the last ten years, and my depression continues chronically without any interruption. Nothing has made it any better—none of the eight drugs I've tried, new and old, none of the psychotherapy, not even shock treatments. This must be what living in hell is like.

Depression is not an emotion, it's a lack of emotion. I feel nothing. Depression is not feeling unhappy, miserable, blue—all healthy reactions to life. Depression is lack of any feeling about outside happenings. It is complete and total absorption with myself. For example, whether I feel hungry or not. I remember not knowing when I'd eaten enough; my insides never felt full. I could eat two platefuls and not realize that I'd eaten anything. There is always excessive involvement with my body functions: Did I or did I not have bowel movements? This obsession takes up a lot of my thinking. I am always aware of dryness in my mouth, a bad taste. I worry whether to answer the phone or not. Should I live the next day or not. If I lived or died, it wouldn't matter to me. I cannot cry, I cannot laugh, a smile is simply a forced and strained movement of my lips. I cannot bring myself to look in anyone's eyes. When I speak, my voice—which I use as little as possible—is unemotional, one pitch, no ups and downs with which normal conversation is sprinkled. I want to lie in bed every day and do nothing. Not one thing.

With superhuman effort I got up and made dinner for my husband and myself last night. The meal was only a hamburger, a frozen vegetable, instant mashed potatoes. Fortunately for me, my husband forced me to cook. He didn't want to let me just stay in bed, at least not until I'd prepared the food, served, eaten and cleared it. This was an overwhelming task, as are all the little daily chores for me. I was able to continue in my job part-time this year, thanks to a kind and caring boss and another secretary who did a lot of my work. I kept to myself at work, and had little motivation, no energy. When I first became ill I wanted to resign, but friends talked me out of it—again, bless them! The job gave a semblance of normality to an otherwise freaky existence.

An extremely great problem that continues to give me a lot of anxiety is the fear of forgetting—forgetting the letters on the typewriter, my phone number, even how to sign my name. Normal, routine actions are hard to perform in this depressed state. I feel slowed down. I wonder sometimes if I'll remember to put one foot in front of the other to walk. I call myself a zombie—I often wish I were dead. Life has no meaning. I take no pleasure from anything. I have finally come to feel that I will simply be this new, different person, and that I will just live my life out this way. This illness called depression is not as obvious to an outsider as the sad, disfigured one of an amputated arm or leg, or blindness, or total paralysis from polio. To the person with it it is a greater torture than solitary confinement for an eternity.

I have treated many of these "hopeless" chronic depressions with new antidepressant medications. Some of these drugs have been used successfully in Europe, Canada, and other countries but may not yet be available in the United States. I have also used other drugs that are in their second, third, and fourth phases of research development in this country. Although they are not available by prescription in local drugstores, and are not yet approved by the Food and Drug Administration, they are available to a limited number of my patients. To qualify for a research drug that has not yet been marketed, the patient must become part of a clinical trial in an FDA approved setting, and be free from medical illness, alcoholism, or drug abuse, and show certain depressive symptoms.

Clinical trials are conducted by major drug companies throughout the United States. They are under careful medical, legal, FDA scrutiny, and the supervision of human rights committees. These drugs are called maverick, or second- or third-generation drugs under development. A psychopharmacologist, such as I, needs government permission, as well as that of the pharmaceutical companies, to use these drugs in premarketing trials for patients who have not responded to traditional antidepressants, or who cannot afford traditional therapy.

To patients of mine who have repeatedly failed with me or other psychiatrists with antidepressant drugs and who often feel hopeless, I offer the possibility that the right drug may be just around the corner. Or if a traditional drug has had overwhelmingly difficult side effects, I stress the possibility that one or more of these new medications may work better. For many, their participation in a clinical trial is like coming to a court of last resort.

To qualify for such a trial, a patient must have a moderate to severe depression that has lasted for weeks, months, or even years. As with the woman who wrote the letter describing her desperation to me, the typical patient is unable to feel pleasure, has difficulty carrying out everyday activities, has little interest in sex, family or friends, and a deep sense of hopelessness, helplessness and worthlessness. Usually he or she loses or gains weight, has difficulty sleeping, or sleeps too much. The chronically depressed patient may have had suicidal thoughts in the past, but if now the thoughts are actively suicidal the patient cannot be part of an antidepressant trial. Usually the typical patient feels worse in the morning dreading the new tasks of the day.

Interestingly, some of the very newest medications are said to work faster than traditional antidepressants. Within even a few days, rather than weeks or months, patients may begin to feel better. They may feel a surge of energy and a lifting of mood for the first time in months or years.

Many of the new drugs being tested are new versions of older tricyclics. Some of the second- and third-generation drugs are called unicyclics, bicyclics, and tetracyclics. Other drugs are completely different chemically and in the way they work. These are called "other biochemical structures." These new drugs put hope on the faces of the 30 percent of depressed patients who have not responded well to other antidepressants or other treatments for depression, be it "talking therapy" or electroshock— which other psychiatrists still frequently use.

Most of the new antidepressants can be used with no dietary restrictions. They are safe even for cardiovascular patients, including those with cardiac arythmias and blood pressure changes. Some of them don't produce weight gain, a side effect some patients fear as much as depression itself. Many women want to stop antidepressant drugs because of fluid retention and an unwanted five pounds. The new drugs usually do not carry the danger of fatal overdose, as do most of the drugs of the past. Suicide is most rare with these new medications, whereas it was a frequent problem with the old tricyclics used in the emergency wards of most hospitals.

These drugs of the future have completely different biochemical structures from the drugs of the past. This is important because we have made progress in diagnosing new subtypes of depression, as well as in developing new biological marker tests and arriving at new genetic findings. And these new findings make it apparent that depression is a spectrum of disorders and may require a spectrum of antidepressant medications as yet undiscovered to treat them.

In order for an investigational drug to be given to depressed, anxious, phobic, or obsessional patients, the sponsoring drug company must submit a safety profile to the FDA and apply for an investigational drug permit (IND). The application contains the results of sometimes years of animal studies, biochemical and biological studies, high-dose studies, and studies showing that the drug can be used safely and reliably by humans. Once the drug company obtains the permit from the FDA, the chief of clinical trials at the company chooses one or more experienced clinical investigators. These investigators have usually had years of experience with the use of investigational and marketed antidepressant drugs in depressed and anxious patients. The pharmaceutical company designs a research protocol that the FDA must approve; the university or clinic then submits the research protocol to its own review board for approval; then both protocols must be submitted to the FDA before the study can begin.

When a depressed patient is interviewed for possible inclusion in a new antidepressant study, he or she is told of the drug's present state of development, its side effects, and potential risks and benefits. The patient must read this information and sign a consent form, which also says the patient may drop out at any time, for whatever reason. For the most part, women of childbearing age are not permitted to participate in most trials with new medications. However, some drugs are given with the provision that depressed women in the study agree to continue contraception. Before entering the trial, the patient receives a complete physical with electrocardiogram and blood chemistries, as well as a psychiatric exam in which the patient must show a certain level of depression.

If the complete physical exam is normal, and all inclusion/exclusion criteria satisfied, the patient may enter the trial. He or she will generally be given the prepackaged medication with instructions on how to take it, and will return once a week to see the research nurse and psychiatrist for biochemical, behavioral, mood, anxiety, and side effect ratings. If a patient has undesirable side effects at any point in the trial, he or she telephones the research psychiatrist, who may ask the patient to come in immediately. The psychiatrist may decide to keep the patient in the study, if the complaints are of no great significance, or may decide to stop the drug and give treatment with a known marketed compound.

For the eight weeks that the trial lasts, constant monitoring is carried out by the nurse and myself, and often by a second treating psychiatrist. The patients and data are consistently reviewed by the drug company monitor who makes frequent trips to the research center. The head doctor keeps in constant contact with his clinical investigators. When the patient finishes the trial, all the data on biochemistry, mood, side effects, and behavior are reviewed by the monitor and sent to the pharmaceutical company—usually in a three-ring notebook with fifty to sixty pages of scrupulous notes that have been kept over the eight weeks.

Once data on twenty to fifty patients have been completed at a center, the drug company pools the results with data from five or ten other centers. Ultimately the information is analyzed in the company's home office and the results are presented to the FDA in a final application demonstrating the effectiveness and safety of the new antidepressant.

The FDA then evaluates, criticizes, and sometimes asks for more data, or else rejects the application to market the drug. Finally the FDA may agree to marketing, usually after years of study and millions of dollars have been spent in preparation for the launching of the new compound.

It is very important for the depressed patient to understand how new medications are developed and tested. Everyone who responds to a medication should be aware of the years of struggle in the laboratory and outpatient clinic for its development and final FDA approval. For those patients who have repeatedly failed with all available medications, it is heartening to know that there is hope that a new antidepressant may be just around the corner.

When these patients are finished with their drug trial, they have several choices: They may, if the drug has been extremely successful and is the only medication that has helped them, apply for a "humanitarian protocol." This means that I will write the drug company to apply for a specific protocol or drug treatment regimen to permit me to keep this patient on the drug and monitor him or her indefinitely. A second option is that the patient may go on another antidepressant that is under investigation. Or the patient may transfer to our Foundation's low-cost Medicaid clinic. Or a patient may transfer to another physician or clinic or to private treatment.

Another avenue being explored is "step-up" treatment, where the action of an antidepressant is strengthened by giving thyroid medication or lithium along with the antidepressant. Lithium and thyroid medications have similar "boosting" properties for antidepressant agents. I use step-up treatments with patients of mine who are not responding to antidepressants at a certain point in time.

As aids in finding the specific antidepressant for a patient, a number of new diagnostic tests are being used or developed. The Dexamethasone Suppression Test (DST) is a method of measuring the type of depression and the expected recovery. Dexamethasone, a small pill that turns the pituitary gland off for twenty-four hours, is given to the patient at bedtime, and the next day at 4 P.M. the amount of cortisol in the patient's blood is measured. If the level is abnormally high, it is likely that the patient is suffering from a major depressive mood disorder. About 25 to 60 percent of patients with major depressive disorders have elevated next-day cortisol, whereas most other psychiatric disorders, including depression of a reactive nature, do not show the elevated cortisol effects. Weeks later, if the cortisol level remains elevated even after the patient appears to be coming out of the depression on medication, then the chances of the patient having a relapse are high. If the cortisol level returns to normal, the patient is likely to remain depression-free.

High technology testing such as Positron Emission Tomography (PET) and Single Proton Emission Computed Tomography (SPECT) hold out hope for more specific diagnosis and treatment in the future. Already researchers are attempting to map out specific PET and SPECT brain scan patterns for manic depression, schizophrenia, drug abuse, and alcoholism.

Genetic counseling is another field in which the mood disorders and their specific treatments are undergoing a revolution. Long-term studies by my research team have established that most manic depression is transmitted in a multifactorial fashion from one generation to the next. This means that genetic predisposition interacts with stress factors in the environment. Our study of more than six hundred manic-depressed patients and their three thousand near relatives lasted for over seven years and found that in a small percentage of patients the illness appears to be transmitted on the X female chromosome. We continue to look for manic-depressives with large family groups—of from fifteen to twenty available relatives—to further study the possibilities of X chromosome linkage or other forms of genetic transmission.

Frequently I am asked what the possibilities are of a parent with manic depression transmitting the illness to a child. We think the tendency is approximately 10 to 15 percent. Among the equivalent illnesses that can be inherited in manic-depressive families are alcoholism, sociopathy, drug abuse, suicide, depression, and manic depression—all part of the depressive disorder spectrum. Patients who wish to understand the risk to offspring or first-degree relatives should ask for genetic counseling. The chance that a first-degree relative of a patient will develop a disorder is eight to ten times higher than it is for the general population. For a parent, the chance is almost 8 percent; for a sibling, almost 9 percent; and for a child, more than 10 percent. For second-degree relatives, such as uncles and aunts, the risk decreases to 1 to 4 percent. When both parents have the illness, the risk is much greater for children, in the range of 20 to 40 percent.

When I speak to adults with mood disorder who are concerned about getting married and having children, I usually recommend that a manic-depressive avoid marrying another manic-depressive if possible, as well as anyone with a strong family history of depression, drug abuse, suicide, or alcoholism.

If my patient already has young children, I take the position that by the time the child is in his or her twenties, which is when manic depression usually first appears, even better treatment than lithium may be available. Promising alternatives to lithium being explored include carbamazapine and valproic acid. Furthermore, our genetic research may one day provide us with an earlier diagnostic method that allows earlier intervention in children and adolescents, before the adult illness has begun.

We are only beginning to understand that the biochemistry of depression in the brain manifests itself by many subtypes of clinical depression.

I have always been fascinated and challenged by the depressed patient who has not responded to any previous treatment. I remain convinced that with the right medication given in the right dosage by the right physician, the patient will respond with hope and confidence.

EPILOGUE

Manic depression is a spectacular disease because of its bizarre, excruciating, and at times beneficial and even ecstatic symptoms. It is spectacular because people who suffer from the illness in its milder forms of moodswing tend to be magnificent performers, magnetic personalities, and true achievers. Many superachievers in business, the arts, and especially in politics are hidden hypomanics. Many forms of manic elation seem to be a genetic endowment of the same order as perfect pitch, a photographic memory, great intelligence, or artistic talent of any sort. Manics have not only fabulous energy when they're not too manic, but a qualitatively different, quicker, more perceptive grasp of others and of their surroundings. They are manipulators par excellence, and they are also the people who get things done. Without them society would be much impoverished.

Although most people recognize that the exuberant drive of the manic depressive is extraordinary, few realize that their superior energy is frequently very costly: it can result in personal disasters such as losing a job, being divorced, being isolated from one's family, or even in breaking the law and going to prison.

Too few people—and too few physicians—recognize that there is often also a painful and dangerous low. These depressions sometimes grow shattering enough to take the terrible toll of suicide.

Fortunately, manic depression, this spectacular disease, has an equally spectacular cure. Lithium was the first drug in the history of psychiatry to so radically and specifically control a major mind disorder. In general medicine, miracle drugs are commonplace. Penicillin, insulin, and antibiotics have spoiled us. But in psychiatry, in which disorders generally mean years lost, lives wasted in emotional agony, untold damage to self, friends, family, and finances, it is truly spectacular to watch this simple, naturally occurring salt, lithium carbonate, return a person from the terrible throes of moodswing to normalcy in one to three weeks.

And now we have developed antidepressant drugs that work alone or in combination with lithium to improve the long-term results in the depressive disorders.

Perhaps psychiatry, having found its lithium, tranquilizers, and its newest antidepressants, is not far behind general medicine. Perhaps more of psychiatry's miracle drugs are on their way, too, and a true revolution in mental health is occurring.

ACKNOWLEDGMENTS

I am deeply indebted to my patients, my professional colleagues, and my research and editorial assistants for help in bringing this book to completion.

The patients whose lives I have described are those I have treated over a twenty-five-year period of clinical practice and research in psychiatry. Their names have been changed and their stories disguised in order to preserve their anonymity.

Lawrence D. Kolb and Shervert Frazier stimulated my early clinical interest in lithium and manic depression. Seymour Kety and Jonathan Cole contributed greatly to my concept of "relevance" in research and to the critical need for scientific controls when evaluating experimental results. William Bunney influenced my interdisciplinary approach to manic depression from his model team at the National Institutes of Mental Health. George Winokur's innovative studies stimulated my interest in the genetics of depression and manic depression and my work with X chromosome markers.

Special credit should be given to the staff and patients at the Foundation for Depression and Manic Depression, who have worked with me and participated in research over the past ten years. Drs. David Dunner, Eric Pesclow, Brian Anderson, Paul Goodnick, Faouzia Barouche, Herbert Meltzer, Ngaere Baxter and Stanley Platman have worked indefatigably with me. Many thanks are due to my head administrative nurse, Cynthia Craft, my former administrative heads, Jo Kolesar, Louise Mussolini, and Barbara Brody, and my head private clinical nurse, Nancy Rao, as well as my drug study research nurses, Annamarie Schlegel, Joanne Ryan, Ann Marie Phillipi, Nathane Brown, and Dee Henry. And very special thanks and deep appreciation to my administrative assistant, Motria Milanytch.

Marguerite Howe helped enormously in researching and rewriting numerous chapters of both editions of this book, and her assistance in preparing the reference notes, as well as her overall suggestions on the manuscript, have been invaluable.

My friend the late Herbert Alexander urged me to write this book and the revision. My wife, Katia, gave me the title and much perceptive advice.

To Jeanne Bernkopf, my editor, I wish to express many thanks for her patience and hard work.

REFERRAL SOURCES

The Foundation for Depression and
Manic Depression
7 East 67th Street
New York, New York 10021

National Depressive and Manic Depressive Association
Merchandise Mart, Box 3395
Chicago, Illinois 60654

National Mental Health Association
1021 Prince Street
Alexandria, Virginia 22314

National Alliance for the Mentally Ill
1901 North Ft. Myer Drive, Suite 500
Arlington, Virginia 22209-1604

National Institute of Mental Health
Public Information Branch
5600 Fishers Lane
Rockville, Maryland 20857

American Psychiatric Association
1400 K Street, NW
Washington, D.C. 20005

REFERENCE NOTES

CHAPTER 1: THE CHEMICAL REVOLUTION

For details on the first and second revolutions in psychiatry I am indebted to *A Short History of Psychiatry,* 2nd edition, by Erwin Ackerknecht, M.D. (New York: Hafner, 1968).

Statistics on mental health in America today are provided in *Discoveries in Biological Psychiatry,* a collection of essays by pioneers in modern psychopharmacology, edited by Frank J. Ayd, Jr., M.D., and Barry Blackwell, M.D. (Philadelphia: Lippincott, 1970).

Also consulted was "Issues in the Development of Statistical and Epidemiological Data for Mental Health Services Research," by Morton Kramer, Sc.D. Presented at the World Psychiatric Association Symposium, Teheran, Iran, May 1974.

Additional information on the history and present uses of lithium can be found in a booklet prepared by the National Institute of Mental Health, entitled *Lithium in the Treatment of Mood Disorders* (National Clearinghouse for Mental Health Information). This is available from the Superintendent of Documents, U.S. Government Printing Office, Washington, D.C.

CHAPTER 2: MOODSWING

The statistics from the Department of Health, Education, and Welfare on the prevalence of affective disorders were cited by Shirley Willner, statistician at the Biometry Branch of the National Institute of Mental Health, in a personal communication, July 5, 1973.

CHAPTER 3: MOODS AND CREATIVITY

Joshua Logan described his moodswing at the American Medical Association Symposium on Depression, New York, June 24, 1974. The excerpts in this chapter are taken from the press release.

Part of the discussion of the problems and treatment of the creative personality is drawn from *The Artist in Society* (New York: Grove Press, 1965), a highly readable study by Lawrence J. Hatterer, M.D.

I am indebted to Myron Marshall, M.D., for his observations in "Lithium, Creativity and Manic-Depressive Illness," published in *Psychosomatics*, 11/5, 1970.

The study at the Iowa Writer's Workshop was conducted by Nancy Andreasen, M.D. It was prepared as "Genius and Insanity Revisited. Psychiatric Symptoms and Family History in Creative Writers," for Vol. 3 of *Studies in Life History Research*. Also see Andreasen's "Creativity and Mental Illness," *American Journal of Psychiatry*, 144/10, 1987. Jamison's work is mentioned in *Time*, October 8, 1984.

Psychoanalytic writings on creativity are legion. Anthony Storr explores most of the traditional theories (wish fulfillment, schizoid defense, obsessional behavior) in *The Dynamics of Creation* (New York: Atheneum, 1972).

The classical psychoanalytical study of an artist's psychosexual development is of course Freud's "Leonardo da Vinci" *(Collected Works*, Vol. 11, London: Hogarth, 1957).

Biographical information on Handel, Rossini, and Balzac is taken in part from Rosamond Harding's *An Anatomy of Inspiration and An Essay on the Creative Mood* (Cambridge, Eng.: Heffer, 1948). More about Balzac's manic depression can be found in *The Infirmities of Genius*, by W. R. Bett (New York: Philosophical Library, 1952). Information on Schumann's disorder, as well as additional details on Balzac, can be found in Storr's *The Dynamics of Creation*.

Some of the information on Van Gogh's enigmatic illness is taken from F. Destaing's "Le soleil et l'orage ou la maladie de Van Gogh," *La Nouvelle Presse Medicale*, 1/46, 1972. Destaing discusses the possible reasons for Van Gogh's suicide, as does F. W. Maire, M.D., in "Van Gogh's Suicide," *Journal of the American Medical Association*, 217/7, 1971.

A detailed study of Van Gogh's life that also proved useful was Humberto Nagera's *Vincent Van Gogh: A Psychological Study* (New York: International Universities' Press, 1967).

Of the many books about Hemingway, the following were particularly useful: *Papa*, by James McLerndon (New York: Popular Library,

1972), a day-to-day account of Hemingway's life in Key West. *My Brother, Ernest Hemingway,* by Leicester Hemingway (Greenwich, Conn.: Fawcett, 1961), provided details of the writer's early years. A particularly valuable psychological study is "Ernest Hemingway: A Psychiatric View," by Irvin Yalom, M.D., and Marilyn Yalom, M.D., in *Archives of General Psychiatry,* 24, 1971.

CHAPTER 4: WALL STREET WIZARDS AND THE MIDAS TOUCH

The genetic basis of gambling is discussed in *Manic-Depressive Illness,* by George Winokur, M.D., Paula Clayton, M.D., and Theodore Reich, M.D. (St. Louis: Mosby, 1969).

The distinction between professional and compulsive gamblers is cited in Edmund Bergler, "Typology of Gamblers," in *The Psychology of Gambling* (New York: Hill and Wang, 1957).

For a first-person account of compulsive gambling, see Fyodor Dostoevsky's *The Gambler,* translated by Victor Terras (Chicago: University of Chicago Press, 1972).

Richard Ney's *The Wall Street Jungle* (New York: Grove Press, 1970) is a lively and cynical insider's account of the stock market.

Psychiatric diagnosis has been revolutionized by the American Psychiatric Association's landmark publication, *Diagnostic and Statistical Manual of Mental Disorders.* The most recent is the revised third edition, *(DSM III-R),* Washington, D.C., 1987.

Observations on the similarity of gambling and the market were made by Charlotte Olmsted, in *Heads I Win* (New York: Macmillan, 1962).

Facts about James Ling are based on *Ling,* by Stanley H. Brown (New York: Bantam, 1973).

Details about Harold Geneen are taken from "Harold Geneen: No Time to Be Nice," by Stanley Brown, *Life,* May 19, 1972.

The information on Charles Bluhdorn comes from "Multimillion Reach of Wall Street's Mad Austrian," by Chris Welles, in *Life,* March 10, 1967.

William Zeckendorf is written up in "A Big Man on a Thin Edge," by Chris Welles, *Life,* February 12, 1965.

Stewart Alsop described "America's Big New Rich" in *The Saturday Evening Post,* July 17, 1965.

Jack Dreyfus's depression is discussed in "10,000-to-1 Payoff," by Albert Rosenfeld, *Life,* September 29, 1967.

CHAPTER 5: BIOLOGICAL CLOCKS

Much of the information on biological clocks in this chapter is taken from Gay Gaer Luce's *Body Time* (New York: Pantheon, 1971). This is a summary of literally thousands of scientific papers into highly readable English, and it is probably the best introduction to periodicity in body chemistry, sleep, mood, growth, drug effects, and so on.

Much valuable information is also provided in Curt P. Richter's pioneer study, *Biological Clocks in Medicine and Psychiatry* (Springfield, Ill.: Thomas, 1965). Dr. Richter discusses biological clocks in animals, cycles of physical and mental disease in humans, besides offering an hypothesis to explain the clock mechanism.

The effects of lithium on premenstrual tension are discussed in detail in the NIMH report, *Lithium in the Treatment of Mood Disorders,* op. cit.

The mechanisms by which switch in mood occurs in manic depression have been studied extensively by Dr. William Bunney and his research team at the National Institute of Mental Health.

The effects of lithium on rapid cyclers have been investigated by Dr. David Dunner at the New York State Psychiatric Institute. Research on seasonal affective disorders has been described by Dr. N. Rosenthal and colleagues in "Seasonal Affective Disorder," *The Archives of General Psychiatry,* 41, 1984. Information on treatments is given in "Phototherapy of Seasonal Affective Disorder," by Dr. T. Wehr and colleagues, *American Journal of Psychiatry,* 144/6, 1987.

CHAPTER 6: COCAINE, ALCOHOL, AND DEPRESSION

The Consumers Union Report *Licit and Illicit Drugs* (Boston: Little, Brown, 1972) was used extensively in the preparation of this chapter. This report by E. M. Brecher and the editors of *Consumer Reports* deals with narcotics, stimulants, depressants, inhalants, hallucinogens, and marijuana—including caffeine, nicotine, and alcohol.

Also consulted were *Alcoholism,* revised edition, by Neil Kessel and Henry Walton (Baltimore: Penguin, 1971) and Harrison Trice, *The Problem Drinker on the Job* (New York State School of Industrial and Labor Relations, Cornell University, Bulletin 40, 3rd printing, 1964).

For more information about cocaine addiction and treatment, see Dr. Mark Gold's *800-COCAINE,* (New York: Bantam, 1985). Also see "The Facts About Drugs and Alcohol," 3rd edition, by Mark Gold, M.D., (Summit, N.J.: Fair Oaks Hospital, 1988).

Information on drugs in the workplace came from *Business Planning*

Quarterly, January 1988, in an article by Norman Jaspan Also see a four-part series by Tom Nutile in *The Boston Herald,* beginning February 1, 1988, and "Drugs in the Workplace," by Peter Bensinger in *Psychiatry Letter,* August 1986.

For cocaine abuse and treatment, see "Implications of Substance Abuse," by Howard Rome, M.D., *Psychiatric Annals,* April 1986. Also instructive is "Cocaine Abuse and Treatment", in *Psychiatry Letter,* August 1985, by David Smith, M.D., Donald Wesson, M.D., and Mark Gold, M.D.; and "Breakthrough Against Cocaine," by Peggy Mann in *Reader's Digest,* April 1987.

Lawrence Golbe, M.D., and Michael Merkin, M.D., have studied severe cocaine damage in "Cerebral Infarction in a User of Freebase Cocaine ('Crack')," in *Neurology,* 36, 1986. Also see "The Adolescent Drug Epidemic and the Chronic Young Adult Patient," in *Psychiatry Letter,* February 1985, by Thomas Gleaton, M.D., and Sheryl Gowen, M.Ed.

Alcoholics Anonymous and the present state of alcohol treatment is discussed by Nan Robertson in her book, *Getting Better: Inside Alcoholics Anonymous* (New York: William Morrow, 1988).

E. M. Jellinek, *The Disease Concept of Alcoholism* (New Haven: Hill House, 1960).

Some of the statistics on alcoholism were supplied by the National Institute on Alcohol and Drug Abuse, National Institute of Mental Health.

Donald Horton's "The Function of Alcohol in Primitive Societies: A Cross-cultural Study" appeared in *Quarterly Journal of Studies on Alcohol,* 4, 1943.

CHAPTER 7: TEENAGE AND ADULT SUICIDE

The following references were consulted for information on suicide:

Margaret Hyde and Elizabeth Forsyth, M.D., *Suicide: The Hidden Epidemic* (New York: Franklin Watts, 1986).

John Langone, *Dead End: A Book About Suicide* (Boston: Little, Brown, 1986).

Sandra Gardner with Gary Rosenberg, M.D., *Teenage Suicide* (New York: Julian Messner, 1985).

Alec Roy, M.D., and Markku Linnoila, M.D., "Alcoholism and Suicide," *The Biology of Suicide,* ed. Ronald Maris (New York: Guilford Press, 1986).

Loren Coleman, M.D., *Suicide Clusters* (Winchester, Mass.: Faber & Faber, 1987).

Lewis Lipsitt, Ph.D., "The 'Development' of Adolescent Suicide," *Rhode Island Journal of Medicine,* 69/10, 1986.

Jane Slupski, "Shattered Lives: The Growing Crisis of Teenage Suicide," *Dental Assistant,* 56/5, 1987.

Diane K. Shrier, M.D., "Teenage Suicide: Causes, Warning Signs and Interventions," *New Jersey Medicine,* 84/5, 1987.

Stanley Aronson, M.D., "Suicide in the Adolescent Population," *Rhode Island Medical Journal,* 69/10, 1986.

CHAPTER 8: MOODS AND GREAT MEN

The major Lincoln biographies on which this chapter is based are:

W. H. Herndon and J. W. Weik, *Herndon's Lincoln: The True Story of a Great Life,* 3 vols. (Chicago: Bedford, Clarke, 1889). A biased but lively account of Lincoln by his Illinois law partner.

J. W. Weik, *The Real Lincoln* (Boston: Houghton Mifflin, 1922).

Carl Sandburg, *Abraham Lincoln: The Prairie Years,* 2 vols. (New York: Harcourt, Brace, 1926) and *Abraham Lincoln: The War Years,* 4 vols. (New York: Harcourt, Brace, 1939). This is the popular biography of Lincoln the folk hero. It incorporates many of the Lincoln legends and is therefore often unreliable as a basis of retrospective diagnosis.

P. M. Angle, ed., *Abraham Lincoln* (New Brunswick, N.J.: Rutgers University Press, 1948).

Richard Current, *The Lincoln Nobody Knows* (New York: Hill and Wang, 1964). This excellent study runs counter to the Lincoln myth.

Particularly useful was E.J.A. Kempf's magisterial biography, *Lincoln's Philosophy of Common Sense* (New York: New York Academy of Sciences, 1965). A compendium of Lincoln scholarship, this follows his life in great detail, although sometimes Kempf accepts the obviously apocryphal as fact. Kempf's thesis is that Lincoln's depressions were the result of a brain injury caused by a fall in childhood.

Also of interest are Milton Shutes' *Lincoln's Emotional Life* (Philadelphia: Dorrance, 1957) and *Lincoln and the Doctors: A Medical Narrative of the Life of Abraham Lincoln* (New York: Pioneer Press, 1953).

William Petersen in *Lincoln-Douglas: The Weather as Destiny* (Springfield, Ill.: Thomas, 1943) maintains that the outcome of the Lincoln-Douglas debates depended on Lincoln's mood, which was affected by the weather.

L. P. Clark explains Lincoln's depressions in classical psychoanalytical terms in *Lincoln: A Psychobiography* (New York: Scribner's, 1933) and in "A Psychoanalytical Study of Abraham Lincoln," in *Psychoanalytic Review*, 8, 1921.

The description of Lincoln at thirty is from Kempf. Lincoln's relationship with Dr. Anson Henry is discussed by Kempf and Herndon.

R. P. Randall, *Mary Lincoln: Biography of a Marriage* (Boston: Little, Brown, 1953).

Lincoln's characteristic slowness is noted by Kempf; the description of Lincoln at forty-nine is from Kempf.

Letter to E. A. Paine (November 9, 1858) in *Complete Works of Abraham Lincoln,* 12 vols. (New Brunswick, N.J.: Rutgers University Press, 1953, Vol. 3).

Lincoln's depressions in the White House are documented in the biography by J. G. Nicolay and J. Hay in *Abraham Lincoln: A History* (New York: Century, 1890).

Lincoln's depression after Willie's death is described by F. B. Carpenter in *The Inner Life of Abraham Lincoln* (New York: Hurd and Houghton, 1877). Carpenter lived in the White House for six months to paint Lincoln's portrait.

Lincoln's moodswing has also been discussed in detail by J. G. Randall in *Lincoln the President: Springfield to Gettysburg,* 2 vols. (New York: Dodd, Mead, 1945).

The possibility that Lincoln's melancholy was caused by the mental strain of his crossed eyes is discussed by T. M. Shastid in "My Father Knew Lincoln," in *The Nation,* February 20, 1929.

Lincoln's letter on suicide in the *Sangamo Journal* was cited by Richard Hudgens, M.D., in "Mental Health of Political Candidates: Notes on Abraham Lincoln," in *American Journal of Psychiatry,* 130/1, 1973.

Lincoln made an amazing number of speeches against Douglas in 1858 (Kempf) and again after his election in 1861, when in a two-week period he made seventy public appearances which included twenty speeches.

The biographical data on Roosevelt have been drawn extensively from Henry Pringle's Pulitzer Prize-winning biography, *Theodore Roosevelt* (New York: Harcourt, Brace and World, 1956, revised edition). First published in 1931, Pringle's biography is disparaging in an attempt to debunk the Roosevelt myth, but it is the best insight into the character and mentality of the boisterous Roosevelt.

William Henry Harbaugh's *Power and Responsibility: The Life and Times of Theodore Roosevelt* (New York: Collier, 1963) is the most comprehensive, fair-minded, and authoritative biography of the twenty-sixth President.

Other biographies consulted were: *The Life and Times of Theodore Roosevelt,* by Stefan Lorant (Garden City, N.Y.: Doubleday, 1959), which assembles a large number of pictures, cartoons, and diaries; and James Morgan's *Theodore Roosevelt, The Boy and the Man* (New York: Macmillan, 1907), an interesting portrait by a contemporary.

A detailed study of TR's youth and early career is undertaken in Carleton Putnam's *Theodore Roosevelt: The Formative Years* (New York: Scribner's, 1958).

Edward Wagenknecht makes an incisive analysis of Roosevelt's thought and the character of his leadership in *The Seven Worlds of Theodore Roosevelt* (New York: Longmans, Green, 1958).

The following anthologies were also consulted:

Theodore Roosevelt, ed. Dewey Grantham (Englewood Cliffs, N.J.: Prentice-Hall, 1971). An excellent collection of essays by historians and contemporaries, this also includes some of Roosevelt's own most representative writings.

Another indispensable collection is *Theodore Roosevelt: A Profile,* edited by Morton Keller (New York: Hill and Wang, 1967).

Roosevelt's *Autobiography* (New York: Scribner's, 1920) is fascinating self-description almost totally devoid of self-consciousness, perspective, or introspection. First published in 1913, it is a convenient summary of his ideas.

Sarah Churchill, *A Thread in the Tapestry* (London: Deutsch, 1967).

Lord Moran (Charles Wilson, M.D.) records his years as Churchill's personal physician in *Winston Churchill: Taken from the Diaries of Lord Moran, The Struggle for Survival 1940–1965* (Boston: Houghton Mifflin, 1966).

A psychoanalytically oriented biography is *Churchill: Four Faces and the Man,* by Anthony Storr (London: Allen Lane, 1969).

Three anthologies of excellent essays were used extensively in the preparation of this chapter:

Churchill, edited by Martin Gilbert (Englewood Cliffs, N.J.: Prentice-Hall, 1967), which also includes selections from Churchill's own writings.

Churchill Revised: A Critical Assessment (New York: Dial Press, 1969). An important collection of articles and memoirs about Churchill by A.J.P. Taylor, R. R. James, J. H. Plumb, B. L. Hart, and Anthony Storr.

Another indispensable collection of essays is *Churchill: A Profile,* edited by Peter Stansky (New York: Hill and Wang, 1973).

The description of young Churchill is by G. W. Stevens, "Born to Lead" (1898), in Gilbert, op. cit.

A. G. Gardiner describes Churchill as childlike in *Prophets, Priests and Kings* (London, 1908), cited in Gilbert. Also see *Pillars of Society* (London, 1916), in Gilbert.

David Lloyd George's description of Churchill is in *War Memoirs of David Lloyd George,* 2 vols. (London, 1938), in Gilbert.

Lord Beaverbrook's description of Churchill is in *Men and Power* (London, 1956), cited in Gilbert.

Harold Nicolson describes Churchill as the most interesting man in England in *Vanity Fair,* 1931, in Gilbert.

Viscount Montgomery's description of Churchill is from *Memoirs,* by Montgomery of Alamein (London, 1958), in Gilbert.

Aneurin Bevan's description of Churchill is in *Hansard,* July 2, 1942, in Gilbert.

H. G. Wells describes Churchill in an article in *The Tribune,* reprinted in Gilbert.

The first-person description of Churchill's life-style as prime minister is given by John Colville, "Churchill as Prime Minister," in *Action This Day,* edited by Sir John Wheeler Bennet (London: Macmillan, 1968), cited in Stansky.

Classification of physiques is the subject of *The Varieties of Human Physique,* by William H. Sheldon, M.D. (New York: Harper and Brothers, 1940).

CHAPTER 9: PSYCHIATRIC INTERVENTION IN GOVERNMENT AND POLITICS

There is a surprising paucity of literature on the problem of psychiatric disability in high office. By far the most comprehensive discussion of the subject is a monograph prepared by the Group for the Advancement of Psychiatry (GAP) Committee on Governmental Agencies, entitled *The VIP with Psychiatric Impairment* (New York: Scribner's, 1973). This short book is virtually the only authoritative treatment of this problem.

Also of interest is Arnold Rogow, M.D., "Psychiatric Disability in High Office," in *Medical Opinion and Review,* 1:16–19, 1966.

An article by Lester Grinspoon, M.D., called "The Psychosocial Constraints of the Important Decision-Maker," in *The American Journal of Psychiatry* (125/8, 1969), deals with the normal pressures on leadership as well as pathological ones.

Jerome Frank, M.D., touches briefly on the question of competence in national leaders as it is affected by illness and aging, in *Sanity and Survival: Psychological Aspects of War and Peace* (New York: Random House, 1967).

The procedures for reviewing the mental health of the judiciary (as well as other branches of government and the military) are discussed in *The VIP with Psychiatric Impairment.*

The controversial question of presidential disability is the subject of a government publication "The United States Congress. Senate Committee on the Judiciary. Subcommittee on Constitutional Amendments. Presidential Inability; hearings before the Subcommittee . . . of the Committee . . . Eighty-eight Congress, first session on S. J. Res. 28, S.J. Res. 35 and S. J. Res. 84 relating to the problem of presidential inability, June 11 and 18, 1963." Washington, D.C.: U.S. Government Printing Office, 1963, 117 pages.

Arnold A. Rogow, M.D., has written extensively on Forrestal's psychiatric disorder, in *James Forrestal: A Study of Personality, Politics* and *Policy* (New York: Macmillan, 1964). See also "Private Illness and Public Policy: The Cases of James Forrestal and John Winant," in *The American Journal of Psychiatry,* 125/8, 1969.

The paranoid commander is mentioned in *The VIP with Psychiatric Impairment,* as are George Washington's depressions.

The best-known exponent of psychiatric screening for political candidates is Arnold A. Hutchnecker, M.D. Several of his articles on "Psychopolitics" were used in preparing the present chapter: "The Stigma of Seeing a Psychiatrist" (*The New York Times,* November 20, 1973) and "The Drive for Power," a five-part series in *The New York Post,* beginning December 30, 1974.

Opposing points of view on the controversial question of psychiatric testing of political candidates are given by George Mishtowt, M.D., and Michael Halberstam, M.D., in "Should Candidates be Screened for Medical and Physical Fitness?" in *Medical World News,* 15, 1974.

The statistics on disagreement in psychiatric diagnosis are from Aaron Beck, M.D., *Depression: Causes and Treatment* (Philadelphia: University of Pennsylvania Press, 1967).

Bruce Mazlish's *In Search of Nixon* (New York: Basic Books, 1972) is a psychohistorical inquiry into Nixon's personality and the ramifications of his presidency.

Good armchair psychiatry is Eli S. Chesen's *President Nixon's Psychiatric Profile* (New York: Wyden, 1973).

R. D. Laing's existential philosophy of treatment is explained in *The Divided Self* (New York: Pantheon, 1966) and *The Politics of Experience* (New York: Pantheon, 1967).

Another advocate of the notion that society is insane and insanity is not is Thomas Szasz, M.D. See *The Myth of Mental Illness* (New York: Dell, 1967), and *Manufacture of Madness: A Comparative Study of the Inquisition and the Mental Health Movement* (New York: Harper and Row, 1970).

Ralph Nader's remarks on General Motors are from a speech given at the Eighth Biennial Divisional Meeting of the American Psychiatric Association, New York State District Branch, New York City, March 16, 1974.

Arthur Schlesinger's remarks on psychiatry were made in the keynote address to the New York State District Branch Meeting of the American Psychiatric Association, New York City, March 15, 1974.

The biographical information on Ralph Nader was taken from "Profile: A Countervailing Force," in *The New Yorker,* October 8, 1973.

Biographical information on Senator Thomas Eagleton was taken from *The New York Times* of July 14, 26, 31, and August 1, 1972.

CHAPTER 10: DOES PSYCHOTHERAPY WORK?

Extremely valuable in preparing this chapter were *Trick or Treatment: How and When Psychotherapy Fails,* by Richard B. Stuart (Chicago: Research Press, 1970), and *The Uses and Abuses of Psychology* by H. J. Eysenck (Baltimore: Penguin, 1953).

The effects of psychotherapy are discussed by Myra Weissman, M.D., and Eugene Paykel, M.D., in *The Depressed Woman: A Study of Social Relationships* (Chicago: University of Chicago Press, 1974).

The Menninger Clinic study was published in the *Bulletin of the Menninger Clinic* (36/1 & 2, 1972) as "Psychotherapy and Psychoanalysis: Final Report of the Menninger Foundation Psychotherapy Research Project."

The Chicago Institute study of 1937 is cited in Stuart, op. cit.

Jerome Frank's comments on the salutary effects of reassurance are from *Persuasion and Healing* (Baltimore: Johns Hopkins University Press, 1961).

The remarks on the many "cures" for neuroses are by A. Myerson, M.D., in "The Attitude of Neurologists, Psychiatrists and Psychologists Toward Psychoanalysis," in *The American Journal of Psychiatry*, 96, 1939.

The deterioration effects of psychotherapy are discussed by C. B. Truax, M.D., and R. R. Carkhuff, M.D., in *Toward Effective Counseling and Psychotherapy* (Chicago: Aldine, 1967).

The study of inpatients was published by G. W. Fairweather, M.D., as "Relative Effectiveness of Psychotherapeutic Programs," in *Psychological Monographs* 74/5, 1967 (Whole No. 492).

Positive results from group therapy in conjunction with drugs were reported by L. Covi, M.D., in "Drugs and Group Psychotherapy in Neurotic Depression," *The American Journal of Psychiatry*, 131/2, 1974.

The problem of relapse is studied by G. Klerman, M.D., in "Treatment of Depression by Drugs and Psychotherapy," *The American Journal of Psychiatry*, 131/2, 1974.

The percentages of improvement with and without drugs are reported by D. Klein, M.D., and J. Davis, M.D., in *Diagnosis and Drug Treatment of Psychiatric Disorders* (Baltimore: Williams and Wilkins, 1969).

The remark of F. C. Redlich, M.D., on Freud is quoted in Stuart, op. cit.

The Wolf Man's autobiography as well as Freud's "The Case of the Wolf Man" is published in *The Wolf Man*, by the Wolf Man (New York: Basic Books, 1971).

Many of the observations on Freud's Wolf Man are from Juan Lopez-Ibor, M.D., "Sergei the Wolf Man: A Mirage of Psychiatry?" *Acta Luso Españolas de Nefrología e Psiquiatría* (1, 1973). Lopez-Ibor points out that the Wolf Man was manic-depressive and that Freud misdiagnosed him.

The survey of psychoanaltyic practice is from an item in *Psychiatric News*, April 4, 1973.

Alfred Freedman, M.D., remarks on the demise of psychoanalysis in *Psychiatric News*, September 5, 1973.

CHAPTER 11: MISDIAGNOSIS OF DEPRESSION AND MANIC DEPRESSION IN AMERICA

Dr. Joseph Zubin planned the cross-national study that was published as *Psychiatric Diagnosis in New York and London,* by J. Cooper, M.D., R. E. Kendall, M.D., B. Gurland, M.D., L. Sharpe, M.D., J. Copeland, M.D., and R. Simon, M.D. (London: Oxford University Press, 1972).

M. Shepherd, M.D., "A Study of the Major Psychoses in an English County," Maudsley Monograph No. 3 (London: Chapman and Hall, 1957).

M. Kramer, "Some Problems for International Research Suggested by Observations of Differences in First Admission Rates to Mental Hospitals of England and Wales and of the United States," in *Proceedings of the Third World Congress of Psychiatry,* Vol. 3 (Montreal: University of Toronto Press/McGill University Press, 1961).

B. Gurland, M.D., et al (United States team) and John Copeland, M.D., et al (United Kingdom team), "The Mislabeling of Depressed Patients in New York State Hospitals," in *Disorders of Mood* (Baltimore: Johns Hopkins University Press, 1972).

The concept of pseudoneurotic schizophrenia originated with Paul Hoch, M.D., and Philip Polatin, M.D., at the New York State Psychiatric Institute in 1949.

Nolan Lewis's "trace of schizophrenia" is found in "Clinical Diagnosis of Manic-Depressive Psychosis" in *Depression,* edited by P. Hoch and J. Zubin (New York: Grune and Stratton, 1954).

CHAPTER 12: WHEN IS HOSPITALIZATION NECESSARY?

The SADS (Schedule for Affective Disorders and Schizophrenia) was developed by Robert Spitzer, M.D., and Jean Endicott, Ph.D., with other participants from the National Institute of Mental Health Research Branch Collaborative Program on the Psychobiology of Depression.

CHAPTER 13: DEPRESSION TREATED AT THE OFFICE

The way I set up my Foundation and clinic and the cost effectiveness of this method is described in Robert M. Daly, "Lithium-Responsive Affective Disorders," *New York State Journal of Medicine,* 78, 1978.

CHAPTER 14: THE LITHIUM BREAKTHROUGH

Portions of the history of lithium, as well as many of the studies mentioned in this chapter, are taken from *Lithium in the Treatment of Mood Disorders,* op. cit.

Research at Rockland State Hospital on the use of lithium in alcoholism is reported in *The New York Times,* June 22, 1973.

Information on Dr. J. Tupin's research on aggression in California prisoners can be found in *Psychiatric News,* October 17, 1973.

E. B. Dawson, Ph.D., "Relationship of Lithium Metabolism to Mental Hospital Admission and Suicide," in *Diseases of the Nervous System,* 33, 1972.

A. Voors, M.D., "Does Lithium Depletion Cause Atherosclerotic Heart Disease?" in *Lancet,* December 20, 1969.

Ronald R. Fieve and Kay Jamison, "Rubidium, an Overview," in *Modern Problems in Pharmacopsychiatry* (Basel: S. Karger, 1982).

CHAPTER 15: HOW TO OBTAIN THE LATEST ANTIDEPRESSANT DRUG

A detailed summary of new antidepressants under various stages of development worldwide can be found in Ronald R. Fieve, "La Récherche pour des nouveaux antidépresseurs: orientations actuelles," *L'Encéphale,* 5 (suppl.): 1979 (Eng. abstr.).

Ronald R. Fieve and Brian Anderson, "New Drugs to Manage Depression," *The Female Patient,* 9, 1984. The authors evaluate the new drugs that were approved for use in the United States in the early 1980s and show their applicability in the management of depression.

Roger M. Pinder, "Antidepressant Drugs of the Future," *Psychopharmacology: Recent Advances and Future Prospects,* edited by Susan D. Iverson (New York: Oxford University Press, 1985). An up-to-date, highly detailed account of new antidepressant agents being developed by laboratory pharmacologists and clinical psychopharmacologists worldwide.

INDEX

From *New York Times* bestselling author
Patty Duke
and Gloria Hochman

A BRILLIANT MADNESS

In this compassionate, moving, and eloquent book, Patty Duke joins with medical reporter Gloria Hochman to reveal fully what it's like to live with manic depression, a powerful, paradoxical, and destructive illness, and how it can be brought under control.

Patty recounts with painful honesty her temper tantrums, crying jags, hospital stays, suicide attempts, panic attacks, crushing depressions, and plunges into near bankruptcy. She frankly reveals how her disease helped to destroy two marriages and deeply hurt her children. But Patty's story has a happy ending: after diagnosis and years of on-again off-again treatment, she was prescribed lithium, which offered a near-miraculous recovery. And it is to lihium that she ascribes her newfound happiness—a loving marriage, healthy family,and the joy she feels as she contemplates a future filled with life's normal ups and downs.

Manic depression is a complex disorder that often masquerades as other illnesses. In alternating chapters, Gloria Hochman reports on the latest findings about its probable causes, its wide range of symptoms, and the most effective treatments. Vivid case histories reveal the many faces of manic depression and demonstrate why some patients resist treatment. She also offers fascinating insights into the link between creativity and manic depression—from the brilliant acting of Patty Duke to its influence on prominent entrepreneurs, politicians, musicians, and writers.

For all those who suffer from mood
disorders, and for the family, friends, and
physicians who love and care for them,
A Brilliant Madness
provides new and profound insight into
the challenge of mental illness.

ON SALE IN JUNE 1991   AN 433 5/92

We Deliver!
And So Do These Bestsellers.